Of Mind and Mat

Central European Studies

Of Mind and Matter

The Duality of National Identity in the German-Danish Borderlands

Peter Thaler

Purdue University Press
West Lafayette, Indiana

Printed in the United States of America.

Library of Congress Cataloging-in-Publication Data

Thaler, Peter
Of mind and matter : the duality of national identity in the German-Danish borderlands / by Peter Thaler.
p. cm.
Includes bibliographical references.
ISBN 978-1-55753-524-5
1. Schleswig-Holstein (Germany)--Ethnic relations. 2. Sønderjyllands amt (Denmark)--Ethnic relations. 3. Minorities--Germany--Schleswig-Holstein--History. 4. Minorities--Denmark--Sønderjyllands amt--History. 5. Ethnicity--Germany--Schleswig-Holstein--History. 6. Ethnicity--Denmark--Sønderjyllands amt--History. 7. Cultural pluralism--Germany--Schleswig-Holstein--History. 8. Cultural pluralism--Denmark--Sønderjyllands amt--History. 9. Nationalism--Germany--Schleswig-Holstein--History. 10. Nationalism--Denmark--Sønderjyllands amt--History. I. Title.
DD801.S63348T438 2009
943'.512--dc22

2009004937

CONTENTS

TABLES

PREFACE

Of Mind and Matter analyzes national identity along the German-Danish border. The study strives to add new angles to the literature on national identity in border areas and to fill a conspicuous gap in English-language historiography, which includes very few contemporary analyses of this region.

I hope that the book will be able to satisfy its two foremost audiences. On the one hand, it is directed at readers with an interest in German and Scandinavian history. On the other, it wants to attract readers with an interest in nationalism, borderlands, and cultural diversity. By applying a comparative and transnational approach and anchoring the analysis in a theoretical framework, the study also tries to make a small contribution to the debate about the nature of history.

During my work on this study, I have profited from the help of many. The libraries at the University of Southern Denmark fulfilled my never-ending requests for additional materials. The Danish national archives in Copenhagen and the regional archives in Aabenraa and Schleswig supplied most of the primary sources. Last, but by no means least, the insightful comments by Hans Schultz Hansen, Frank Lubowitz, Kurt Goblirsch, Tina Thaler, Gary Cohen as well as the editors and referees at Purdue University Press improved the study in content and style. I am glad to be able to acknowledge these contributions.

FOREWORD

When historians of modern Europe have written about the relationship of Sleswig and Holstein to the modern Danish and German national states, the subject has typically arisen in connection with great events in politics and diplomacy: the upheavals of 1848, the wars of German unification in the 1860s, the cession of northern Sleswig to Denmark in 1920, and the organizing of Schleswig-Holstein in 1949 as a state in the Federal Republic of Germany. Alongside the tangled geopolitical and dynastic questions, however, is the equally interesting and significant question of how loyalties of the inhabitants of these territories to crown, state, region, and nation developed through all the conflicts over sovereignty. Peter Thaler offers here a penetrating treatment of how national identities have evolved over the last two centuries among the population, analyzed in terms of regional, urban-rural, and class differences as well as politics and ideology.

From the mid-nineteenth century through the mid-twentieth century, Danish and German nationalist activists and ethnographers often made broad claims about the character and trends of development in ethnic and national loyalties in these territories. A substantial body of serious scholarship has arisen since 1945 on the evolution of culture and politics in Sleswig and Holstein, written mostly by Danish and German scholars; but little of that work has achieved the international scholarly attention which, in contrast, discussions of the western and eastern border areas of Germany have attracted. Thaler's thoughtful examination of the changing patterns of national identification in the Danish-German borderlands over the course of the nineteenth and twentieth centuries should remedy that neglect.

In recent years historians have produced many fresh and original social analyses of developing national identification and nationalist political mobilization in various borderlands of modern Europe. To avoid the essentialist perspectives on ethnicity and national identity of many older studies which focused on broad discussions of cultural differences and national ideas, scholars have increasingly focused on how national loyalties have been socially and politically constructed, with a strong emphasis on the performance of those loyalties in everyday life. Fruitful as those studies have been, they have sometimes neglected the ideas which animate national loyalties and nationalist political action and undervalued the cultural nuances which distinguish members of diverse groups who cohabit in particular territories. Thaler's work traces the social and political construction of national loyalties and the performance of national differences in the everyday, but he also takes seriously the impact of contending nationalist political ideas and ideologies as well as government policies, laws, and administrative structures. Nationalist activists and leaders, after all, have asked populations in these territories, as part of the process of aligning with one or another nationalist cause, to subscribe to particular political ideas and to live within particular governmental and legal frameworks–or to want to be part of alternative state frameworks. In these territories, where many of the inhabitants long held multiple, layered loyalties, convincing people that they belonged to either a distinct Danish or German nation and should retain an exclusive loyalty to that nation despite the vicissitudes of war and changes of borders was no simple process.

Interestingly, the evolution of national identities in these territories did not find any easy, neat, and definitive resolution with the reaffirmation of northern Sleswig's inclusion in the Kingdom of Denmark after World War II and the 1955 Bonn-Copenhagen Declarations about minority rights on both sides of the Danish-German border. Thaler shows that national loyalties continued to evolve in complex and not easily predictable ways even after 1945. National political loyalties in the post-World War II era increasingly reflected individual and group political sentiments which might not be connected to actual language usage or direct familial descent. Essentialist notions of identity based on ethnic descent failed to explain the realities of Danish and German loyalties for many people through the late twentieth century just as they failed to explain loyalties during the early or mid-nineteenth century. The conditions and circumstances of Danish and German loyalties have continued, as Thaler explains, to be affected by ideas as well as concrete cultural, social, and political realities, to be matters of both mind and matter.

—Gary B. Cohen
Series Editor

BILINGUAL TOPOGRAPHIC GLOSSARY[1]

South of 1920 Border

German	*Danish*
Achtrup	Agtrup
Angeln[2]	Angel
Bredstedt	Bredsted
Eiderstedt	Ejdersted
Flensburg	Flensborg
Friedrichstadt	Frederiksstad
Gottorf (also Gottorp)	Gottorp
Idstedt	Isted
Leck	Læk
Niebüll	Nibøl
Rodenäs	Rødenæs
Schlei	Slien
Schleswig	Slesvig
Schwansen	Svans
Schwesing	Svesing
Süderlügum	Sønder Løgum
Sylt	Sild
Viöl	Fjolde

North of 1920 Border

Danish	*German*
Aabenraa	Apenrade
Emmerlev	Emmerleff
Haderslev	Hadersleben
Højer	Hoyer
Kongeå	Königsau
Ribe	Ripen
Sønderborg	Sonderburg
Tinglev	Tingleff
Tønder	Tondern
Ubjerg	Uberg

Notes

1. This list covers Sleswig topographic designations that occur in the text, but does not include dynastic names and designations that are identical in both languages or merely differ in spelling conventions.
2. The text uses the English/Latin term Anglia.

MAP OF SLESWIG (1943)

LANGUAGES IN SLESWIG ACCORDING TO GEERZ (1838)

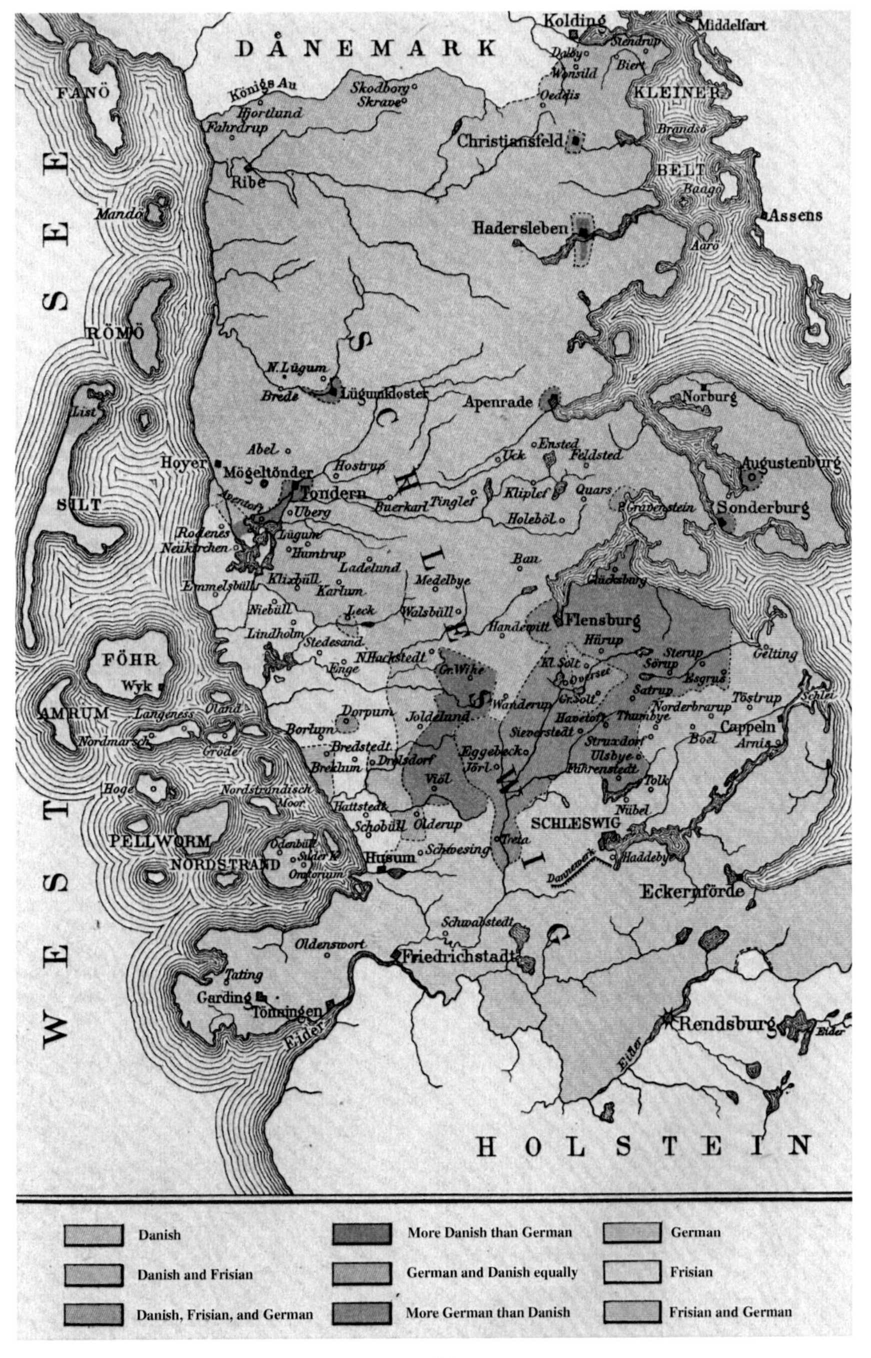

PLEBISCITES 1920

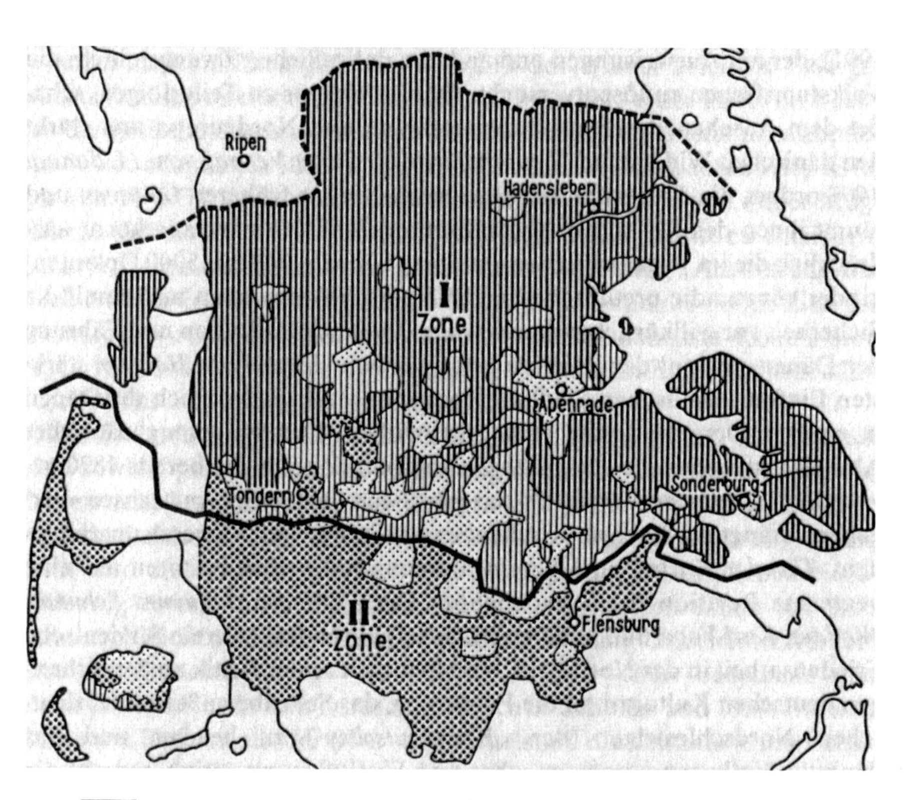

75%-100% German votes

50%-75% German votes

Border 1864-1920

75%-100% Danish votes

50%-75% Danish votes

Border today

CHAPTER ONE

Identity in the Borderlands

A Conceptual Introduction

For many centuries, the duchy of Sleswig constituted a vital link between the German and the Scandinavian world.[1] Extending 9,000 square kilometers between the North Sea and the Baltic Sea, it dominated the southern portion of Jutland. Whereas the base of this large peninsula merges naturally into the north German plains, its tip points toward the coastlands of western Sweden and southern Norway.

Today, the duchy of Sleswig is but a historical memory. Its territory has been divided between the modern nation-states of Denmark and Germany, and even its name has widely disappeared from official use. The southern half forms a component of the German federal state of Schleswig-Holstein, but there are only a few legal and administrative matters in which the specific character of the Sleswig region comes to bear.[2] The northern half of the former duchy has reassumed the early designation of Sønderjylland, which is generally translated into English as South Jutland. The Danish national movement considered this designation, which emphasizes the connection with Jutland's north, more Danish-sounding than a name derived from the now German-speaking city of Schleswig.

At first glance, it may seem ironic that the name Sleswig has been kept alive most visibly by the national minorities left behind on both sides of the border. Whereas the German inhabitants of Flensburg and Husum see themselves predominantly as inhabitants of Schleswig-Holstein, the members of the German minority north of the border describe themselves unambiguously as North Sleswigers. And whereas the Danes of South Jutland at most connect the term Sleswig with their own region in a historical context, the Danish-minded population of the southern part of the old duchy has proudly embraced it.[3]

Upon closer inspection, this seeming paradox becomes less puzzling. After all, it is in these minorities that the old Sleswig identity has survived. By emphasizing that they are not outsiders in a nation-state called Denmark or Germany, but Sleswigers in the historically bicultural Sleswigian realm, these minorities claim their place as equal and perhaps even more traditional components of regional society.

Of Mind and Matter analyzes national identity along the German-Danish border. It highlights the composite and changeable nature of this identity and explores what has motivated local inhabitants to define themselves as Germans or Danes. The analysis focuses especially on national self-identification, because it was self-identification rather than palpable differences in color, creed, or lifestyle that guided the nationalization process. At the same time, this personal decision-making did not occur in a political and cultural vacuum. Not even the respective national minorities, among whom the transitional and flexible aspects of Sleswig identity surface most clearly, remained untouched by the tension between subjective and objective markers of nationhood.

Unlike a number of significant new studies of European borderlands, the current investigation primarily applies a macrohistoric approach. This choice seemed most fruitful for a subject matter characterized by a dearth of up-to-date English literature. The macrohistoric angle more readily reveals the historical framework within which the process of nationalization took place; if successful, it might inspire microstudies in its wake. In order not to lose sight of the individual experience, however, one chapter focuses exclusively on intellectual life stories. A further chapter puts Sleswig into a comparative context by drawing on related developments in other Central European settings. This comparative angle highlights underlying structures and thus creates a natural transition from empirical analysis to theoretical categorization and interpretation.

Finally, I would like to address the use of geographic names in this study. Their politicized nature has complicated the choice of appropriate designations. Outside Sleswig, the study generally introduces bilingual locations with both names and proceeds with the period's prevalent designation. In so composite a setting as Sleswig, this approach proved elusive; therefore, the names of towns and municipalities are rendered in their current official form. This division could not be upheld in regard to an overarching term such as Sleswig. The Danish designation Sønderjylland not only lacks an unambiguous and generally understood English equivalent, but has undergone a change of meaning as well. Whereas it referred to the entire territory in early medieval time and in the language of nineteenth-century Danish nationalism, it has now been restricted to the northern, Danish section. The term Schleswig, in turn, which is commonly used in English today, corresponds directly to current German usage. Thus, it seemed most appropriate to utilize the form Sleswig, which occasionally appears in older English usage, does not correspond to the current official designation in either Denmark or Germany, and allows a straightforward distinction between North and South Sleswig. In direct reference to the current German federal state, the term Schleswig-Holstein is retained, however.

By the same token, such terms as German or Dane have connoted varying concepts throughout the long time frame of this study. In particular, their association with nation-states is of more recent origin. In his much-lauded monograph on multilingual regions in Habsburg Austria, Pieter Judson decided to resolve this dilemma by reserving such terms for individuals who had publicly expressed a national inclination and addressing all others as speakers of a specific language.[4] I have chosen a different approach because the disparity between native tongue and national orientation has formed so significant an aspect of the Sleswig experience. I entrust the reader with the task of understanding these terms in the context within which they are used. Thus, a reference to Danes in a paragraph examining medieval linguistic divisions implies a different kind of Danishness than an allusion to the Danish self-identification of postwar German speakers in Flensburg. In this manner, we can also remain truer to the diction used by the people we examine.

Sleswig in the Scholarly Debate

Seldom has so much been written about so few, the Danish South Sleswiger Martin Klatt observed in regard to his own community, and this tongue in cheek *apercu* could be applied to other aspects of the region's history as well.[5] Up-to-date literature on the specific question examined in this study, by contrast, is much rarer. In earlier periods, many scholars designed their works as contributions to the political debate. Up to World War II, at the least, a substantial part of the research delivered arguments for the national conflict. Recent writings, in turn, have not so much focused on Sleswig in its entirety, but more specifically on the respective Danish or German provinces or their national minorities. Finally, almost all of this literature has been written in German and Danish and has thus remained inaccessible to an international readership.

In the early 1800s, the scholarly debate revolved primarily around the constitutional aspects of Sleswig history. Danish-oriented historians wanted to prove that Sleswig formed an integral part of Denmark and had done so throughout history. Their German-minded colleagues, in contrast, described the duchy as an independent political entity, inseparably connected with Holstein, while merely affiliated with the Danish kingdom through a joint monarch. These parameters are visible in Christian Paulsen's *Über Volkstümlichkeit und Staatsrecht des Herzogthums Schleswig* and C. F. Allen's *Haandbog i fædrelandets historie* on the Danish side as well as in Nicolaus Falck's *Das Herzogthum Schleswig in seinem gegenwärtigen Verhältnis zu dem Königreich Dänemark und zu dem Herzogthum Holstein* and *Die historischen Landes-Rechte in Schleswig und Holstein urkundlich* on the German.[6]

Both Paulsen and Allen included ethnographic aspects; the latter especially in his widely read *Det danske sprogs historie i hertugdømmet Slesvig eller Sønderjylland* from the middle of the century.[7] It was mainly after the incorporation of Sleswig and Holstein into Prussia, however, that this ethnolinguistic line of argument became truly prevalent. In agreement with thoughts promoted by prominent historians such as A. D. Jørgensen and Aage Friis, Peder Lauridsen strove to identify the southernmost extension of Danish settlement.[8] H. V. Clausen relied on personal observations as well as a network of local informants to establish a dividing line between Danish and German in Sleswig.[9] These contributions were included in Franz von Jessen's large compilation *Haandbog i det nordslesvigske spørgsmaals historie*, which tried to document Denmark's claim to the northern half of the duchy.[10] On the German side, August Sach underlined the area's West Germanic prehistory and the assimilatory powers of the German-speaking upper classes to uphold Sleswig's inclusion in a German framework.[11] Countering H. V. Clausen, J. G. C. Adler analyzed linguistic conditions in Sleswig based on census results instead of personal calculations.[12]

The publication of encyclopedic handbooks on the national conflict persisted in the interwar era. Karl Alnor worked for one and a half decades on his voluminous compilation; Franz von Jessen continued his earlier research into the twentieth century.[13] At the same, regional surveys appeared in both Denmark and Germany. Otto Brandt finished the first edition of his often republished *Geschichte Schleswig-Holsteins* in 1925; Vilhelm La Cour and others brought out a five-volume history of South Jutland in the 1930s.[14] Like most other contemporary works, these provincial histories largely analyzed Sleswig history from their respective national premises, that is, they put the territory either into a Dano-Jutlandish or a Sleswig-Holstein tradition. As an echo of the large-scale linguistic surveys, Paul Selk examined the status of the Danish dialect in interwar South Sleswig.[15]

In the early postwar years, at least part of the literature still reflected evident national goals, which revolved especially around the nature of Danish identity in southern Sleswig. From the 1950s on, however, a new perspective began to take root. Increasingly, the Sleswig experience was put into a context of European reconciliation and integration. Generous public support led to the establishment of such institutions as the Danish Institute of Border Region Studies in Aabenraa and the research department of the Danish library in Flensburg.[16] Together with the provincial archives of South Jutland, these institutions became major centers for the investigation of identity questions in Sleswig. On the German side, the Institute for Contemporary and Regional History of Schleswig-Holstein participated in analyses of border identities, as did smaller institutions affiliated with the German minority in North Sleswig and with non-governmental border associations.

The ensuing scholarly production has been impressive. Danish historians such as Troels Fink, Johan Peter Noack, and Henrik Becker-Christensen meticulously investigated the minorities on both sides of the border, especially during the first half of the twentieth century.[17] Lorenz Rerup not only published the most significant Danish survey of newer Sleswig and Holstein history, but also contributed more detailed studies of select aspects.[18] Hans Schultz Hansen focused especially on the growth of national consciousness in the nineteenth century, as well as on the special characteristics of the national conflict in rural areas.[19] Social scientists such as Jørgen Elklit used public opinion surveys to identify the nature of national self-identification in North Sleswig.[20]

Although the history of national identity in Sleswig no longer seemed quite as central to German researchers, a number of publications appeared south of the border as well.[21] An older generation of Sleswig-Holstein regional historians such as Alexander Scharff and Erich Hoffmann retained an interest in this subject matter.[22] It also surfaced in large-scale provincial histories, such as Olaf Klose's multi-volume *Geschichte Schleswig-Holsteins* and Ulrich Lange's 700-page work with the same title.[23] Jürgen Rohweder examined the connection between language and nationality in nineteenth-century Sleswig, whereas Jürgen Zeh, Gösta Toft, and Kai Detlev Sievers analyzed the social and cultural parameters of the German minority in North Sleswig from a social-science perspective.[24] A number of Ph.D. dissertations shed further light on the history of minority populations on both sides of the border.[25] Finally, the establishment of the North Frisian Institute in Bredstedt provided a more secure basis for research on this small cultural community, which has expressed itself not least of all in the groundbreaking publications of Thomas Steensen.[26]

International researchers have not played a prominent role in the analysis of the German-Danish borderlands. Kim Salomon's innovative *Konflikt i grænseland*, which analyzes the relationship between Danes and Germans in interwar North Sleswig with the tools of conflict theory, does not fully belong into this category, since the author is a native Dane, albeit teaching in Sweden.[27] His Swedish colleague Sven Tägil has examined the German minority in the same period.[28] Significant publications in English are rare. In 1933, Sarah Wambaugh included a thorough investigation of the 1920 plebiscites in Sleswig in her still valuable *Plebiscites since the World War*.[29] At about the same time, Lawrence Steefel examined the German-Danish conflict over the duchies in the 1860s.[30] In 1963, William Carr looked at the origins of this conflict in the first half of the nineteenth century.[31] And in one of the few newer book-length studies in English, Michael Byram studied the importance of the educational system for the identity of German North Sleswigers.[32]

In recent years, cooperative ventures between Danish and German scholars have become more common. A 1998 study edited by Henrik Becker-Christensen and Ulrich Lange examined select aspects of the region's history from the early Middle Ages to 1920.[33] As director of the Institute of Border Region Studies, the Danish South Sleswiger Jørgen Kühl promoted transnational research projects. The fundamental outlook of these Danish-German ventures is reflected in the title of the recent *En europæisk model?*[34] With the 1955 Bonn-Copenhagen Declarations as the turning point, Sleswig is described as an example from which other countries can learn how to overcome historic animosities and establish harmonious interethnic relations. Many scholars on both sides of the border have converged on this consensus paradigm, in which the Sleswig experience serves as a model for successful conflict resolution.[35]

National Identity: An Assessment

In the last decades, the concept of identity has become a central component of historical and social-science research. In a world in which borders become porous and transnational interactions omnipresent, this might seem puzzling. Yet the growing interest in questions of identity in an age of multicultural societies as well as economic and cultural globalization forms part of a natural dialectics. The constant challenge by the Other reinforces reflection about the self. For isolated human communities, social norms and behaviors constitute largely unquestioned certainties. It takes the confrontation with alternative conceptions to turn these modes of conduct into expressions of a distinct identity.

The dictionary defines identity among other things as "the condition of being oneself and not another" and "as the sense of self, providing sameness and continuity in personality."[36] These definitions reflect the dual dichotomy of identity. Identity refers to the self in relation to an Other and is rooted in both subjective and objective characteristics.

In this examination of the German-Danish borderlands, the foremost focus is on national identities. Although analyzing these concepts has been an important scholarly enterprise since the nineteenth century, it has not led to convincing, generally applicable models. The divergent historical experiences of different populations resulted in divergent perceptions of nationhood, even if experiences as well as perceptions have become increasingly similar over time. Originally, concepts of nationhood tended to differ along political and geographical lines, but the analytical threads can be more easily pulled together now. The growing importance of non-Western experiences has blurred the once prevalent juxtaposition of Western and Eastern European models and can serve as a starting point for more universal viewpoints.

In many countries, not least of all in Central Europe, the conceptual dichotomy of *Staatsnation* and *Kulturnation,* introduced into the scholarly debate by Friedrich Meinecke, continues to dominate the theoretical discussion—notwithstanding its theoretical expansion and critical revision.[37] The *Staatsnation*, which signifies the political or civic nation, is constructed around the citizenry of a politically organized territory, in other words, a state, regardless of the ethnic and cultural composition of this citizenry and of possible ethnocultural continuities beyond the existing political borders.[38] It is sometimes defined as a constitutional nation when it demarcates the nation by the reach of a liberal constitution; this reach will normally correspond to the political frontiers of a state. Its dependence on a specific constitutional content gives this conceptual variation a normative rather than empirical character, since even internal revisions of the political structure would terminate the existing constitutional nation. The concept resembles the comparably ideology-based, if politically diametrically opposed, class nation, which periodically provided the theoretical foundation of the German Democratic Republic and was envisioned to create a structure of coherence for *Soviet Man*. National community was tied to the (premised) identity of class interest, which would create a common consciousness. Both the constitutional nation and the class nation can be viewed as ideologically superstructured political nations.

By contrast, the typology of the *Kulturnation*, the cultural or ethnic nation, has personal rather than institutional foundations. According to this conception, the nation is a community of people who share cultural attributes, the most prominent of which is a common language. These cultural and linguistic criteria can be supplemented with images of a common ancestry or of shared historic experiences.[39] The ethnocultural concept of nationhood stresses noninstitutional criteria—political frontiers do not universally create or disjoin nations.

In the contemporary international debate, the juxtaposition of civic/political and cultural conceptions surfaces in critical differences between the instrumentalist and the ethnocultural school of nationalism. Due to the central role of these two interpretive traditions in the current academic debate, the relationship between them is of fundamental importance. During the recent decades, the theoretical discussion of nationalism was dominated by the instrumentalist or modernist school; ethnocultural concepts provided the most persistent scholarly challenge.

The proponents of instrumentalism merged an essentially Marxian focus on socioeconomic interests with a subjectivist intellectual tradition that criticized nationalism from a standpoint of conservative universalism. This cross-pollenization of Marxist and non-Marxist scholarship on nationalism had been a recurrent feature of modern nation theory. The classical contributions of Marxist scholarship to the theory of nationalism, such as Otto Bauer's psychologically and historically oriented definition of a nation as an "aggregate of people bound into a community of character by a common destiny" and Joseph Stalin's criterion-based approach that defines a nation as a "historically evolved, stable community of people, formed on the basis of a common language, territory, economic life, and psychological make-up manifested in a common culture" were to a larger degree informed by than opposed to non-Marxist theory of the time.[40] This interrelationship with non-Marxist scholarship became even more pronounced with the postwar academic ascent of the social sciences, which stimulated fresh interpretations of nationalism. The most important new concept in the explanation of nationalism in the early postwar era was modernization, which produced numerous models and began to dominate the theoretical debate.[41]

Modernization theorists reject descriptive explanations of nationhood and nationalism, which assign nation status to political entities that fulfill specific objective criteria. They see the idiosyncrasies of nation-building, which render any universal criterion-based definition difficult, as incompatible with a theoretical focus on such objective requirements. Nations arise out of fundamental changes that transform traditional into modern societies. Based upon this common assumption, various models of nation-building emerged.

One of the most influential interpretations derived from Karl Deutsch's study *Nationalism and Social Communication*, which first appeared in 1953.[42] Deutsch ascribes central importance for the development of national identity to the social mobilization that followed increasing urbanization, industrialization, education, and political participation and focuses especially on the communicational integration initiated by the emergence and spread of mass media. Another important submodel of modernization applies the popular social-science dichotomy of center versus periphery to the nation-building process. Territorial or social centers expand their influence to the periphery, which becomes integrated into a national structure through assimilation and coalition-building. Finally, functionalist submodels stress the role of national identity in fulfilling the need for cohesion arising from the collapse of traditional communities under the impact of social change; nationalism develops in periods of social crisis at the onset of modernity.

The neo-Marxist theories of nationalism that developed in the 1960s built on rather than replaced modernization theory. The academic success of neo-Marxist scholarship increased the significance of Marxian concepts for the discussion of nationalism outside the countries of the Communist world. Apart from contributing to the ideology of national liberation that dominated the period of decolonialization, Marxist scholars focused predominately on the role of class interest in the development of nationalist thought. Like modernization theorists, they were not satisfied with interpretative approaches that relied on premised cultural idiosyncrasies; for them, socio-economic conditions and interests determined the specific development of nationalism.

Nation theory took a new turn when a group of scholars from a broadly defined Marxist or post-Marxist tradition opened themselves to a more subjectivist strand of interpretation and laid the groundwork for the instrumentalist interpretation of nationhood.[43] The roots of this intellectual influence can be traced back to the nineteenth century, when traditionalist thinkers expressed opposition to the emerging focus on individual and national self-determination. Refining this interpretation with his acclaimed 1960 study *Nationalism*, Elie Kedourie earned preeminence among conservative critics of nationalist ideas. Kedourie describes nations as constructs of alienated intellectuals and nationalism as a doctrine invented in early nineteenth-century Europe.[44] Although this paradigm is hostile to nationalism, *inter alia*, because it classifies it as an outgrowth of the Enlightenment and the French Revolution, it also appealed to less conservative scholars who looked for a broader theoretical approach and wanted to add cultural and intellectual components to their economic analysis. Focusing on the mythical superstructure that frequently surrounds the national self-image, these authors developed and refined modernist theories of nationalism: they argued that nations are social constructs rooted in the self-interest of nationalist elites.

One of the pioneers of the new concept was Ernest Gellner, who explained the emergence of nationalism with the need for homogeneity arising in modern industrial societies.[45] Whereas different social groups in feudal agrarian societies were separated by too deep a gulf to permit the development of national community, the industrial state required interchangeable, culturally standardized populations that could be transferred according to economic needs. Nations are not inherent or natural institutions, and they did not engender the age of nationalism; instead, it was nationalism that gave rise to nations. In these new nations, unified high cultures take the place formerly held by local cultures. Although nationalism relies on the symbolism of traditional community, it ultimately erodes this community by building up an industrial mass society.

Benedict Anderson's *Imagined Communities: Reflections on the Origin and Spread of Nationalism* expands further the concept of constructed identity.[46] Anderson defines the nation as a cultural artifact, as an "imagined community," as his now famous expression goes. However, the author emphasizes the distinction between invented and fabricated; he ascribes very real and deeply felt reality to the nation and reminds the reader of the sacrifices it has been able to inspire.

Anderson aligns nationalism not with ideologies such as liberalism or socialism, but with cultural systems. Nationalism grew out of the demise of two cultural systems that preceded it—the religious community and the dynastic realm. National identity provides a form of continuity lost through the disappearance of religious certainties. When people lost their belief in holy script languages such as Latin, in divine rulers, and in cosmic concepts of history, the void was filled by national ideas.

Why was it the nation that took the place of earlier cultural systems? Anderson upholds the received view that the convergence of capitalism and print technology created the possibility of a new community based on language. He does not consider this point a sufficient explanation, however, because the nation-states of Spanish-America and the "Anglo-Saxon family" were not established along linguistic lines. As a consequence, Anderson attributes primary importance for the rise of nationalism in the New World to the local-born European—also called Creole—elites that dominated the mid-levels of colonial bureaucracy. Their realm of experience—the administrative colonial subdivision—became the new nation-state. Because of the relative underdevelopment of Spanish-America, no encompassing Spanish-American nationalism was viable. In Europe, nationalism was carried by the bourgeoisie, which, contrary to the cosmopolitan nobility, based its professional and social coherence on linguistic communality. Both Creole functionaries and the European educated classes created nations along the lines of their professional universe.

Anderson asserts that this populist nationalism, which endangered the traditional role of pre-national elites, could be countered by an "official nationalism" devised by social groups in power. The latter form of nationalism tended to conceal a discrepancy between the nation and the existing territorial configuration and tried to assimilate minority populations into the dominant national group.

New postcolonial nations could also resort to this "official nationalism." They inherited the artificial boundaries of colonial conquest, which rarely coincided with ethnic and linguistic borders, and embarked on the creation of a common national identity within these territories. Anderson delineates how westernized intelligentsias that received their education in European-led schools developed nationalist dreams informed by Western models. They saw the maps of European colonialism as their own guideposts and shared the Creole experience of professional development along colonial administrative lines. Therefore, languages did not represent a cultural heritage or symbol, but a practical means to generate imagined communities. In these new nations, colonial or newly created languages could serve as national languages.

This instrumentalist theory of nationalism, which bases nationhood on constructed traditions that serve the particular interests of the elites who generate them, found its most comprehensive expression in the work of Eric Hobsbawm. In his contributions to *The Invention of Tradition,* which he co-edited with Terence Ranger, and in his study *Nations and Nationalism since 1780*, Hobsbawm documents the adaptations and innovations that surround national symbols such as folk dances, national dress, and ethnic festivals.[47] Hobsbawm deconstructs such tradition-carrying symbols by pointing to their conscious creation or transformation and applies the implicit lesson to the concept of the nation in general. Much of the subjective content of national identity is the outcome of careful social engineering. The underlying motivation of this invention of tradition lies in the political and economic interests of ruling classes and elites. Thus, Hobsbawm combines modernist cultural theory with a more traditionally Marxist concept in which the class interests of the elites are the determinants of nationalist agitation.

In spite of his pronounced skepticism about the claims and motives of nation-builders, Hobsbawm acknowledges a populist element in the development of national consciousness. Before the beginning of true nations, which the author assigns to the time period following the French Revolution, "popular proto-nationalism" formed a net of cohesion that could serve as a building block in the subsequent development of nationalism proper. And even this nationalism, in spite of its constructed nature, cannot be understood without considering the hopes and desires of ordinary people in the emerging nation.

Much of modernist or instrumentalist theory relativized the power of nationalism and predicted its increasing supersession by alternative loyalties. When Walker Connor presented a collection of his articles on nationalism titled *Ethnonationalism* in 1994, the resurgence of nationalist sentiments that had characterized the preceding years had put much of current scholarship into question.[48] Connor's essays, in contrast, although first published between the 1960s and the early 1990s, seemed to have stood the test of time.

Connor argues that the terminological chaos that surrounds the concepts of nationhood and nationalism has precluded a realistic assessment of their relevance and their political potential. Although scholarship has in principle accepted the premise that the nation is not in and of itself identical to the sovereign state, the widespread identification of these key terms in popular and political usage—such as in the case of the *United Nations*—resulted in a fundamental lack of clarity even in academic writing. Too often, the development of a centralized state was termed nation-building, and nationalism was defined as loyalty to the state. Thus, the phenomenon that Connor sees as true nationalism—which frequently developed in outright opposition to the existing state—had to be described in different terms. Such substitute terms—among others, Connor lists tribalism, primordialism, and regionalism—evoke images of peripheralness and antiquatedness vis-à-vis the implied primary allegiance of state nationalism. As a consequence, most theorists of nationalism were unprepared for the strength of ethnonational consciousness when it openly expressed itself in such places as Eastern Europe.

Connor's oeuvre forms part of a less visible but persistent scholarly opposition to concepts of nationalism that neglect the role of ethnicity. Anthony D. Smith is the preeminent representative of a school that stresses the necessity of ethnic roots for the subsequent development of national identity.[49] Not only were most nations built upon preexisting ethnic foundations, but the absence of such foundations would constitute a serious impediment to the intended creation of a nation. While acknowledging the modernity of the nation-state and nationalism in their contemporary meanings, Smith underscores the continuity of cultural communitarianism.[50] In this focus, he echoes John Armstrong's allusion to the existence of "nations before nationalism," which tries to disengage the concepts of modern nationalism and culture-based group cohesion.[51]

In the sophisticated form represented by Smith and his closest associates, ethnist theory does not ignore the differences between traditional ethnies and modern nations. John Hutchinson sees modern cultural nationalists as moral innovators that stake out a medium path between universalist modernizers and isolationist conservatives by embracing development but insisting on following an autonomous path.[52] And Smith himself acknowledges the pivotal role of ethnic intellectuals, who turn a largely unreflected cultural affiliation into a conscious political reality.[53] In pursuing this objective, these ethnic intellectuals might indeed instrumentalize traditional symbols to gain legitimacy for their reformist agenda. Smith insists, however, that this selective reading of an ethnic past could only function within the limits set by living traditions.[54]

The Subjective Nature of Identities on the Margins

If one carefully analyzes the various concepts of nationhood, their demarcations frequently prove to be fluid, and their rigid juxtaposition becomes less persuasive. Most nations display characteristics found in a variety of theoretical models, and conceptual variances among national self-images tend to be based on the particular historical circumstances more than on irreconcilable ideological differences.

French nationalism, which is generally seen as the archetype of a state-centered conception, was not content with mere political loyalty; on the contrary, ethnic minorities enjoyed fewer cultural rights in France than in most other European countries. For the Corsicans and Bretons, French political nationalism essentially entailed an adaptation to French language and customs that left little room for autochthonous cultural traditions.[55] As Eugen Weber demonstrated in his magisterial *Peasants into Frenchmen*, this process was not simply left to popular initiative, but relied on a thorough policy of national mobilization.[56]

Civic participation, in turn, does not inherently conflict with cultural definitions of nationhood. Civic life frequently functions more smoothly in culturally homogenous societies, and it was hardly coincidental that the egalitarian social policies of the welfare state had their earliest and most comprehensive expressions in the countries of the Scandinavian north, in which a high degree of cultural coherence strengthened the sense of responsibility toward society's less fortunate.[57]

Conscious policies of nation-building and long-term cultural processes form a theoretical dichotomy that can be reflected in political reality. These factors can reinforce each other or compete with each other. A stress upon ethnocultural continuities dating back centuries that overlooks the fundamental change in societal interconnectedness that began in late eighteenth-century Europe is just as incomplete as the exclusive reference to the recentness and inventedness of national concepts and symbols that ignores genuine cultural continuities.

But there is another aspect to consider. While representing the leading interpretations, ethnoculturalism and instrumentalism are not the only ones. In addition to these most visible schools, and in a variable and ambiguous relationship to them, one can also find a voluntaristic conception. This conception is commonly traced back to Ernest Renan's classic dictum that the nation is a daily plebiscite.[58] Often, it is seen as a subcategory of the *Staatsnation*, because the nation-creating will of this concept has commonly been tied to the population of a preexisting territorial unit. Its basic premise, however, is compatible with other theoretical models as well. An abstract understanding of the voluntaristic nation would even provide for individuals spread across the globe to merge into a nation through a common will; such broader approaches have not been given serious consideration, though.

Thus, voluntarism remained within distinct boundaries. Renan developed his argument to a large degree in order to demonstrate that it was inappropriate of Germany to reannex Alsace in 1871, even if the local population might have had German cultural roots. He claimed the Alsatians for the French nation, because they did not identify with the German. The decision was seen as personal and subjective, but the choices were predetermined. It had to be the existing nation-states of Germany or France; there was no third option, although later developments, particularly in the interwar period, indicated that the most natural point of reference for many Alsatians might have been Alsace itself.[59]

The subjectivity of identity can also express itself in a more fundamental manner, however. The recent movement toward globalism and transnationalism, whereby the former is defined as largely detached from specific national territories and the latter as rooted in but transcending them, has added new facets to this phenomenon. Ever larger numbers of people live outside the state of their birth but retain social and emotional ties to it. Their identities tend to be influenced by both their native and their host cultures, from which they pick and receive in varying and eclectic ways. Diasporan communities try to preserve a sense of uniqueness in their new country and an active interest in their old.[60] Tourism both highlights and levels cultural differences. The youth culture of MTV reaches almost every corner of the world. Culture becomes deterritorialized, because people living next to each other are no longer necessarily participating in one and the same.[61]

Subjectivity and fluidity need not be connected with migratory processes. In more than a few border regions, too, a clear-cut determination of national identity proved to be challenging.[62] In such cases, local identities did not conform to the national paradigm, be it based on political or linguistic standards. It is this specific border environment with its ambiguities and interdependencies that forms a focal point of this study.

The geographical literature, for which the question of political demarcations has the most immediate relevance, has developed its specific terminology. J. R. V. Prescott distinguishes frontiers, zones of transition that used to represent the traditional separator of adjacent territories, from boundaries, which are the lines of demarcation with which we are currently familiar.[63] The primary American usage of the term frontier, namely, the furthest extent of a country's settled territory, reminds us of the origins of territorial deliminations. Territories were separated by largely uninhabited wilderness areas. Reinhard Schneider has documented that linear borders were not unknown in medieval Europe, but only in modern times were the former zones of transition cultivated universally and replaced by tangible demarcations.[64]

The term border can refer to both the political boundary and the area adjacent to it. The dictionary defines a border as the line that separates one country, state, or province from another and as the district or region that lies along the boundary line of another.[65] The latter meaning of the word is expressed less ambiguously in the term borderland(s). Borderlands are hence those strips along the border line in which the influence of the border is clearly present. As a consequence, such zones can vary in depth, depending on the cultural and socioeconomic conditions that characterize the border.

In earlier periods, borders tended to be analyzed from a conflictual perspective. A focus on politics and boundaries placed border disputes in the center of investigation. Borderlands appeared as potential sources of international conflict, not as zones of integration. In the course of recent decades, however, the investigation of interactive border identities has made visible progress.

Oscar J. Mártinez has developed a typology of borderlands.[66] In his categorization, Mártinez employs the nature and frequency of crossborder interaction as the crucial criterion. The border type with the least interaction is defined as an alienated borderland. Rigid border controls and popular enmities keep crossboundary interaction to a minimum. In coexistent borderlands, tensions have been reduced to a more manageable level. The border dwellers on both sides interact with each other, but this interaction is strongly influenced by the guidelines emanating from the respective central governments and remains on a formalized level. Interdependent borderlands, by contrast, are characterized by a greater flow of goods and people and by the formation of an economic subsystem that ties the regions on both sides together. Central governments still take an active interest in supervising crossborder interactions they consider harmful to their national interests, but in general, interaction is friendly and cooperative. Finally, in relatively few cases, the neighboring states reduce the relevance of their political boundary to such an extent that an integrated borderland can take shape. Virtually all restrictions on crossborder movement have been removed; in fact, a transnational ideology actively encourages it. Border dwellers on both sides consider themselves as part of a single social system.[67]

Mártinez is aware of the fact that most real-life borderlands will not fit neatly into distinct categories, but he emphasizes the analytical usefulness of his typology. He argues, furthermore, that these border types do not occur in a completely arbitrary fashion. Instead, he observes an internal logic and diagnoses a tendency toward increased interaction in recent history, which—for areas thus defined—turns the different categories of borderlands into sequential stages. Many borderlands have developed from the disjointed and hostile types to the more open and interacting ones. These interdependent borderlands with their transitional and connecting quality will be examined in the current study.

The conditions along the boundaries between the United States and Mexico, in particular, have given rise to a distinct literature about borderlands.[68] Along the Rio Grande and continuing to the Pacific Ocean, a fascinating environment full of contradictions attracted scholarly interest.[69] On the one hand, this border features a socioeconomic clash of rare proportions, where the developed and the developing world face each other unmitigated along a line stretching almost 2,000 miles across a whole continent. On the other hand, the political boundary is frequently just a marker on the map, whereas the cultural patterns have become increasingly similar on both sides. Special economic incentives, especially the so-called *maquiladora* program, have drawn American companies to northern Mexico and have tied this region closer to the economic sphere of its northern neighbor. By the 1990s, more than half a million Mexicans worked in one of the foreign-owned assembly plants close to the U.S. border. In turn, extended migratory processes have reinforced the Mexican cultural presence north of the Rio Grande and have given an unmistakable Mexican appearance to a broad belt on the American side of the border.

Below the surface, the picture of this borderland is even more complex. There are not only Anglos and Mexicans, but also Amerindians. And while an outsider may only see Mexicans, locals distinguish the well-established Tejanos and their more modest cousins in New Mexico, American-born Chicanos and Mexicanos, Spanish speakers and English speakers of Mexican descent, as well as citizens, green carders, and illegals, to name just a few fault lines within a seemingly homogenous population.

Yet borderlands have not only been investigated in the western hemisphere. Due to its colonial past, the African continent, and especially its subsaharan segment, contains an unusually large share of interactive borderlands. Since the political boundaries of the postcolonial state system largely adhered to the often arbitrary lines drawn by the colonial powers, they frequently cut across established or potential cultural spheres.[70] Rather than reflecting cultural or even geographical realities, the majority of African boundaries follow astronomical or geometrical lines. As a consequence, African borderlands are often characterized by strong cross-boundary affiliations, which can also express themselves in such economic forms as shared pastoral lands or internationally attended markets and fairs. A Hausa cultural sphere ties together the regions along the boundary between Nigeria and Niger just as much as the Yoruba-inhabited districts further south create an interactive borderland in Nigeria and Benin. And through the civil wars in Ruanda and Congo, the transboundary ties among the Tutsi people of East Africa have become known in parts of the world that are otherwise unfamiliar with the nature of ethnicity and nationhood on the African continent.[71]

Additional factors contribute to the permeability of African boundaries. The lines and arcs that neatly visualize boundaries on the map are often invisible on the ground. Many of the rivers used as boundary markers are easily crossed; sometimes, they dry up for part of the year. The official border crossing points are few and far between; the approximately 50,000 miles of international boundaries are guarded by fewer than 400 official road crossing points, which results in one for more than 100 miles of boundary.[72] The remainder of many boundaries is little marked and even less guarded. These borders are easily crossed, particularly by migratory pastoralists on their seasonal search for grazing lands, for whom international state lines represent an unwelcome intrusion into their economic sphere of life.[73]

At the same time, the idiosyncrasy of African borders should not be overstated. Wilderness areas and wildlife refuges constitute formidable hindrances to population movement in such areas as Sierra Leone and South Africa. Since many of the colonial acquisitions were based on treaties with local African rulers, they sometimes retained the outlines of historical African subdivisions. Paul Nugent points out that even seemingly artificial lines could be in harmony with local interests.[74] Moreover, the imposition of international boundaries on interrelated border populations has been a frequent occurrence in other parts of the world as well. As Anthony Asiwaju argues, the partitioning of the Catalan Pyrenees between France and Spain was just as much an expression of external intervention as the division of Yorubaland by France and Britain.[75] While African boundaries may face more than their fair share of challenges, these challenges are not uniquely African but representative of global transborder *problematiques*.[76]

In Western Europe, the focus has shifted to transnationalism during recent decades. For centuries, many European borders had been marked by conflict and frequent, often violent, change. Attempts to create a more representative state system in the aftermath of World War I only led to new conflicts. Since the 1950s, however, a new development has taken root, and the cooperation between border regions has been actively encouraged as part of the European unification process. Especially in the economic field, but not restricted to it, such institutions as the

Council of Europe and what is now called the European Union have promoted interaction across the boundaries of member states. This cooperation is not confined to EU member states, as can be seen in the cooperative framework along the Upper Rhine, which ties together the Swiss city of Basel with its natural upland in the German province of Baden-Württemberg and in the French region of Alsace.[77] As early as 1963, the association Regio Basiliensis started a process that led to an ever more extensive framework of cooperation in this culturally interrelated but politically divided region. In 1991, deputies from all three countries began to meet regularly in an Upper Rhine Assembly, and in 1995, the individual national associations formed the Council of the RegioTriRhena. This council, which has representatives from regional municipalities as well as from the local business and university communities, wants to broaden the popular appeal of mostly government-sponsored initiatives.

It was no coincidence that the Regio Basiliensis was pathbreaking for transboundary cooperation. The push for such cooperations was most pronounced along the Rhine axis at the center of the evolving European Community. In 1958, a group of German and Dutch municipalities formed a transnational body called euregio for the purpose of deepening both the sociocultural and the socioeconomic integration, and additional euregios sprouted up in the area during the following years.[78] Other parts of Europe followed suit. One of the largest and most international efforts is the arge alp, the cooperation of Alpine regions, which contains 11 German, Austrian, Swiss, and Italian provinces with a combined population of 23 million people. In 1971, ten such transboundary initiatives founded the Association of European Border Regions (AEBR).[79] This association, which by the year 2000 had grown to more than sixty members, among them many from the former east bloc, has set its agenda to work "toward a common future in a Europe without borders." The regional administrative bodies along the Dano-German border, such as the counties of Schleswig-Flensburg and South Jutland, also joined the AEBR.[80]

◆ ◆ ◆

The scholarly interpretation of nationalism and identity has increasingly highlighted their constructed nature. This growing consensus has also met criticism, however.[81] Most relevant for the current study were the very dissimilar concerns raised by Miroslav Hroch on the one hand, Rogers Brubaker and Frederick Cooper on the other. Pinpointing his major disagreement with Ernest Gellner's theory of nationalism, Hroch insisted that the relation between nation and national consciousness is not unilateral but complimentary.[82] Nationalist agitation was not predestined to succeed; its impact depended on the extent to which it reflected a perceived reality. Nation-building required both a viable entity and its mobilization, Hroch argued, and the discussion about the respective primacy of these preconditions should be left to philosophers and ideologues.

Brubaker and Cooper shook up the scholarly community when they challenged not only the essentialist rhetoric inherent in much of identity politics, but also the radical constructionism so popular in recent scholarship.[83] Distinguishing between categories of practice and categories of analysis, they questioned the conceptual value of identity. Essentialist interpretations define identity as indispensable for both groups and individuals. Although this imagery continues to influence popular usage, international scholarship has increasingly converged on a constructionist model. In the eyes of Brubaker and Cooper, however, this shift has not resolved the underlying problem. If identity is as malleable and ephemeral as many scholars have argued, how useful is it as an analytical category? Are soft concepts of identity capable of accounting for the power it holds over the minds of so many? Can a single concept such as identity account for both rigid and interchangeable understandings of social coherence? These legitimate questions will have to be addressed in a study of national self-identification in a once hotly disputed border province. Objectivist as well as subjectivist interpretations, instrumentalist as well as ethnonationalist ones must all be measured by their ability to account for national identity in all its facets.

The experience of transitional and border identities puts established interpretations of collective identities to the test. Marginal settings take many aspects of identity formation to their limits. The remoteness of the center and the ready availability of alternative identifications provide congenial conditions for individual decision-making. At the same time, this choice and changeability raises questions about the nature of the phenomena it brings forth. Identities invoke a variety of subjective and objective criteria, whose standards do not necessarily coincide. The impact of such divergent identity markers on identity in the German-Danish borderlands constitutes the conceptually most significant subject of investigation in this study.

The Structure of the Book

The history of modern Sleswig has been examined before. Much of the research has centered on creating a historical chronology and, just as often, on using this chronology to demonstrate the preferred national character of the region. The current study has a completely different focus. It investigates national sentiments in a transitional region from a theoretical perspective and places their malleability in the framework created by the modern literature on nationalism and on borderlands. For this purpose, it relies on diverse forms of historical evidence to establish the contribution of both objective and subjective criteria to the formation of national identity in Sleswig. This historical evidence includes quantitative sources such as language statistics and election results, but also more subjective sources such as personal life stories and interviews.

The introductory chapter describes focus and purpose of the study. It summarizes the historiography of Sleswig and delineates the theoretical framework in which the study is embedded. For this purpose, the chapter discusses the central theories of national identity, with a special focus on the nature of this sentiment in border regions.

Chapter two delineates the course of Sleswig political history and the central debates that derived from it. It follows the development of the region from Danish border territory via increasingly independent duchy intertwined with neighboring German Holstein to contested borderland in the age of nationalism. Chapter three supplements this constitutional investigation with a long-term perspective on cultural and linguistic conditions.

Chapters four and five form the core of the study. Chapter four explores the nature of national identification in Sleswig by examining three cultural communities at different points during the nineteenth and twentieth centuries. It develops typologies of group identity and highlights the coexistence of various forms of identity within individual communities. Chapter five supplements this macro-analysis with individual biographies in order to illuminate the personal aspects of identity formation.

Chapter six puts Sleswig border identities into a comparative context. The chapter examines the forming of national identities in East Central European zones of transition. This analysis serves to contrast identity formation in Sleswig with wider European phenomena and thus enables us to determine the distinct characteristics of this process in the German-Danish borderlands.

In the final chapter, the different threads of analysis are pulled together. The chapter assesses the nature of national identity in Sleswig and views it from the broader perspective of identity formation on the margins. Before the eyes of history, the sharp edges of national boundaries begin to blur, and several layers of identity surface side by side. This composite character gives national identity in Sleswig special relevance for the international political and scholarly discussion.

Notes

1. The use of the term "Sleswig" is discussed below.
2. The German *Länder* correspond to American states and have extensive legislative and administrative competencies. Between 1867 and 1946, Schleswig-Holstein was not a separate federal state but an administrative subdivision of Prussia.
3. The Danish minority almost universally refers to its home region as South Sleswig (Sydslesvig).
4. Pieter M. Judson, *Guardians of the Nation: Activists on the Language Frontiers of Imperial Austria* (Cambridge, Mass., 2006), xiii.

5. This Shakespearean witticism can be found in Martin Klatt, "Det danske mindretal 1945-1955: Hjemstavnsbevægelse—flæskedanskere—flyktningefjender?" in *En europæisk model? Nationale mindretal i det dansk-tyske grænseland 1945-2000*, ed. Jørgen Kühl (Aabenraa, 2002), 135.
6. Christian Paulsen, *Über Volksthümlichkeit und Staatsrecht des Herzogthums Schleswig* (Kiel, 1832); C. F. Allen, *Haandbog i fædrelandets historie* (Copenhagen, 1840); Nicolaus Falck, *Das Herzogthum Schleswig in seinem gegenwärtigen Verhältnis zu dem Königreich Dänemark und zu dem Herzogthum Holstein* (Schleswig, 1816); and idem, *Die historischen Landes-Rechte in Schleswig und Holstein urkundlich* (Kiel, 1842).
7. C. F. Allen, *Det danske sprogs historie i hertugdømmet Slesvig eller Sønderjylland,* 2 vols. (Copenhagen, 1857-58).
8. Peder Lauridsen was best known for his voluminous *Da Sønderjylland vaagnede*, 8 vols. (Copenhagen, 1909-22), which looked at the origins of the Danish national movement in Sleswig. He researched the ethnographic conditions in his essay "Vort folks sydgrænse," *Sønderjyske Årbøger* (1893): 28-50; 106-148; 253-289. A. D. Jørgensen not only inspired younger researchers but had a deep impact on the Danish sense of self among North Sleswigers through his popular Danish history *Fyrretyve fortællinger af fædrelandets historie* (Copenhagen, 1882). Aage Friis actively supported the Danish North Sleswigers and subsequently published *Det nordslesvigske spørgsmaal, 1864-1879: Aktstykker og breve til belysning af den danske regerings politik*, 6 vols. (Copenhagen, 1921-48).

   Many Danish personalities are known by the initials rather than the full forms of their first and middle names. This practice has largely been retained in this study so as to avoid confusion.
9. For the final delineation of Clausen's border line at the end of World War I, see H. V. Clausen, *Før afgørelsen* (Copenhagen, 1918).
10. Franz von Jessen, ed., *Haandbog i det nordslesvigske spørgsmaals historie* (Copenhagen, 1901).
11. August Sach, *Das Herzogtum Schleswig in seiner ethnographischen und nationalen Entwicklung*, 3 vols. (Halle, 1896-1907).
12. J. G. C. Adler, "Die Volkssprache in dem Herzogthum Schleswig seit 1864," *Zeitschrift der Gesellschaft für Schleswig-Holstein-Lauenburgische Geschichte* 21 (1891): 1-135, and idem, "Die Volkssprache in dem vormaligen Herzogtum Schleswig auf Grund der Sprachenzählung vom 1. Dezember 1905," *Zeitschrift der Gesellschaft für Schleswig-Holsteinische Geschichte* 45 (1915): 55-85.
13. Karl Alnor, *Handbuch zur schleswigschen Frage,* 4 vols. (Neumünster, 1926-41); Franz von Jessen, ed., *Haandbog i det slesvigske spørgsmaals historie*, 3 vols. (Copenhagen, 1935-38).
14. Otto Brandt, *Geschichte Schleswig-Holsteins* (Kiel, 1925); Vilhelm La Cour et al., eds., *Sønderjyllands historie: Fremstillet for det danske folk*, 5 vols. (Copenhagen, 1931-33).
15. Paul Selk, *Die sprachlichen Verhältnisse im deutsch-dänischen Sprachgebiet südlich der Grenze: Eine statistisch-geographische Untersuchung,* 2 vols. (Flensburg, 1937-40).
16. In the meantime, the Institute of Border Region Studies has merged into the University of Southern Denmark and relocated to Sønderborg.
17. See Troels Fink, *Da Sønderjylland blev delt*, 3 vols. (Aabenraa, 1978-79); Johan Peter Noack, *Det tyske mindretal i Nordslesvig under besættelsen* (Copenhagen, 1975); idem, *Det danske mindretal i Sydslesvig 1920-1945*, 2 vols. (Aabenraa, 1989); idem, *Det sydslesvigske grænsespørgsmål 1945-1947*, 2 vols. (Aabenraa, 1991); and idem,

Det danske mindretal i Sydslesvig 1920-1945, 2 vols. (Aabenraa, 1997); Henrik Becker-Christensen, *Dansk mindretalspolitik i Nordslesvig* (Aabenraa, 1984), and idem, *Det tyske mindretal i Nordslesvig 1920-1932*, 2 vols. (Aabenraa, 1990).

18. See Lorenz Rerup, *Grænsen: Fra grænsekamp til sameksistens* (Albertslund, 1969), and idem, *Slesvig og Holsten efter 1830* (Copenhagen, 1982).
19. Hans Schultz Hansen, *Det nordslesvigske landbrug og den danske bevægelse 1880-1914* (Aabenraa, 1985); idem, *Danskheden i Sydslesvig 1840-1918 som folkelig og national bevægelse* (Flensburg, 1990); idem, *"Dansk jord på danske hænder": Foreningen Landeværnet og den nationale jordkamp i Sønderjylland 1927-2002* (Aabenraa, 2002); and idem, *Hjemmetyskheden i Nordslesvig 1840-1867,* 2 vols. (Aabenraa, 2005).
20. See Jørgen Elklit, Johan Peter Noack, and Ole Tonsgaard, *Nationalt tilhørsforhold i Nordslesvig* (Århus, 1978). In English, see also Jørgen Elklit and Ole Tonsgaard, "The Policies of Majority Groups towards National Minorities in the Danish-German Border Region: Why the Differences?" *Ethnic and Racial Studies* 6:4 (1983): 477-491.
21. It might be an interesting exemplification of this tendency that the single contribution by a Danish historian to a recent multi-author history of Schleswig-Holstein is titled "nationalism or democracy" and focuses predominantly on the rise of the national movements. See Hans Schultz Hansen's chapter in Ulrich Lange, ed., *Geschichte Schleswig-Holsteins* (Neumünster, 1996).
22. See Alexander Scharff, *Schleswig-Holstein in der deutschen und nordeuropäischen Geschichte* (Stuttgart, 1969); and idem, *Wesen und Bedeutung der schleswig-holsteinischen Erhebung 1848-1850* (Neumünster, 1978); Erich Hoffmann, *Die Herkunft des Bürgertums in den Städten des Herzogtums Schleswig* (Neumünster, 1953). Hoffmann, born in 1926, is in many ways located between the generations, which also expresses itself in recent publications. Among these, one should list Erich Hoffmann, *Das Nationalitätenproblem in Schleswig* (Neumünster, 1995), which appeared as volume 8:2 of Olaf Klose and Erich Hoffmann, eds., *Geschichte Schleswig-Holsteins*, 8 vols. (Neumünster, 1958-), as well as his contributions to Andreas Kappeler, ed., *The Formation of National Elites* (Aldershot, 1992).
23. Olaf Klose and Erich Hoffmann, eds., *Geschichte Schleswig-Holsteins*, 8 vols. to date (Neumünster, 1958-); Ulrich Lange, ed., *Geschichte Schleswig-Holsteins: Von den Anfängen bis zur Gegenwart* (Neumünster, 1996; 2d ed., 2003).
24. Jürgen Rohweder, *Sprache und Nationalität: Nordschleswig und die Anfänge der dänischen Sprachpolitik* (Glücksburg, 1976); Jürgen Zeh, *Die deutsche Sprachgemeinschaft in Nordschleswig: Ein soziales Gebilde im Wandel* (Stuttgart, 1982); Gösta Toft, *Die bäuerliche Struktur der deutschen Volksgruppe in Nordschleswig* (Flensburg, 1982); Kai Detlev Sievers, ed., *Beiträge zur Frage der ethnischen Identifikation des Bundes Deutscher Nordschleswiger* (Flensburg, 1975).
25. Among those dissertations, some of which were subsequently published in book form, one could list Hilke Lenzing, "Die deutsche Volksgruppe in Dänemark und das nationalsozialistische Deutschland (1933-1939): Ein Beitrag zur Problematik deutscher Volksgruppen während des Dritten Reiches" (Ph.D. diss., University of Bonn, 1973); Carl Boehm, *Die jüngere politische und kulturelle Entwicklung der dänischen nationalen Minderheit in der Bundesrepublik Deutschland und der deutschen nationalen Minderheit im Königreich Dänemark unter besonderer Berücksichtigung des friesischen Bevölkerungsteils in der Bundesrepublik* (Hamburg, 1991); and Sabine Lorek, *Rechtsabrechnung—Retsopgør: Politische Säuberung nach dem Zweiten Weltkrieg in Nordschleswig* (Neumünster, 1998).
26. See Thomas Steensen, *Die friesische Bewegung in Nordfriesland im 19. und 20. Jahrhundert,* 2 vols. (Neumünster, 1986). For a broad introduction to Frisian studies, see

Horst Haider Munske, ed., *Handbuch des Friesischen/Handbook of Frisian Studies* (Tübingen, 2001).

27. Kim Salomon, *Konflikt i grænselandet: Sociale og nationale modsætninger i Sønderjylland 1920-33* (Copenhagen, 1980).
28. Sven Tägil, *Deutschland und die deutsche Minderheit in Nordschleswig: Eine Studie zur deutschen Grenzlandpolitik 1933-1939* (Stockholm, 1970).
29. Sarah Wambaugh, *Plebiscites since the World War* (Washington, D.C., 1933).
30. Lawrence Steefel, *The Schleswig-Holstein Question* (Cambridge, 1932).
31. William Carr, *Schleswig-Holstein 1815-48: A Study in National Conflict* (Manchester, 1963).
32. Michael Byram, *Minority Education and Ethnic Survival: Case Study of a German School in Denmark* (Clevedon, 1986). Another recent publication in English, Norman Berdichevsky's *The Danish-German Border Dispute: Aspects of Cultural and Demographic Politics 1815-2001* (Bethesda, Md., 2002), is more of an opinion piece than a scholarly analysis.
33. Henrik Becker-Christensen and Ulrich Lange, eds., *Geschichte Schleswigs vom frühen Mittelalter bis 1920* (Aabenraa, 1998).
34. Jørgen Kühl, ed., *En europæisk model? Nationale mindretal i det dansk-tyske grænseland 1945-2000* (Aabenraa, 2002). Another cooperative effort was Robert Bohn, Uwe Danker, and Jørgen Kühl, eds., *Nationale mindretal i det dansk-tyske grænseland 1933-1945* (Aabenraa, 2001).
35. Brief overviews that reflect this paradigm have also been published in English. See Jørgen Kühl, *The "Schleswig Experience": The National Minorities in the Danish-German Border Area* (Aabenraa, 1998), and idem, *The National Minorities in the Danish-German Border Region* (Aabenraa, 2003). Useful also for its many quantitative data is Jørgen Kühl and Marc Weller, eds., *Minority Policy in Action: The Bonn-Copenhagen Declarations in a European Context, 1955-2005* (Flensburg and Aabenraa, 2005).
36. Random House Unabridged Dictionary, 2d ed., s.v. "identity."
37. Friedrich Meinecke, *Weltbürgertum und Nationalstaat* (Munich, 1907).
38. For a more recent pronouncedly political definition of nationalism, see John Breuilly, *Nationalism and the State* (New York, 1982).
39. Otto Bauer stressed the historical experience; Walker Connor delineated the importance of ancestry myths.
40. Otto Bauer elaborated extensively on the nationality question in his study *Die Nationalitätenfrage und die Sozialdemokratie* (Vienna, 1907); for his definition, see Otto Bauer, "Die Nationalitätenfrage und die Sozialdemokratie," in *Werkausgabe*, ed. Arbeitsgemeinschaft für die Geschichte der österreichischen Arbeiterbewegung (Vienna, 1975), 1:194. The Stalin quote is taken from his 1913 essay "Marxism and the National Question," printed in English in Joseph Stalin, *The Essential Stalin: Major Theoretical Writings, 1905-52,* ed. by Bruce Franklin (Garden City, N.Y., 1972), 60.
41. Prior to the emergence of modernization theory, the Anglo-American discussion of nationalism had been dominated by a more traditional criterion-based approach. After earlier beginnings with scholars such as Carlton Hayes, research expanded greatly after the end of World War II. [For Hayes, see his study *The Historical Evolution of Modern Nationalism* (New York, 1931).] Hans Kohn interpreted nationalism as "a state of mind, in which the supreme loyalty of the individual is felt to be due the nation-state," which underscored the psychological factors that form a central part of national community. [Hans Kohn, *Nationalism: Its Meaning and History* (Princeton, N.J., 1955), 9.] Louis Snyder defined it as "a condition of mind, feeling, or sentiment of a group living in a well-defined geographical area, speaking a common language, possessing a literature

in which the aspirations of the nation have been expressed, attached to common traditions and common customs, venerating its own heroes, and, in some cases, having a common religion." [Louis Snyder, *The Meaning of Nationalism* (New Brunswick, N.J., 1954), 196f.] Definitions of nationhood that are organized around specific objective prerequisites, such as common territory, language, historical experience, and heritage, represented—and to a certain extent still represent—the most common approach to the theory of nationhood. These definitions can be called "criterional definitions."

42. Karl Deutsch, *Nationalism and Social Communication* (Cambridge, Mass., 1953).
43. This does not mean that the foremost representatives of instrumentalism were necessarily practicing Marxist scholars but rather that their work was visibly influenced by Marxian concepts and methodologies. Instrumentalists such as Gellner could indeed be quite critical of Marxism, particularly on a political plane; at one point, Gellner referred to himself as a "post-Marxist." [Ernst Gellner, "An Alternative Vision," in *Encounters with Nationalism* (Oxford, 1994), 185.]
44. Elie Kedourie, *Nationalism,* 4th ed. (London, 1993).
45. Ernest Gellner, *Nations and Nationalism* (Oxford, 1983). Gellner refined his argument subsequent to the publication of his seminal work and allowed more room for genuine traditions that predate modern nationalism. He remained adamant about his central argument, however, which links nationhood and industrialization. See his thoughts in "From Kinship to Ethnicity," in *Encounters with Nationalism* (Oxford, 1994), 34-46, and in "Nationalism and Marxism," in ibid., 1-19.
46. Benedict Anderson, *Imagined Communities* (London, 1983).
47. Eric Hobsbawm, *Nations and Nationalism since 1780* (Cambridge, England, 1990); and Eric Hobsbawm and Terence Ranger, eds., *The Invention of Tradition* (Cambridge, England, 1983).
48. Walker Connor, *Ethnonationalism* (Princeton, N.J., 1994).
49. See his studies *The Ethnic Origins of Nations* (Oxford, 1986) and *National Identity* (London, 1991).
50. Smith develops this approach most explicitly in his essay "The problem of national identity: ancient, medieval and modern?" *Ethnic and Racial Studies* 17:3 (July 1994): 375-395.
51. John Armstrong formulated his views in a study with the programmatic title *Nations before Nationalism* (Chapel Hill, N.C., 1982).
52. See John Hutchinson's study *The Dynamics of Cultural Nationalism* (London, 1977).
53. See Anthony D. Smith, *National Identity* (Reno, Nev., 1991), 64.
54. Anthony D. Smith, "The Origins of Nations," *Ethnic and Racial Studies* 12:3 (1989): 356.
55. Ernest Renan's belittling attitude toward the French minority languages, which have traditionally been addressed as mere *patois*, can be seen in Eugen Weber, *Peasants into Frenchmen: The Modernization of Rural France, 1870-1914* (Stanford, 1976), 89.
56. Eugen Weber, *Peasants into Frenchmen: The Modernization of Rural France, 1870-1914* (Stanford, 1976).
57. Over the last decades, in turn, the increasing individualization and cultural diversification of the Scandinavian societies was echoed by intensified resistance to policies of income redistribution.
58. Ernest Renan, *Qu'est-ce qu'une nation* (Paris, 1882), 27. See also Anthony D. Smith, "Nationalism and the Historian," in *Ethnicity and Nationalism*, ed. Anthony D. Smith (Leiden, Netherlands, 1992), 61.
59. For a more detailed analysis of interwar Alsatian identity questions, see Philip Bankwitz, *Alsatian Autonomist Leaders 1919-1947* (Lawrence, Kans., 1978).

60. Nancie L. González, *Dollar, Dove and Eagle: One Hundred Years of Palestinian Migration to Honduras* (Ann Arbor, Mich., 1992), 31.
61. For an overview of the anthropologic literature about these developments, see Michael Kearney, "The Local and the Global: The Anthropology of Globalization and Transnationalism," *Annual Review of Anthropology* 24 (1995): 547-565.
62. For examples from other transitional European settings, consult Jeremy King's analysis of Bohemian České Budějovice/Budweis, Richard Blanke's study of Masuria, and Margit Feischmidt's research on Transylvania. See Jeremy King, *Budweisers into Czechs and Germans: A Local History of Bohemian Politics, 1848-1948* (Princeton, 2002); Richard Blanke, *Polish-speaking Germans? Language and National Identity among the Masurians since 1871* (Cologne, 2001); Margit Feischmidt, *Ethnizität als Konstruktion und Alltagskultur im siebenbürgischen Cluj* (Münster, 2003). See also Maria Bucur and Nancy M. Wingfield, eds., *Staging the Past: The Politics of Commemoration in Habsburg Central Europe, 1848 to the Present* (West Lafayette, 2001).
63. J. R. V. Prescott, *Political Frontiers and Boundaries* (London, 1987), 1.
64. See Reinhard Schneider, "Lineare Grenzen: Vom frühen zum späten Mittelalter," in *Grenzen und Grenzregionen*, ed. Wolfgang Haubrichs and Reinhard Schneider (Saarbrücken, 1994), 51-68.
65. *Random House College Dictionary*, 2d ed., s.v. "border."
66. For the categorization below, see Oscar J. Mártinez, *Border People: Life and Society in the U.S.-Mexico Borderlands* (Tucson, Ariz., 1994), 5-10.
67. C. S. Momoh's categorization into minimal borderlands, zero borderlands, and maximal borderlands parallels certain aspects of Mártinez's typology. See C. S. Momoh, "A Critique of Borderland Theories," in *Borderlands in Africa*, ed. Anthony I. Asiwaju and Peter O. Adenyi (Lagos, 1989), 51-61.
68. Among the foremost authorities on the U.S.-Mexican borderlands is Oscar J Mártinez; see especially Oscar J. Mártinez, *Border People: Life and Society in the U.S.-Mexico Borderlands* (Tucson, 1994). For multidisciplinary overviews of the various issues and approaches, consult Oscar J. Mártinez, ed., *U.S.-Mexico Borderlands: Historical and Contemporary Perspectives* (Wilmington, Del., 1996); Stanley R. Ross, ed., *Views across the Border* (Albuquerque, 1978); and David Spener and Kathleen Staudt, eds., *The U.S.-Mexico Border: Transcending Divisions, Contesting Identities* (Boulder, Colo., 1998). For an introduction to the special conditions faced by undocumented immigrant populations, see Linda Chavez, *Shadowed Lives: Undocumented Immigrants in American Society* (Fort Worth, 1992).
69. In the United States, the Association of Borderlands Scholars (ABS) was established in 1976; it began publishing the *Journal of Borderlands Studies* in 1985. Additional institutions can be found in Milton H. Jamail and Margo Gutiérrez, eds., *The Border Guide: Institutions and Organizations of the United States-Mexico Borderlands* (Austin, 1992).
70. As a consequence, there have been many suggestions for a fundamental redrawing of African boundaries. See for example Makua wa Mutua, "Redrawing the Map along African Lines," *Boston Globe,* 22 September 1994.
71. For an introduction to the wider theoretical and empirical aspects of Africa's borders and state system, see Paul Nugent and Anthony I. Asiwaju, eds., *African Boundaries: Barriers, Conduits and Opportunities* (London, 1996), and Anthony I. Asiwaju and Peter O. Adeniyi, eds., *Borderlands in Africa: A Multidisciplinary and Comparative Focus on Nigeria and West Africa* (Lagos, 1989). For an examination of transboundary ties, see W. F. S. Miles, *Hausaland Divided: Colonialism and Independence in Nigeria*

and Niger (Ithaca, N.Y., 1994), and Anthony I. Asiwaju, ed., *Partitioned Africans: Ethnic Relations Across Africa's International Boundaries, 1884-1984* (London, 1985).

72. Ieuan Griffiths, "Permeable Boundaries in Africa," in *African Boundaries: Barriers, Conduits and Opportunities,* ed. Paul Nugent and Anthony I. Asiwaju (London, 1996), 70.
73. The identity of one of the best-known pastoralist people in Africa is examined in Thomas Spear and Richard Waller, eds., *Being Maasai: Ethnicity and Identity in East Africa* (London, 1993).
74. See Paul Nugent, "Arbitrary Lines and the People's Minds: A Dissenting View on Colonial Boundaries in West Africa," in *African Boundaries: Barriers, Conduits and Opportunities,* ed. Paul Nugent and Anthony I. Asiwaju (London, 1996), 35-67.
75. See his essay "Borderlands in Africa: A Comparative Research Perspective with Particular Reference to Western Europe," in *African Boundaries: Barriers, Conduits and Opportunities,* ed. Paul Nugent and Anthony I. Asiwaju (London, 1996), 253-265.
76. For a comparison of African and European transboundary issues, see also Anthony I. Asiwaju, ed., *Transfrontier Regionalism: Perspectives on the European Union and Post-Colonial Africa with Special Reference to Borgu* (Ibadan, Nigeria, 1999).
77. For a look at the framework of such cooperative ventures, consult Bernd Groß and Peter Schmitt-Egner, *Europas kooperierende Regionen: Rahmenbedingungen und Praxis transnationaler Zusammenarbeit deutscher Grenzregionen in Europa* (Baden-Baden, 1994).
78. In their own writings, euregio and some of the other regional cooperations spell their names in all capital letters, but since these names are not acronyms, this practice does not seem appropriate in scholarly contexts.
79. For focus and membership of the association, see its Web site, currently at http://www.aebr.net.
80. For an introduction to German-Danish transborder initiatives, see Hayo Herrmann, "Situation und Entwicklung der deutsch-dänischen Grenzräume und insbesondere des Grenzraumes Sønderjylland-Schleswig," *Grenzfriedenshefte* 53:3 (2005): 227-236.
81. Some important challenges and modifications to instrumentalist theory are gathered in John A. Hall, ed., *The State of the Nation: Ernest Gellner and the Theory of Nationalism* (Cambridge, England, 1998),
82. Miroslav Hroch, "Real and Constructed: The Nature of the Nation," in *The State of the Nation,* ed. John A. Hall (Cambridge, England, 1998), 91-106. Hroch had already voiced his concerns about contemporary theories of nationalism in "From National Movements to the Fully-Formed Nation," *New Left Review* 198 (1993): 3-20.
83. Rogers Brubaker and Frederick Cooper, "Beyond 'Identity'," *Theory and Society* 29:1 (2000): 1-47.

CHAPTER TWO

Political Evolution and Points of Contention

The Course of Sleswig History

The history of Sleswig and its relations to Holstein and Denmark holds a reputation for being all but intractable. In the nineteenth century, the so-called Schleswig-Holstein question marred the lives of diplomats and politicians, and British statesman Lord Palmerston is widely quoted as calling it "so complicated that only three men in Europe have ever understood it. One was Prince Albert, who is dead. The second was a German professor, and he became mad. I am the third, and I have forgotten all about it."[1] This reputation may explain why modern analyses of this subject in English are exceedingly rare and international familiarity with its intricacies remains correspondingly small. At the same time, it makes it all the more important to introduce an investigation of identity formation in Sleswig with a cogent delineation of its political and cultural framework.

Yet the need to provide the requisite empirical knowledge is not the only rationale for this chapter. The past formed a crucial aspect of the national debate in the nineteenth and twentieth centuries. Not only scholars, but also politicians, journalists, and—following a period of educational mobilization—everyday people debated the fine points of territorial dependencies and feudal vassalage. "Denmark to the Eider" and "Sleswig-Holstein undivided" became the battle cries of competing national movements, and in the minds of their propagators, these were not merely present-day political demands, but ancient rights anchored in the medieval origins of the Kingdom of Denmark on the one hand and the almost equally distant Treaty of Ribe on the other. Past and present merged in the political debate, and without understanding the historical origins of the political arguments used, we might feel as overwhelmed and exasperated as the contemporaries of Lord Palmerston.

This does not mean that we must take the historicist slogans at face value. When this chapter examines the formation of an increasingly autonomous political entity within the medieval Danish kingdom, the integration of this entity with the neighboring German territory of Holstein under the roof of the Danish composite monarchy, and the subsequent implications of this bridging of political—as well as cultural—boundaries in an era of nation-states, it does not assign historical legitimacy. The national conflict of the 1800s was not about history, but about contemporary interests and identities. These interests and identities, however, cannot be understood without their social and political preconditions. By examining the historical background, we also increase our understanding of the actions and arguments of the political actors that invoked it.

Before There Was a Sleswig: South Jutland at the Dawn of History

In the Jutland peninsula, the European mainland projects far into the Scandinavian world, which is otherwise separated from the continent by the Baltic Sea and the North Sea. This geographical location has also expressed itself in the area's historical experience.[2] Prior to the period of migrations, much of Jutland formed a zone of passage between West and North Germanic populations.[3] In fact, the peninsula and its immediate vicinity formed the center of prehistoric Germanic Europe. From this core area, northern Europe's major cultural group gradually expanded in all directions and became a significant factor in the continent's political and cultural development.

The tumultuous centuries that followed the incursion of the Huns and the decline of Roman authority witnessed the transformation of northern Europe and the origins of medieval society. Many Germanic population groups left their homelands, usually to move toward the south and west into the disintegrating Roman empire. As a consequence, western Slavs gradually took over regions that had become more sparsely populated.

The Jutland peninsula, too, felt the impact of these developments. The departure of populations that came to be known as Anglo-Saxons on the British Isles removed an important link in the dialectal continuum of the Germanic linguistic sphere. The partially depopulated landscapes of southern Jutland were replenished with new arrivals, predominantly from the north. At the same time, the Slavic Obotrites reached the northwestern apex of their expansion, as they pushed into the neighborhood of Saxons and Dano-Jutlanders and settled in eastern Holstein.[4] The result was the most visible linguistic divide within Germanic Europe, establishing a marked line between the budding Scandinavian and German cultural zones.

At that historic juncture, the territory later designated as Sleswig fell squarely into the Scandinavian political sphere. Around the year 800, the differences between the continental Germanic populations and their northern neighbors became further accentuated when the Saxons, bordering Denmark to the south, were subjugated and Christianized by the Frankish king Charlemagne. In 811, the Eider River was mentioned as the boundary between the realms of Charlemagne and the Danish king Hemming. Southward all the way to Italy and Spain, a powerful new political structure had taken shape. Toward the north, the gradually forming Danish monarchy came to encompass the lowlands of southern Scandinavia.

The later Sleswig formed the southern border region of the Danish realm. Although it was inhabited predominantly by Danish Jutlanders, the growing Frisian population along its southwestern seashore set it slightly apart from the rest of Denmark. Even more important for the formation of distinct political structures, however, was the area's location at the border. Jutland separated into two administrative entities, which were centered on the important assembly places of Viborg in the north and Urnehoved in the south. The area between the river Kongeå and the southern border was increasingly referred to as Sønderjylland, or South Jutland. It contained the important defensive structure called Dannevirke, which was gradually expanded between the eighth and twelfth centuries to prevent incursions from the south.[5]

The Beginnings of the Duchy of Sleswig

South Jutland's proximity to the powerful Frankish and subsequently Holy Roman Empire on the one hand and the unruly and bellicose Wagrian Slavs on the other made it advisable to establish an efficient regional administration. Since the eleventh century, the sources mention counts, or jarls, of South Jutland. When Knud Lavard rose to this position in 1115, he soon distinguished himself as one of the foremost political figures of early South Jutland history.[6] By assuming leadership of the neighboring Slavic groups, he came into conflict with his own king, on whose behest he was murdered in 1131. For the territory's constitutional development, it was most important that Knud Lavard assumed the title of duke. Even though this position was not yet affixed specifically to South Jutland, it furthered the transformation of the border region into a self-sufficient political entity.

From the early thirteenth century, at the latest, South Jutland was universally recognized as a duchy.[7] The exact meaning of this new status remained open to interpretation, as did the relationship between ducal and central authority. The dukes were commonly Danish princes and held the ambition to achieve parity with their royal siblings. Following the death of King Valdemar II in 1241, Duke Abel, in particular, enhanced the standing of his dynasty.

The dukes increasingly asserted their independence. The powers of the Danish king were continually reduced, and South Jutland changed from being an integral part of the Danish kingdom to an autonomous territory intertwined with it. Following the defeat of King Christopher II at the battle of Hesterberg in 1326, the new Danish monarch Valdemar III even had to pledge that kingdom and duchy never would be united under a common ruler (*constitutio valdemariana*).[8] Although this concession born out of defeat did not endure, it marked a further stepping stone in the autonomization of South Jutland.

The designation Jutland or South Jutland was gradually overshadowed by the designation Sleswig, in which the name of the capital city was extended to the entire territory. At first, the various labels existed side by side. Even though Danish historians such as Saxo Grammaticus and Svend Aggesen used Sleswig as a territorial name around 1200, the term became truly prevalent in the late 1300s.[9]

At the same time, the Danish border territory became politically intertwined with its German counterpart to the south. Common interests prevailed among the political elites. The dukes of South Jutland needed outside support in their conflict with the Danish crown. The counts of Holstein gladly provided this support, since they preferred a medium-sized duchy for a neighbor, instead of a powerful kingdom.

Aristocrats from Holstein expanded their influence, which entailed growing migration and cultural penetration from the south. Germanization was accelerated when Holstein's Schauenburg dynasty directly assumed the governance of Sleswig in 1386. Sleswig and Holstein were thus united under the same ruler. This transnational integration gave reason for concern in Denmark, whose political elites attempted to reassert their sovereignty over Sleswig. Although Duke Adolf won hereditary status for his fief in 1440, his childless death nineteen years later reopened the discussion about Sleswig's position within the Danish realm and about its relationship with Holstein.

Sleswig and Holstein United within the Danish Composite Monarchy

In 1459, the continued integration of Sleswig and Holstein faced a serious challenge. There was no common heir to all the dominions left behind by Adolf VIII. Different inheritors stood to assume power, and the duchy of Sleswig could easily have reverted to the Danish crown. At this critical juncture, the joint noble representatives of Sleswig and Holstein, the so-called *Ritterschaft*, moved to the forefront. They had a political and economic interest in preserving the close ties between the territories and took up negotiations with heirs and potential successors.

In March 1460, the noble councils elected Denmark's King Christian I duke of Sleswig and count of Holstein. In exchange, the new ruler granted extensive privileges to the territories and especially their estates.[10] Sleswig and Holstein retained wide autonomy, including separate taxation, currency, and jurisdiction. Only indigenous aristocrats were to be eligible for government positions. In all important matters, the ruler was to consult the noble council. Finally, in a stipulation that received its foremost impact when the nineteenth-century Sleswig-Holstein movement transferred it into a very different political context, the territories were to remain "forever united and indivisible."[11] Thus, the nobles had secured their vital role in the future administration of the territories in exchange for electing their ruler—although they had no constitutional mandate for this act.

Subsequent to the Treaty of Ribe and its accompanying Kiel amendment, Sleswig and Holstein were united in a personal union with the Danish kingdom. They were also linked with each other and—following Holstein's elevation to the rank of a duchy in 1474—increasingly seen as the German duchies within the wider Danish realm. German assumed the role of official language in Sleswig, although Danish remained the dominant vernacular in the northern and, for a long time, also in the middle sections of the duchy.

Not all the stipulations of the Treaty of Ribe remained in force. Just as the election of the Danish king as duke of Sleswig had negated the *constitutio valdemariana*, the guarantees issued at Ribe could not prevent the subsequent partition of the duchies between various princes and dynastic branches. In 1490, the reign of the duchies was shared between the two sons of Christian I, Frederick and John, and in 1544, the duchies were even divided threefold.[12] The legal provisions nonetheless helped the estates preserve a basic level of coherence and integration amongst the often-shifting political domains. Particularly the diet, the common estates of clergy, nobility, and towns, remained an integrative force in the period of territorial division.

In 1581, the complicated administrative structure in the duchies was simplified. Governance of the duchies was restricted to two main branches—a royal and a ducal. Other branches of the Oldenburg dynasty retained minor independent domains, but they no longer governed the duchies and effectively descended to the rank of local magnates. Thus, the kings of Denmark ruled one segment of Sleswig and Holstein and the dukes of Gottorp the other.[13] The ensuing rivalry dominated domestic affairs for the following centuries and repeatedly rose to the level of Scandinavian and even European politics.

The two ruling houses in the duchies pursued diametrically opposed long-term goals. The royal branch tried to reestablish central control over the ducal lands and reduce the house of Gottorp to a feudal vassal under the Danish crown. The dukes, in contrast, desired full sovereignty for their possessions, in line with the increasing independence enjoyed by the territorial princes of the Holy Roman Empire.

In this conflict, the much weaker dukes were dependent on outside support, which they received from Denmark's long-time adversary, Sweden. Throughout much of the seventeenth century, the dukes of Gottorp profited from their ally's military victories. Following the disastrous Treaty of Roskilde in 1658, in which Denmark forfeited Skåne and its other historic possessions on the Scandinavian peninsula, the Danish king had to grant full sovereignty to ducal Sleswig in the Treaty of Copenhagen.[14] In turn, the king also lifted the feudal bonds for his own possessions in the duchy, making it sovereign in its entirety.

The successes achieved by the dukes of Gottorp reinforced their dependence on Sweden, however, because they served as a constant irritant to the Danish crown. In 1675, King Christian V of Denmark compelled the ducal councils to surrender the territory's sovereignty, and in 1684, he declared its outright annexation. Both times, the dukes were only restituted due to the favorable turns of wider international conflicts.

At the beginning of the eighteenth century, the good fortune of the house of Gottorp came to an end. Sweden's defeat in the Great Northern War also meant the end of Gottorp rule in Sleswig. In 1713, King Frederick IV annexed all Gottorp lands, and in the peace treaties of 1720, the international powers confirmed this act in respect to Sleswig. Thus, Sleswig was reunited under the Danish king, whereas Holstein remained divided in a royal and a ducal section.

Like the Treaty of Ribe, the absorption of ducal Sleswig formed a major point of contention during the national conflict of the nineteenth century. In August 1721, Frederick IV issued a decree of incorporation, in which he declared his intention to unite and incorporate the ducal parts of Sleswig with his own.[15] The following month, prelates, knights, and noble estate owners were assembled to affirm the new order. Whether this act merely signified the unification of ducal and royal Sleswig, in other words, the consolidation of Sleswig as an autonomous possession of the Danish king, or entailed an outright incorporation into Denmark, remained long disputed among Danish and German scholars.

The king clearly wanted to establish his rule as comprehensively as possible. Officials from the central government initially replaced many local dignitaries, and numerous reforms modernized Sleswig—and royal Holstein—along the same lines as Denmark proper. Yet no full homogenization of Danish and Sleswigian conditions took place, and the duchy retained an autonomous legal, administrative, and—with respect to such important aspects as customs and currency—also economic status. The German Chancellery in Copenhagen was the king's foremost instrument in the governing of Sleswig as well as of royal Holstein. The nexus between the noble representations of Sleswig and Holstein was downgraded, however, and their privileges were confirmed separately. By establishing a "continual deputation" of prelates and nobles from both duchies in 1775, the estates, in turn, emphasized their unity.

In the course of the eighteenth century, the Danish crown consolidated its control of the duchies. Until 1779, the possessions of the non-governing Sønderborg branch of the Oldenburgs were incorporated into royal Sleswig. Even the dispute with the dukes of Gottorp was resolved in Denmark's favor. Initially, this outcome had seemed unlikely. Duke Karl Frederick never resigned himself to the loss of his Sleswigian possessions. He was able to establish dynastic ties to Sweden and, more ominously for Denmark at this historical juncture, the czars in St. Petersburg. When his son assumed the Russian throne in 1761 as Peter III, he seemed poised to reclaim his paternal dominions. Peter's swift overthrow and assassination opened the door for an understanding, however. In the 1773 Treaty of Czarskoje Selo, the Russian grand prince Paul exchanged his possessions in Holstein for Oldenburg and Delmenhorst in northwestern Germany. With insignificant exceptions, the Danish monarch again ruled directly over all of Sleswig and Holstein.

The final decades of the eighteenth century marked the autumn glow of the Danish composite monarchy. The duchies were joined with the kingdoms of Denmark and Norway in a geographically far-flung dynastic conglomerate, in which the central government in Copenhagen became more determined and successful at initiating parallel developments and thus increasing commonality. The period of recurrent wars seemed to have passed. Political reforms as well as new enterprises contributed to an economic upswing, which supported a growth in population as well. The abolishment of serfdom opened new opportunities for hitherto restricted segments of the rural population. These developments reinforced popular attachment to monarchy and realm.

The Tumultuous Long Century: Sleswig from the French Revolution to World War I

The seeming consolidation of the Danish composite monarchy came to an end when it was drawn into the encompassing European conflict that followed the French Revolution. During the initial phase of the war, the Danish economy continued to flourish, because the country's neutrality and the increased demand for its goods and means of transportation expanded opportunities for trade and economic growth. Denmark forged alliances with other neutrals, initially Sweden, subsequently also Russia, to protect its shipping interests against encroachments from the major warring powers.

In the long run, however, the country proved unable to remain neutral in a confrontation that engulfed the continent. The trade wars between Britain and France affected everyone. In 1801, in a step directed against vigorous neutral cooperation, a British fleet crossed the sea passages to the Baltic and successfully confronted the Danish defenders outside Copenhagen. A more dramatic encounter was to follow six years later. Trying to preempt possible French ambitions to avail themselves of Danish naval capacities, the British revisited Copenhagen, bombarded the city, and captured most of the Danish fleet. As a consequence, Denmark was driven into an alliance with Napoleonic France, against which, deprived of its navy, it could no longer have put up noteworthy resistance.

Denmark thus shared the fate of France and found itself on the losing side of the Napoleonic Wars. This defeat exacted a bitter price. In order to compensate Sweden—in the end among the victors—for the loss of Finland, Denmark had to surrender sovereignty over Norway in the 1814 Treaty of Kiel. After four centuries, the union between Denmark and Norway had ended. Denmark was downgraded to a minor power, ever watchful of the foreign-policy constellations in its geographic vicinity. The economic collapse of 1813, in which the legal tender was devalued to one-tenth of its value, only completed the tribulations that had befallen Danish society.

In more ways than one, the changing fortunes of the international war reverberated in the duchies. The dissolution of the Holy Roman Empire in 1806 left the fate of Holstein unclear. King Frederick VI decided to avail himself of this opportunity to amalgamate also this duchy more directly with the Danish crown. Although this action aligned the constitutional status of Sleswig and Holstein, its real intent was the assimilation of both duchies into the Danish orbit. This objective expressed itself in attempts to strengthen the role of the Danish language, especially in Sleswig. Wartime priorities soon prevented further implementation of such measures, however.

In 1815, Holstein regained its distinct position by being included in the German Confederation. This body was a concession to the national-liberal forces in the German states, whose calls for a rejuvenated German empire went unheeded. In the Treaty of Chaumont, the allies had expressed their intent to create a "Germany composed of sovereign princes unified by a federal bond that shall assure and guarantee the independence of Germany."[16] Thus, Holstein and the tiny duchy of Lauenburg on the lower Elbe—the only compensation Denmark received for its extensive territorial losses—became members of a loose association of German states, subject to its laws and regulations.

This political affiliation assumed immediate relevance as the confederation's legal framework, the Federal Act, had demanded the implementation of estatist constitutions in all member states. The ambiguous stipulation, which was alternately interpreted as a return to the medieval estate system or a call for popular representation, became interwoven with the budding conflict between the Danish government and the Sleswig-Holstein movement. The local nobility used this federal obligation to call for a common constitution for Sleswig and Holstein. The Danish court was merely ready to negotiate about Holstein and Lauenburg.

In the ensuing controversy, the nobility managed to forge bonds with German-oriented liberals of middle-class background, who shared the former's interest in common institutions for both duchies. The Danish king profited from the conservative turn in European diplomacy. When the nobility sought the support of the German Confederation and turned to its federal assembly in 1822, its request was denied. The major German powers did not yet follow national priorities, but were more concerned with preserving the existing monarchic order.

For the next few decades, the overall appearance of public life in the duchies remained calm, and the basic political and administrative structure changed little. Through decrees in 1831 and 1834, the king finally instituted the long-debated estatist constitution, which provided for separate assemblies for the Danish islands, Jutland, Sleswig, and Holstein. These bodies had predominantly consultative powers and were elected by a tiny minority of the overall population. Still, they witnessed the formation of a structured and informed political debate.

Not least of all, it was the national question that surfaced both within and outside the new political institutions. Previously, the cultural diversity of Sleswig had not created much tension. In the nineteenth century, however, the duchy became the center of a drawn-out conflict. In 1830, news from the upheavals on the continent reached the duchies, and Uwe Jens Lornsen's demands for a dual monarchy with equal status for a Danish kingdom and German-dominated duchies foreshadowed subsequent confrontations.[17] The Sleswig-Holstein movement spread rapidly among the teachers and students at the university in Kiel. Its protagonists emphasized the distinction between the united duchies on the one hand and the Danish kingdom on the other and frequently sympathized with the drive for German unification. At the same time, Danish North Sleswigers began to make their voices heard. They rejected the equation of German and Sleswigian that so often characterized Sleswig-Holstein activism and demanded equal status for German and Danish in the duchy's public life, as well as a common constitution for Sleswig and the kingdom.[18]

In 1848, the conflicting visions clashed openly. Again, a revolutionary wave spread from France to many European regions. It reached the duchies from both the north and the south. In Denmark, a national-liberal government ended the absolutist reign; it desired to integrate Sleswig as fully as possible into the kingdom. At the same time, the Sleswig-Holstein movement attached itself to the revolutionary upsurge in the German lands. On 24 March, a provisional government was formed in Kiel. Although it claimed to defend the monarchy as well as the traditional rights of the duchies against the revolutionary developments in Copenhagen, the latter lay closer to its heart. The provisional government found support in Holstein, in the southern half of Sleswig, and in many of the urban centers. Most Danish-speaking North Sleswigers rejected it, however, as did many inhabitants of Flensburg.

Before long, the Sleswig-Holstein debate rose to the level of European politics. On their own, the Sleswig-Holsteiners proved no match militarily for the better-trained Danish troops. Whenever units from other German territories intervened in the conflict, the tide turned. Thus, the fortunes of the German revolution and the intervention of international powers decided the outcome of the three-year conflict.

After initial support for the Sleswig-Holstein cause, the Prussian king returned to a more conservative position, which reflected the reversals of the revolutionary forces in Prussia and Germany. At the same time, Russia, in particular, pressured the German states to withdraw their support for the insurgent duchies. After repeated international agreements and ceasefires, Danish and Sleswig-Holstein forces met in a final encounter in the summer of 1850. Militarily, the Danish victory at Idstedt sealed the fate of the uprising.

In the international London Protocol of 1852, as well as in preceding communications between Denmark and the German powers of Austria and Prussia, the nature of the Danish composite monarchy was delineated.[19] The integrity of the monarchy as well as its line of succession was guaranteed; the German Confederation resumed its role in Holstein and Lauenburg. Sleswig was not to be incorporated into the kingdom of Denmark. To a large extent, the future meant a return to the past.

Neither Danish- nor German-oriented liberals could be satisfied. In regard to the Sleswig-Holstein movement, this assessment is unequivocal. Its hopes for independence were dashed, most of its officials and military leaders replaced, sometimes even forced into exile. Sleswig was more detached from Holstein, not to mention Germany, than it had been in a long time.

The new situation contained some bright spots for the Eiderdanes, who desired Sleswig's separation from Holstein and its ultimate amalgamation with Denmark proper.[20] The administrative ties between the duchies were reduced. Sleswig received a common currency with Denmark, and in August 1850, the customs border was moved from the Kongeå to the Eider.[21] This tied Sleswig more closely to the Danish economic sphere and temporarily divided the duchies through a customs border.[22] In addition, the government's new language policy attempted to reverse the linguistic trend in central Sleswig through political measures in support of Danish.

Nonetheless, the Danish national-liberals remained discontented. They had hoped that Denmark's apparent military victory would be used to reintegrate Sleswig fully into the Danish kingdom. More so than the conservative establishment, they understood that a return to the composite monarchy did not solve the national conflict but only delayed its resolution. At the same time, the national-liberals misjudged the international framework of Denmark's political restitution. It was primarily the diplomatic intervention of the great powers, especially Russia, that had saved the Danish monarchy, and without this support, control of the duchies would be imperiled anew.

For the next decade, the royal government attempted to consolidate its power and to steer a course tolerable to public opinion in Denmark, in the duchies, and abroad. Attempts to establish a common constitution in accordance with the postwar agreements failed. German-minded deputies in the Holstein and Sleswig assemblies demanded the restoration of close ties between the duchies, and the German Confederation watched over the developments in its member states of Holstein and Lauenburg. The Danish national-liberals, in turn, continued their efforts toward a closer union of Sleswig and the kingdom.

In 1863, the Danish government, under Prime Minister Carl Christian Hall, regarded conditions favorable for a unilateral solution of the conflict. The path of negotiation with the Sleswig-Holsteiners seemed exhausted. The Polish revolt promised to keep Russia occupied and divert the attention of Prussia and other European powers. Fueled by a spirit of Scandinavianism, leading Swedish political figures, including King Karl XV and his foreign secretary Manderström, advocated closer political and military ties between the Scandinavian powers. In March, Holstein and Lauenburg were officially excluded from the Danish constitutional framework, and on 13 November, parliament adopted the government's proposal for a new joint constitution for Denmark and Sleswig.

The negative international reaction was predictable. The situation was complicated further when Denmark's King Frederick VII died two days later, extinguishing the male lineage of the family. Although the line of succession had been settled by the major powers in the London Protocol, the Augustenburg branch of the ruling house, pragmatically cooperating with the Sleswig-Holstein movement, asserted its own right to the duchies. Whereas Christian IX of Glücksburg reluctantly signed the November constitution and was identified with the Danish cause, the Augustenburg claim became a *cause célèbre* among German liberals.

In December, troops from Hanover and Saxony occupied Holstein in the name of the German Confederation. It was Prussia's Prime Minister Otto von Bismarck, however, who dominated the subsequent developments. Whereas the German public favored a largely independent Sleswig-Holstein under Augustenburg rule, Bismarck's policy followed the agreements of 1851/52. On 16 January 1864, Prussia and Austria demanded that the common constitution be revoked within 48 hours. When Denmark proved unable and unwilling to fully comply with this demand, the die had been cast. Last minute efforts by the international powers, especially Britain, to solve the dispute through multilateral negotiations failed. On 1 February, Austrian and Prussian troops advanced into Sleswig.

The military campaign proceeded quickly and lopsidedly. By late April, the Danish troops had withdrawn from mainland Sleswig. The signatories of the 1852 London Protocol assembled anew in the British capital. The Danish government had not yet fully recognized the severity of its predicament, however, and no agreement could be reached. The collapse of the London conference in late June also brought the accompanying truce to an end. When Prussian troops conquered the island of Als and threatened the country's core islands, Danish resistance collapsed. A more conservative new government tried to save what could be saved, but it was too late. In the Treaty of Vienna, Denmark had to cede sovereignty over Sleswig, Holstein, and Lauenburg to Austria and Prussia. Only a few northern border districts fell to Denmark in exchange for the royal enclaves further south.[23]

The war of 1864 gave rise to a Danish national trauma. Not only did it mark the final step in the reduction of Denmark from a sizable multinational empire to a peripheral nation-state with North Atlantic outposts, but it also convinced the Danes of their powerlessness vis-à-vis their increasingly more integrated German neighbor to the south. That Denmark was in no position to antagonize this neighbor, unless it enjoyed the full support of great powers, became an axiom of Danish foreign policy for almost a century to come.

Through the Treaty of Vienna, Sleswig had for the first time completely left the Danish political framework. Its future position was yet undetermined and intimately tied in with the larger German question. For the following two years, Prussia and Austria shared uneasily in the administration of Sleswig and Holstein.[24] Public opinion throughout the duchies and most of Germany favored the creation of an independent principality under Augustenburg rule. When Austria, frustrated about Prussian unwillingness to provide adequate compensation for concessions in the duchies, took up this popular cause, Bismarck opted for a military solution. The Prussian victory at Königgrätz in the summer of 1866 decided the future not only of Germany in its entirety, but also more specifically of Sleswig and Holstein.

In the Treaty of Prague that concluded the war, the Austrian emperor ceded all rights in Sleswig and Holstein to the king of Prussia.[25] In the subsequent year, the duchies were formally incorporated into Prussia. They joined the newly formed German empire as a Prussian province in 1871.

For almost half a century, all of Sleswig shared in the ups and downs of the German nation-state. The province of Sleswig-Holstein underwent a thorough modernization of its administrative structure. Accelerated industrialization and investment improved the economic base. The Kiel Canal placed the area in the center of northern European sea transport.

Politically, the picture was more complex. Sleswig enjoyed the universal male suffrage established in the German empire. A broad and flourishing party system ensued. The government, however, did not yet rest on the principle of parliamentarism; the political parties controlled rather than determined governmental policy. In contrast to the federal parliament, the Prussian diet rested on a three-class system of voting that favored the wealthy and the landed aristocracy.

Politics in Sleswig-Holstein were long dominated by parties in opposition to the central government. The Progressives stood in the tradition of liberal Sleswig-Holsteinism and were reluctant to accept incorporation into Prussia. The Social Democrats established themselves early. After the restrictions on their activities were lifted in 1890, they became the strongest electoral force. North Sleswig politics was dominated by the unwavering opposition of the Danish minority to the new border.

It was this last conflict that reverberated beyond regional politics. At the insistence of Emperor Napoleon III, the 1866 Treaty of Prague made allowances for border adjustments in agreement with popular sentiment.[26] Initial negotiations between Prussia and Denmark failed to reach agreement on the area affected as well as on possible protections for a German minority, and in 1878, Prussia and Austria resolved to lift the clause. To the Danish minority, however, it remained an unalterable legal confirmation of its right to self-determination.

In the elections of 1867, Danish candidates prevailed all the way down to the southern environs of Flensburg. In 1871, they still attained more than twenty percent of the provincial vote.[27] Due to such factors as migration, changing social and ideological priorities, as well as political adaptation and resignation, this strong position could not be defended. After 1884, the Danish vote never again passed the ten percent mark. The decline was especially steep in Flensburg and the remainder of central Sleswig, whereas the Danish movement largely retained its hold over rural North Sleswig. German governmental pressure weakened the minority numerically but strengthened its resolve.

In the early twentieth century, Sleswig had experienced several decades under German rule. The Danish minority had consolidated itself in its northern domains, but expectations of an imminent border revision seemed unrealistic. Both Danish-oriented Sleswigers and nationalist circles in Denmark retained such hopes, but official Denmark acted pragmatically and relented on the plebiscite question in exchange for better protections for Danish Sleswigers.

One Sleswig No More: The Borderlands since World War I

The outbreak of World War I changed the international situation. As long as German troops were victorious, Denmark had to contain the widespread displeasure with the sacrifices inflicted on Danish-minded conscripts and the ensuing calls for border revisions. The impending German defeat in 1918, however, put the Sleswig question back on the table of European politics.

In the fall of 1918, Danish and German political circles began to discuss the future of North Sleswig. On 14 November, the republican German government expressed its willingness to apply the principle of national self-determination in North Sleswig. Urged on by the Danish minority, Denmark subsequently turned to the victorious Allies in Versailles, who included the Sleswig question in the German peace settlement.

Articles 109-114 of the Treaty of Versailles provided for separate plebiscites in northern and central Sleswig.[28] The first zone, which was located north of a line connecting the northern suburbs of Flensburg with the southern outskirts of Tønder and Højer, supported inclusion in Denmark in an *en bloc* vote on 10 February 1920. The majority amounted to almost 75 percent. On 14 March, approximately 80 percent of the voters in zone 2 opted for Germany. In this region, which included the city of Flensburg, the results were to be considered on a local basis. Due to near universal German majorities, the local focus had no territorial repercussions. The international powers divided Sleswig along the line of demarcation between the two zones. Around 4,000 square kilometers with a population of 163,000 were turned over to Danish sovereignty.

Following the peace settlement of World War I, the unified history of Sleswig had come to an end. After many centuries as a multiethnic link between different cultural spheres, the old duchy had been torn asunder by modern concepts of nationalism. Nonetheless, the ties were not completely broken. Sleswig history was also henceforth not just ordinary German and Danish history, because there were people on both sides of the border whose self-identification transgressed the political divide.

In the two plebiscites, approximately 20 to 25 percent of the voters had supported a different outcome. These groups formed the starting point for the German minority in Denmark and the new Danish minority in Germany. In the interwar era, the German minority was most relevant numerically and politically. Its continued strength in border regions that had produced German majorities in the plebiscites sustained its hope for eventual border revisions. The Danish minority south of the border, on the other hand, had to regroup on a more modest level following its separation from Danish North Sleswig. Finally, the Frisian population experienced an internal division. Whereas most Frisians continued to identify with a German-oriented Sleswig-Holsteinism, a minority of so-called national Frisians began to define itself as a separate ethnonational group and expected greater support for this identity within a Danish political context.[29]

The National Socialist take-over in Germany in 1933 raised hopes and fears in the borderland. Danish minority institutions were left intact, but the political climate in a nationalist one-party state complicated the activities of any national minority. The German North Sleswigers, in turn, anticipated new initiatives in the border question. It soon became clear, however, that the Berlin government prioritized tolerable relations with Denmark and Scandinavia.[30] The Sleswig Party, the parliamentary representation of the German minority, expanded its voter base in the elections of 1939.[31] This strong mobilization simultaneously created a Danish countermovement, however, so that the minority only insignificantly increased its percental share.

It took another war to fundamentally challenge the status quo. This time, the hostilities also reached Denmark. On 9 April 1940, German troops moved into the country. For the next five years, Denmark was occupied. Initially, the relationship between the two governments retained a semblance of pragmatic cooperation, but from August 1943 on, it became more openly confrontational. In order to preserve some form of understanding, however, the occupying power did not assume legal sovereignty over North Sleswig.

War and occupation had an especially deep impact on the German minority. Its fate became intertwined with the fortunes of the German war effort, especially when many of its members were recruited into the German armed forces. Only a small segment withdrew to form an internal opposition. In November 1943, the Haderslev Circle formulated thoughts for a future coexistence between the nationalities.[32]

The end of World War II opened the arguably most remarkable chapter in Sleswig identity history. The Danish majority in North Sleswig was liberated and no longer had to fear border revisions. The German minority, in contrast, paid a heavy price for its wartime stance. It took years for the minority to reestablish its institutional basis on a more moderate level. More fundamental yet were the developments south of the border. The existing order had collapsed. The expulsion of the German population from the Prussian east brought more than a million refugees to Sleswig-Holstein and increased the population from 1.6 million in 1939 to 2.6 million in 1946.[33] No one knew whether it would be possible to provide for locals and refugees in the prevailing chaos. The future of Germany was unclear.

In this exceptional situation, a large-scale shift in self-identification took place. Many Sleswigers joined Danish organizations. Often, this expressed a desire to escape the tribulations of postwar Germany, but attempts to reopen the border question remained unsuccessful. A larger percentage of the Frisian population than before supported the pro-Danish movement, which especially in the early postwar years also defined itself as a regionalist alternative for Danish, Frisian, and German Sleswigers alike.

In Denmark, reaction was split.[34] Nationalist associations agitated in favor of boundary changes. Some center-right politicians, led by Prime Minister Knud Kristensen, supported them. Many on the left were more skeptical about the national reorientation in South Sleswig and its long-term implications. Thus, official Danish policy coalesced upon securing the rights of Danish South Sleswigers and revisiting the border question after the reestablishment of normal conditions. When the economic recovery led many Danish sympathizers back into the German mainstream, the issue became moot. The minority consolidated itself on a level that lay considerably below the early postwar, but also noticeably above the interwar level.

In the early postwar era, the German authorities were reluctant to accept the German-speaking converts to the Danish movement as genuine minority members. Increasingly, however, self-identification became the core principle. The Kiel Declaration of 1949 and the Bonn-Copenhagen Declarations of 1955 marked important milestones in the official recognition of minority rights.[35] The Schleswig-Holstein constitution of 1990 explicitly confirmed that everyone can freely choose to identify with a national minority and guaranteed the Danish and Frisian minorities official protection and support.

Since the final echoes of the border conflict have passed, the Danish minority has established a visible and well-respected presence in Germany's northern province of Schleswig-Holstein. The Danish minority party, the South Sleswig Electoral Association, is an active participant in the province's political life. Schleswig-Holstein defines itself as Germany's bridge to Scandinavia and has embraced the Danish components of its cultural heritage. Many Danes on both sides of the border nonetheless feel that this openness toward Danish culture expresses itself predominantly on a rhetorical plane. Since few Germans speak Danish, the communicational patterns in the border region, both literally and symbolically, continue to reflect cultural and political imbalances.

The gradual passing of border activism and wartime antagonism also led to a gradual reintegration of the German minority into the region's public life. With the assistance of both the German and Danish governments, it was able to rebuild its organizational structure. This normalization of ethnic relations has not been without problems for the minority, however, as younger generations of German North Sleswigers are increasingly defining their German identity as only one element of a wider South Jutland identity. Thus, the German minority in Denmark, which derives its origins predominantly from a sense of self and not from visible physical or cultural markers, faces the continuous challenge of imparting this sense of self to new generations that are widely integrated into the larger Danish society.

Conclusion

During the past decades, the once acerbic debate about borders and identities in Sleswig has become more conciliatory. The German-Danish borderlands are now seen as a promising example of how to solve national conflicts. Indeed, the Danish, German, and Frisian communities in this region enjoy a high degree of freedom and public support. At the same time, the special nature of minority identity and minority rights in Sleswig has largely internalized their activities. To the outside observer, the border today separates two very distinct cultural spheres.

The history of Sleswig may be called a not atypical expression of European border experiences—with an atypically happy ending. If we look at medieval Europe, webs of feudal dependencies and exemptions, overlapping political allegiances, and linguistically diverse subjects constituted if not the norm then at least a commonplace occurrence. In an era of nation-states, many of these political entities came to be seen as outdated. The price for adapting them to the new standard tended to be high. Alsace became a mere object of conflicting state interests, until it surrendered much of what being Alsatian had been all about. Bohemia resolved its duality by eradicating it. In Sleswig, by contrast, the conflicting parties ultimately understood that compromise not only prevents full victory, but also total defeat. When Sleswig no longer seemed able to be Danish and German as one, it at least proved able to be German and Danish as two.

Notes

1. The quip is rendered in a number of slightly different versions. What is interesting is not whether or not it is authentic, but how far-spread it became. Its sheer popularity confirms that the public definitely considered the Schleswig-Holstein question intractable. For one version, see Christian Degn, *Schleswig-Holstein: Eine Landesgeschichte,* 2d ed. (Neumünster, 1995), 15.
2. In the long-term perspective applied in this chapter, it would be impractical to document every statement with a note. Therefore, such notes have been restricted to especially important or controversial aspects. The general outlines of Sleswig history can be verified in many of the works cited in the bibliography. Useful introductions are Hans Valdemar Gregersen, *Slesvig og Holsten før 1830* (Copenhagen, 1981); Lorenz Rerup, *Slesvig og Holsten efter 1830* (Copenhagen, 1982); Alexander Scharff, *Schleswig-Holsteinische Geschichte*, 4th and rev. ed. by Manfred Jessen-Klingenberg (Freiburg, 1984); Jann Markus Witt and Heiko Vosgerau, eds., *Schleswig-Holstein von den Ursprüngen bis zur Gegenwart* (Hamburg, 2002); and Ulrich Lange, ed., *Geschichte Schleswig-Holsteins: Von den Anfängen bis zur Gegenwart,* 2d ed. (Neumünster, 2003).

   For a brief English-language introduction to the present minority question, see Jørgen Kühl, *The National Minorities in the Danish-German Border Region* (Aabenraa, 2003).
3. In accordance with proper linguistic usage, the term Germanic is used in this study to designate a branch of the Indo-European family of languages. This northern European language group includes not only German and varieties thereof, but also Dutch, Scandinavian, and English, although the last has subsequently integrated numerous non-Germanic words. Unfortunately, it is common practice in English to also use Germanic as a synonym for German or German-speaking and thus blur the distinction between German proper and the larger language family of which it forms just one element. Sometimes, the ensuing gap is filled with the term Teutonic. However, the sometimes peculiar connotations of this term and its occasional usage as yet another synonym for German made it seem more advisable to retain the correct linguistic term, which also corresponds to the usage in other Germanic languages.
4. The designation "Saxon" is originally attached to a northwestern German population that inhabited modern-day Lower Saxony and surrounding areas rather than modern-day Saxony farther to the east. The northernmost subgroup of the Obotrites is also

known as Wagrians, and the peninsula they settled between the modern cities of Lübeck and Kiel is still referred to as Wagria.

5. See H. Hellmuth Andersen, *Danevirke og Kovirke: Arkæologiske undersøgelser 1861-1993* (Århus, 1998).
6. See also Erich Hoffmann, *Die heiligen Könige bei den Angelsachsen und den skandinavischen Völkern* (Neumünster, 1975), 139-146.
7. See Thomas Riis, "Wann entstand das Herzogtum Schleswig?" in *Geschichte Schleswigs vom frühen Mittelalter bis 1920*, ed. Henrik Becker-Christensen and Ulrich Lange (Aabenraa, 1998), 9. For an analysis of the early Danish monarchic system, see also Erich Hoffmann, *Königserhebung und Thronfolgeordnung in Dänemark bis zum Ausgang des Mittelalters* (Berlin, 1976). For an introduction to the rulers of Sleswig, see Carsten Porskrog Rasmussen, Inge Adriansen, and Lennart S. Madsen, eds., *De slesvigske hertuger* (Aabenraa, 2005).
8. For the core passages of the *constitutio valdemariana*, see Flensburger Arbeitskreis für Stadt- und Regionalforschung, ed., *Quellen zur Geschichte Schleswig-Holsteins* 1 (Kiel, 1987), 83.
9. Hans Schultz Hansen, "Det danske navn Sønderjylland og det tyske navn Slesvig," in *19 myter i Sønderjyllands historie*, ed. Axel Johnsen and Birgitte Thomsen (Aabenraa, 2002), 33.
10. For the core passages of the charter known in English as the Treaty of Ribe, see Flensburger Arbeitskreis für Stadt- und Regionalforschung, ed., *Quellen zur Geschichte Schleswig-Holsteins* 1 (Kiel, 1987), 86ff.
11. For a recent critical examination of this clause, see Carsten Jahnke, "'dat se bliven ewich tosamende ungedelt': Neue Überlegungen zu einem alten Schlagwort," *Zeitschrift der Gesellschaft für Schleswig-Holsteinische Geschichte* 128 (2003): 45-59.
12. They are known as Frederik and Hans in Danish and as Friedrich and Johann in German.
13. These segments should not be understood as contiguous territories, but as conglomerates of separate and often geographically disjunct domains.
14. Whereas the genuinely Danish regions of the Scandinavian peninsula were lost to Sweden, Denmark's union with Norway was preserved. Thus, the composite monarchy still dominated the western half of the peninsula.
15. For the core texts, see Flensburger Arbeitskreis für Stadt- und Regionalforschung, ed., *Quellen zur Geschichte Schleswig-Holsteins* 1 (Kiel, 1987), 180ff.
16. Enno Kraehe, *Metternich's German Policy: The Congress of Vienna, 1814-1815* (Princeton, N.J., 1983), 16.
17. See Uwe Jens Lornsen, *Ueber das Verfassungswerk in Schleswigholstein* (Kiel, 1830).
18. See, for example, Christian Paulsen, *Ueber Volksthümlichkeit und Staatsrecht des Herzogthums Schleswig*, in *Samlede mindre skrifter* (Copenhagen, 1857), 2:355-429.
19. The diplomatic exchange between Denmark and the German powers is published in *Aktstykker betræffende det Tydske Forbunds Intervention i Hertugdømmet Holsteen* (Copenhagen, 1852).
20. They received their name for their aspiration to make the river Eider, which separated Sleswig and Holstein, the southern border of Denmark.
21. In his proclamation of 28 August 1850, the royal commissioner for Sleswig announced:

> The southern border of the duchy of Sleswig constitutes the customs border of this duchy for the moment. In regard to customs matters in the duchy of

Sleswig, the duchy of Holstein is, for the moment, to be treated like a foreign country...

"Bekjendtgjørelse, angaaende Hertugdømmet Slesvigs Toldforhold," in *Chronologisk Samling af de i Aarene 1848, 1849 og 1850 udkomne Love og Bekjendtgjørelser for Hertugdømmet Slesvig* (Copenhagen, 1851), 102.

22. In 1853, however, the customs border was moved to the river Elbe and ceased to divide the duchies.
23. For the text of the Treaty of Vienna, see Fred Israel, ed., *Major Peace Treaties of Modern History, 1648-1967* (New York, 1967), 1:611-627.
24. Following the 1865 Gastein Convention, tiny Lauenburg was affiliated directly with Prussia in exchange for an indemnity paid to Austria.
25. For the text of the Treaty of Prague, see Fred Israel, ed., *Major Peace Treaties of Modern History, 1648-1967* (New York, 1967), 1:629-633.
26. Fred Israel, ed., *Major Peace Treaties of Modern History, 1648-1967* (New York, 1967), 1:630.
27. More detailed elections results are presented in Chapter 4.
28. See Fred Israel, ed., *Major Peace Treaties of Modern History, 1648-1967* (New York, 1967), 2:1342-1346.
29. For an introduction to the formation of modern North Frisian identities, see Thomas Steensen, *Die friesische Bewegung in Nordfriesland im 19. und 20. Jahrhundert,* 2 vols. (Neumünster, 1986).
30. Local Schleswig-Holstein activists tried to raise the border question in 1933 but were soon stopped by Berlin.
31. The electoral wing of the German minority was officially called Sleswig Electoral Association in the interwar period. Since it contested elections under the designation Sleswig Party, which also became the sole designation after World War II, it will always be addressed as Sleswig Party in this study.
32. See the text of the so-called Haderslev Declaration in Ernst Siegfried Hansen, *Disteln am Wege* (Bielefeld, 1957), 117f.
33. Statistisches Landesamt Schleswig-Holstein, *Das Flüchtlingsgeschehen in Schleswig-Holstein infolge des 2. Weltkriegs im Spiegel der amtlichen Statistik* (Kiel, 1974), 10.
34. For an in-depth investigation of the border debate in postwar Denmark, see Johan Peter Noack, *Det sydslesvigske grænsespørgsmål 1945-1947*, 2 vols. (Aabenraa, 1991).
35. For a recent assessment of the Bonn-Copenhagen Declarations, see Jørgen Kühl and Marc Weller, eds., *Minority Policy in Action: The Bonn-Copenhagen Declarations in a European Context, 1955-2005* (Flensburg and Aabenraa, 2005).

CHAPTER THREE

Both Argument and Building Block

A History of Language and Culture in Sleswig

Politics was not the only point of contention in the debate about historical legitimacy and national entitlement in Sleswig. Although surprisingly many eventually felt called to argue constitutional law and dynastic succession, historical presence and cultural traditions were issues closer to the heart of most national activists. The question as to who had arrived in the region first was never far from the surface, because in an era of national romanticism, duration of stay seemed to allot special claims to possession. Rather than challenging this rationale, both sides tended to focus their efforts on enhancing their local genealogy.

Of course, Sleswig was by no means unique in this respect. Even a liberal statesman such as Tomáš Masaryk felt justified in designating his Bohemian-German compatriots as mere colonists because they could only trace their roots back to the 1200s.[1] Up to the present, Palestinians and Israeli Jews bolster their rights to the land with conflicting standards of historical precedence and continuity. And enlightened cosmopolitans who consider themselves above this type of atavistic quibble tend to apply different standards to a term such as Native American, which was clearly introduced to emphasize the longer presence and special status of the population formerly designated as Indians on the American continent.

Most modern-day scholars take a different approach to cultural continuity. Social identities and the groups they engender are neither innate nor immutable. The Germans and Danes of the nineteenth century are not identical with the ones recorded in medieval documents, and the same is true for the Poles and Lithuanians examined in a later chapter. This does not mean that previous forms of social organization possess no relevance and have left no marks. They did have an impact on the course of nation-building by leaving both a set of sociocultural conditions and a legacy that could be invoked.

This chapter explores central questions of Sleswig cultural history. The prehistory of Jutland, the medieval interpenetration of Sleswig and Holstein, the rise of German to predominant medium of administration, the partial separation of high culture and low culture, and the ultimate partition of Sleswig into two also linguistically distinct sections not only influenced identity formation in Sleswig, but at the same time constituted topics of discussion and political strife. Culture formed a building block of identity formation, but it also served as an argument employed to shape this identity. This dual role gives it special significance for the study of Sleswig identity.

Angles and Saxons, Jutes and Danes: The Early Cultural History of Jutland

The cultural origins of Jutland have long been a part of the political debate. The advances in philological and historical scholarship during the early 1800s occurred during a period in which the differences between the Danish and German national movements took shape. This even politicized the research of historically remote eras.

A central point of disagreement concerned the indigenous population of Jutland prior to the immigration of the *Dani*.[2] It was largely undisputed that the latter had arrived from southern Sweden and the islands in between. There was disagreement, however, as to the population they encountered on the peninsula.

Germans as well as Danes highlighted facets that strengthened their own national tradition. Complex matters received straightforward answers. Thus, the famous golden horns of Gallehus near Tønder appeared unproblematically in both a distinctly German and a distinctly Scandinavian pantheon.[3] One of these treasures from the earliest Middle Ages contained an inscription, which is rendered as *ek hlewagastiz holtijaz horna tawido* or, especially in Scandinavia, *ek hlewagastiR holtijaR horna tawido.* It tends to be translated as "I, Hlewagast, son of Holte, made the horn."

As Hans Frede Nielsen has shown, the language of the text differs noticeably from the medieval standards of both central and northern Europe.[4] A reconstructed Old Norse **ek hlégestr hyltir horn gørða* and its Old Saxon counterpart **ik hleogast hulti horn toida* constitute a later stage of development. Thus, the inscription cannot easily be placed in either a North or a West Germanic tradition. Nielsen designated the text as Northwest Germanic and assigned it to a period during which only Gothic had departed from an otherwise still unbroken dialectal continuum within the Germanic world.

If such ephemeral objects as the Gallehus horns, which might have originated far from the place they were found, triggered national controversy, the debate about the Angles had to be more acerbic yet. The modern Sleswigian region of Anglia evokes historical and toponymical associations. Tacitus already mentioned *Angli* in his *Germania* and located them close to the Langobards of the Elbe estuary.[5] Several centuries later, Angles participated in the conquest of Britain and lent their name to the kingdom of England.

Some Danish scholars denied the Sleswigian roots of the Angles.[6] They used evidence of Anglian settlements in central and northwestern Germany to argue that they had never dwelt in Jutland.[7] This line of reasoning had to turn the exception into the rule, however. The place name of Anglia, whose long-term continuity holds importance in itself, is reinforced by additional sources. Next to Tacitus' *Germania*, the most significant is Bede's *Ecclesiastical History of the English People* from the first half of the eighth century. Bede relates that the Angles in Britain came from "that country which is called Anglia and from that time to this is said to stand deserted between the provinces of the Jutes and the Saxons."[8] Although Bede's narration also contains mythic and erroneous elements, it further corroborates the toponymical, linguistic, and anthropological evidence.

Why was the Anglian homeland so ardently debated? Few linguistic sources from the predominantly oral culture of early Jutland have survived. Their evidentiary value was limited. The attribution of premedieval place names to specific Germanic subgroups remained speculative. One fact was indisputable, however: the Angles in Britain spoke a West Germanic idiom. If those Angles according to contemporary authors originated in the south of Jutland, where place names seem to confirm their presence, and resembled the Saxons linguistically, a West Germanic prehistory in parts of the peninsula becomes more likely. As a consequence, many newer Danish works on the subject start their analysis in the year 811, in which the river Eider has indisputably become the border between Denmark and the Frankish empire.[9]

Earlier German scholarship politicized historical research in a different manner. It did not restrict itself to highlighting the evidence for Sleswig's Anglian roots, but put all of Jutland into a German historical context.[10] Again drawing on Bede, it postulated a West Germanic origin of the Jutes, too. Since Bede equated the *Iuti* in Britain with the Jutes of Denmark and ascribed them a major role in the colonization of such linguistically indistinguishable regions as Kent and the Isle of Wight, they could not have been North Germanic in origin.

Logically consistently, some Danish researchers turned this argument on its head. If one premises that the Jutes had always been North Germanic, the Angles might not have been West Germanic either. Neither the Anglian nor the Jutish districts of Britain displayed northern features, because both groups had been outnumbered by the Saxons. Thus, Old English derived solely from Saxon and reveals nothing about the background of other populations.[11]

Yet the history of the *Iuti* or *Yte* of southern England is more intricate. They played a smaller role in the settlement of England than the Angles, which suggests an early intermingling with the surrounding Saxons. Furthermore, archeological and dialectal findings as well as the location of their settlement areas in the very south of England raised serious questions about Bede's equation of Jutes and *Iuti*. As a consequence, the Jutish population of Britain cannot provide much support for either line of argument.

More significant for the politicization of the Jutish question has been its transfer to a modern context. Using the lack of a suffixed definite article as his main argument, Jacob Grimm postulated a continuous differentiation between Jutland and the north. He promoted the incorporation of the peninsula into the desired German nation-state, whereas the Danish isles were to belong to a future Scandinavian union.[12]

Grimm's line of reasoning reflects a tendency that has not been restricted to a specific era or nationality. Remote historical periods are instrumentalized in modern political disputes. Danish scholars corrected Grimm factually and assigned the article differentiation to a time period during which Jutland undoubtedly belonged to the North Germanic sphere.[13] More important, however, is the realization that prehistoric settlement patterns cannot change the fact that most of Jutland had become Danish-speaking by the Middle Ages.

In light of the research by such renowned linguists as Hans Frede Nielsen and Elmer Antonsen, it seems most convincing to view early Jutland as the center of a Northwest Germanic or North Sea Germanic core area, which linked the still closely related dialect continuums of Scandinavia and Central Europe. In fact, a growing body of literature sees no clear demarcation within the western Germanic-speaking sphere prior to the sixth century. Not least of all, it was the partial emigration of this intermediary population and the subsequent arrival of *Dani* from the north and Slavs from the south that introduced a sharper linguistic demarcation on the peninsula. The subsequent incorporation into larger polities, whose centers on Rhine and Sound lay far removed from Jutland, further accentuated the divide.

Thus, the prehistory of southern Jutland is not so unambiguously embedded in a Danish cultural tradition as an earlier Danish historiography made it appear. This does not mean, however, that the later Germanization of southern Sleswig was anchored in historical tradition. In the early Middle Ages, Jutland north of the Dannevirke was not only politically but also linguistically Danish. Only the southwestern littoral, which became increasingly dominated by Frisians, represented an exception.

From South Jutland to Sleswig: A Cultural Landscape in Transition

When the Danish realm was consolidated in the tenth century, the later Sleswig had long been affiliated with this cultural sphere. This does not entail that Danes, which term by that time also includes the Jutes, inhabited its entire territory. Frisians occupied the southwestern coast. Between the political border along the Eider and the southern rim of Danish settlement along Dannevirke and Schlei extended largely uninhabited woodlands, whose name has been reported as Isarnho and Jarnvith, that is, the Iron Forest.

The remainder of the region, however, was populated by Danes. This basic fact is not challenged by the presence of Saxons and Slavs in the cosmopolitan trading town of Haithabu or by the short-lived rule of Viking chieftains from other parts of Scandinavia. Only the spread of Frisian settlement from the margins—visible in the designation *Utland*—into more central areas foreshadowed a development that was to revert the south of Jutland into a zone of passage.

Significant changes in these ethnolinguistic parameters could only arise from a direct interaction between Germans and Danes. A first step was the colonization of the borderlands between Eider and Schlei, which gained significance in the 1200s and removed the historical buffer zone. The colonization proceeded primarily from the south and established Low German as the vernacular of southernmost Sleswig. The former Iron Forest never contained a noteworthy Danish element, whereas the Schwansen peninsula was Germanized both by immigration from Holstein and by the assimilation of Danish speakers.[14]

The resulting linguistic differentiation can still be seen in Caspar Danckwerth's *Newe Landesbeschreibung der zwei Herzogthümer Schleswich und Holstein* from 1652. Danckwerth expounded:

> In our times, Danes or Jutes, Saxons, and Frisians inhabit the duchy. The Jutes possess the largest share, since everything from Kolding to the Schlei and the city of Schleswig is Jutish, i.e., of Danish peoples, who use the Danish language, with the exception of the city of Flensburg, in which Danes and Germans intermingle…
>
> The city of Schleswig and everything else that stretches from the Schlei to the Eider and Levensau is largely inhabited by Saxons, who use the Lower Saxon language, as do the inhabitants of the island of Fehmarn. Along the western coast from the border, the Skodborg River, to Tønder there live Jutes again. Thereafter come the North Frisians, however, who do not only occupy the marshlands from Tønder to the Eider, but also a part of the high plains we know as the geest. This part used to be called the Frisian foregeest.[15]

Thus, the early modern period already displayed the linguistic division of Sleswig that still characterized the countryside around 1800. Low German dominated south of a line that followed the Schlei in the east and continued across the country to Husum. The westernmost sector of this region, the Eiderstedt peninsula and its outer islands, had only adopted Low German in the 1600s; previously, the population had spoken Frisian. The Frisian language area extended along the coast north of Husum. It comprised the islands and the coastal lowlands all the way to Sylt and Rodenäs, but it also reached into the high plains, where it collided with the South Jutland dialect of Danish. The remainder of the countryside was still Danophone, and interspersed later arrivals from German-speaking regions, such as the Moravian Brethren of Christiansfeld and the peasant colonists of the interior heath, soon dissipated in their linguistic surroundings.[16]

This relatively clear demarcation of the rural vernaculars constituted only one aspect of the duchy's linguistic composition, however. In the spheres of education and administration, German gained increasing importance; first in its Low German, subsequently in its High German form. The political ties between Sleswig and Holstein triggered the northward expansion of the Holstein nobility. The military defeat of Denmark's King Christopher II in 1326 and the rule of Holstein aristocrats in Sleswig between 1386 and 1459 further deepened German influence.[17] Although this initially only altered vernacular conditions on the Schwansen peninsula, German increasingly established itself as the language of public life throughout the duchy.

The mutual integration of Sleswig and Holstein elites fell into a period during which Low German flourished as the language of the Hanseatic League. As Latin lost significance in public life, Low German assumed its role. Town charters and even the historic Jutish Law were translated into Low German; the records of the cathedral chapter and the episcopal chancellery in Schleswig were increasingly kept in that language. By the mid 1400s, at the latest, Low German had become the duchy's language of government, even though Danish survived in the lower courts of northern Sleswig until the 1700s.[18]

The role of German as the language of the law also surfaced in the village charters, which touched the common people most directly. Martin Rheinheimer found German village charters further north than warranted by vernacular or ecclesiastic practice.[19] As a rule, the language of local jurisdiction was echoed in the charter. One also has to assume, however, that at least the leading strata of the village must have understood the language in which their charters were composed.

The public position of the Low German language also in Danish and Frisian vernacular regions was not the only factor that prevented a clean separation of linguistic spheres. Language use in the cities represented another. During the late Middle Ages, North German merchants and craftsmen settled throughout Scandinavia. The German presence in many cities led to the bilingualism of public life. In the long term, this may have triggered an adaptation process reminiscent of the Anglo-French accommodation that brought forth Middle English. The Scandinavian languages of the mainland adopted numerous Low German loanwords and simplified their grammatical structure.[20] Only the idioms of the remote North Atlantic islands, especially Iceland, remained insolated from this development.

Whereas the German immigrants ultimately assimilated in the cities of central Scandinavia, they encountered a different situation in Sleswig. The proximity of the contiguous German language area, but especially the function of German as the language of government and administration, resulted in the gradual replacement of Danish for official business. In the southern cities, this affected everyday speech as well.

The transformation commenced in Schleswig. The city's location on the late-medieval linguistic divide gave it partially German-speaking environs. Even more important was its role as the seat of education and politics. The German dominance in these fields gained special significance in the capital.

Although Schleswig's advance role in the language change was undisputed, there was disagreement about its date and extent. In contrast to August Sach, who located it in the late 1300s, C. F. Allen did not consider the conversion completed as late as the 1700s.[21] These divergent assessments can be explained by the standards applied. Sach described the moment at which public life in Schleswig became German. Allen, by contrast, demonstrated that the Danish language did not completely disappear from the city. As long as adjacent Anglia was Danish-speaking, the continual immigration from Schleswig's northern hinterland replenished the Danish element. This process did not end until Anglia itself had switched to German.

If the language development in Schleswig, which by the outbreak of the national conflict undoubtedly was German-speaking, could trigger politically charged interpretations, conditions in Flensburg were bound to be controversial. Whereas Schleswig formed an extension of the contiguous German language area since the late Middle Ages, Flensburg continued to be an urban island within a Danish rural environment. In this respect, Flensburg resembled the market towns of the north more than the core city of Schleswig in the south.

Nonetheless, Flensburg turned into a predominantly German municipality. In the political field, this dominance became so lopsided that few examples of Danish official usage after 1400 have survived.[22] In the fifteenth century, the town charter was translated into Low German, which also was the language of contemporary town hall records and the guilds' bylaws. Danish disappeared quite early from public life.

Everyday communication displayed a different pattern. The analysis of Flensburg personal names in the 1400s shows a preponderance of Danish forms.[23] Even if local adolescents increasingly were socialized in Low German, migration from the exclusively Danish surroundings kept the Danish language alive. These Danish surroundings also made it advisable for Flensburg merchants and businessmen to acquire a basic knowledge of the rural vernacular in order to communicate with customers and suppliers. At the same time, regular migration from Germany proper reinforced southern ties, especially among the economically leading strata. The resulting culture clash gave the inhabitants of Flensburg the reputation of using a hard to understand hodgepodge of languages.[24]

If Flensburg was a city in which German predominated, although the Danish language survived through constant influx from surrounding communities, the situation in Tønder was different again.[25] Tønder did have close ties to the south through its proximity to North Frisia and through a town charter based on Lübeck law. Therefore, it cannot surprise that Latin was mainly replaced by Low German as the language of public life. The local citizenry also identified with the German side during the nineteenth-century national conflict. At the same time, South Jutland Danish remained the predominant vernacular. Only much later, in the Prussian period, did German seem poised to assume that position. Otherwise, it functioned as the main public language and as an important second language for many local citizens. Unlike Flensburg, however, Tønder was too small to withstand, not to mention shape, its rural surroundings.

In the other towns of northern Sleswig, in Aabenraa, Sønderborg, and Haderslev, German remained primarily an acquired formal language. Some families spoke it in daily life, and there were always newcomers from the south. The leading role of German in education and administration further increased its familiarity. The bulk of the population, however, used Danish in everyday situations.

Finally, this period experienced the establishment of unified standard languages and the decline of formal Low German. In the older literature, the differences between written standards and vernaculars figure prominently. Many researchers emphasized the variations within the other language community. They suggested that segments of the national Other used a mixed language and therefore should not be associated with the cultural spheres of Denmark or Germany. Thus, C. F. Allen referred to a "so-called Low German," which was spoken in southern Anglia and so far removed from standard German that the students could more easily acquire standard Danish.[26] August Sach, for his part, deplored that the true nature of South Jutish as a distinct language was not universally understood.[27]

These sharp demarcations between standard and dialect cannot be maintained, not only in respect to the political conclusions drawn. In spite of the distinctions, which both major vernaculars display vis-à-vis their national standards, they are unmistakably affiliated more closely with one or the other. Therefore, these dialectal idiosyncrasies had limited relevance for the relationship between German and Danish—with one possible exception.

Some scholars have argued that the introduction of High German as the written standard, which largely occurred in Sleswig during the 1600s, weakened the public position of Low German in the still Danish-speaking regions of central

Sleswig.[28] Since the latter lost its status as a language of education and turned into just another vernacular, it no longer enjoyed superior prestige vis-à-vis the South Jutland dialect. High German, in turn, lacked a popular basis and was too different from Danish to permit an easy transition. This might have slowed down the spread of Low German as the idiom of the village leaders in those rural communities in which Danish predominated in the vernacular and German in the official sphere.

Between Two Worlds: The Language in Church and School

The language of religion formed the link between the language of administration and jurisprudence on the one hand and the language of everyday life on the other. The dignitaries of the church were trained in similar institutions as the governmental leaders. They were a part of the political elite and exercised many public functions, which connected them to a German written culture.

The lower strata of the church hierarchy operated in a different linguistic environment. The political and administrative elites exercised most of their functions far removed from the common citizenry. Even the courts interacted increasingly with lawyers or relied on interpreters. Ecclesiastical life after the Reformation, in contrast, presumed that the congregation understood the pastor. Therefore, the linguistic competence of the population was more important in the religious than in the political domain.

The language question rarely presented itself to the church until modern times. In the Middle Ages, Latin dominated as the holy language, and the theological understanding of medieval Catholicism ascribed little significance to the vernacular. It had an impact, however, that most of the duchy was subject to the cathedral chapter of Schleswig, in which German established itself early on. Only the west of Sleswig, from Tønder northward, belonged to the diocese of Ribe. The district of Barved in the northeast also retained some autonomy from Schleswig and subsequently gained its own collegial chapter in Haderslev.[29] In these two regions, Danish could widely assert itself in the religious sphere.

The Protestant Reformation largely replaced Latin with local languages, which tended to favor Low German in Sleswig. The Reformation reached Denmark from the south and was accompanied by German cultural impulses. In addition, it was implanted by the political authorities, who already preferred Low German.

The church was therefore soon administered in German. The Sleswig-Holstein Church Ordinance of 1542 was not only composed jointly for both duchies in Low German, but consistently treats this language as the native counterpart to Latin.[30] This did not truly aim at the general introduction of Low German throughout Sleswig, which the significance of the sermon for Lutheran services did not permit. Standard Danish succeeded Latin in the monolingually South Jutish districts of northern Sleswig. In the German south as well as the Frisian west, which did not develop its own written standard, Low German was introduced without further ado.

More problematic were those regions of central Sleswig in which dialectal Danish formed the vernacular, whereas Low German dominated in public life. A large part of this transitional zone used German in church. This marked the beginning of a development in which a line connecting Flensburg in the east and Tønder in the west established itself as a still very tentative separator of predominantly German and Danish districts. To the north, the rural language of the church was primarily Danish; to the south, it tended to be German.[31] The dividing line often ran somewhat to the south of the twentieth century border in the high plains, whereas it ran further north in the vicinity of Flensburg. Finally, one should not forget that many congregations held both German and Danish services.[32]

Troels Fink suggested an explanation for this dividing line, which did not correspond to any contemporary administrative demarcation. The ecclesiastical boundaries only approximated it in the far west, where the jurisdiction of the diocese of Ribe ended near Tønder. Farther east, the authority of the bishop in Schleswig reached far to the north. On the political level, the dividing line initially partitioned both Tønder and Flensburg counties, although most of Flensburg county subsequently switched to German.

Fink argued that individual pastors strongly influenced the linguistic conditions in their parishes. Direct interference from upper echelons did occur, as during the tenure of Westphalian-born church superintendent Stephan Klotz, whom Danish historiography regularly criticized for this intrusion.[33] Yet according to Fink, it was the educational system that played the most important role, even prior to the Reformation. If pastors were trained at the German cathedral school in Schleswig, they tended to use that language for their pastoral duties. Where the bulk of the clergy was educated in Schleswig, German predominated as the language of the church.[34]

The significance of this approximate line of division, which continued to shift and never turned into a rigid boundary, was further increased by the introduction of compulsory schooling. The educational institutions were closely tied to the church, because the teachers were either clergy themselves or subject to ecclesiastic supervision.[35] The so-called chaplain schools constituted the core of the rural educational system. Therefore, the language of instruction largely followed the language of the church.[36] Initially, there were also informal rural schools established by the local population, which as late as the mid 1700s still constituted a majority of all schools in North Sleswig.[37] The authorities disparaged these institutions, however, and tried to replace them with centrally administrated ones.

In the cities and towns, school was held in German or sometimes in Latin. Thus, all higher education in the duchy was German, including the tertiary level, which took place at the University of Kiel in Holstein. The rural chaplain schools were initially little more than an auxiliary to and extension of the church service. Even when certified teachers became more common in the 1700s, instruction was characterized by personal and locational instability. The royal edict of 1761, which tried to establish permanent educators and school buildings, brought no immediate remedy. Due to the teachers' limited command of the standard languages, moreover, the instruction often occurred in the Low German, South Jutish, or Frisian vernaculars.[38]

In view of these conditions, the schools initially did not alter the basic language distribution in Sleswig. In the nineteenth century, however, better-trained teachers improved mass education and deepened the knowledge of literary German and Danish. At that time, the language question had already become a political point of contention.

Toward a Political Border: The Linguistic Development from 1800 to the End of World War II

At the onset of the nineteenth century, the linguistic fundamentals in Sleswig had not changed much for centuries. The language of administration and court was German, which by then universally meant High German. Higher education used that language, too. Rural schools and churches preferred German up to a line that approximated the later border, and Danish further north. Everyday language in the countryside was still South Jutland Danish all the way to the Schlei, as always excepting the Frisian southwest, whereas towns and cities were predominantly German-speaking up to Flensburg. Further north, the towns were bilingual, with a preponderance of Danish especially in the lower strata.

Until that time, the languages had developed largely outside the political sphere. This does not mean that there had not been interventions. The central administration, not least of all the German Chancellery in Copenhagen, had repeatedly encouraged the teaching of German. Yet the motives for the use of German in the administration of Danish vernacular regions were primarily pragmatic. The political elites had a palpable interest in the linguistic integration of the duchies. The languages of administration and public life were to coincide. Since the overall linguistic distribution in the duchies and German monolingualism in Holstein made it impossible to reach this homogeneity on the basis of Danish, they promoted the teaching of German in Sleswig. Notwithstanding this pragmatism, however, many civil servants also considered German a superior language of culture and administration.

The nineteenth century brought a fundamental change. Linguistic conditions became a part of the political debate, increasingly defined in national terms. At the same time, the rural inhabitants of central Sleswig adopted a new vernacular. Although that process had prenational roots, it could not be separated from the national conflict. Both developments contributed to a sharper demarcation of German and Danish linguistic spheres.

In the southeastern district of Anglia, German dominated in churches and schools. C. F. Allen documented the sporadic use of Danish in church registers, but public life was overwhelmingly conducted in German.[39] For everyday purposes, most people preferred the Anglian Danish dialect.

This southern outpost developed a specific form of bilingualism very early. Church and school provided a basic command of German. The village charters were composed in German as well.[40] These broader cultural influences, however, which also existed in neighboring districts, were supplemented with economic and geographical ones. Anglia protrudes like a peninsula into the Baltic Sea between the Schlei and the Flensburg sound. Along the Schlei, it bordered on the district of Schwansen, which had become German-speaking in the Middle Ages. Thus, the southern rim of Anglia touched the contiguous German language area. At the northern and southern starting points of the peninsula lay the two main cities of the duchy, the politically leading Schleswig and the economically and demographically important Flensburg. This made Anglia a rural link between two German-dominated urban centers, closely integrated with both of them.

Anglia's exposed location gave its Danish-speaking rural inhabitants a different relationship to German than prevailed in regions farther north. German was not merely a lifeless language of authority that lacked everyday significance. German, especially in its Low German form, was at the same time the idiom that the Anglites encountered in their centers of economic and cultural interaction. An insufficient knowledge of German marked them as ignorant peasants.[41]

The flourishing economy of Anglia drew the local farmers toward the German middle-class culture they encountered in the cities of Flensburg and Schleswig.[42] The educational advances of the 1800s reinforced these considerations. The school ordinance of 1814 improved the attractiveness of the teaching vocation and professionalized the educational system. This deepened the impact of school on the students and raised the status of a good education in the eyes of the public. Both aspects had special importance in a district where Danish served as the vernacular and German as the medium of instruction. For one, the younger generations acquired a deeper knowledge of the High German standard. For the other, the increased status of education convinced many Anglites to give their children a head start by communicating with them in the local Low German dialect.[43] This often discussed development also documents, however, that Low German was already established as a second language in Anglia.

In the course of the nineteenth century, Low German became the Anglian vernacular. The language maps by Geerz (1838), Koch (1839), and Biernatzki (1848) concurrently depict a broad strip of southern Anglia along the Schlei as monolingually German. The remaining peninsula is described as bilingual, which increasingly meant that Danish was still widely understood by the older generations, whereas it was gradually disappearing among young people. The Anglian pastor Hans Nicolai Andreas Jensen predicted in his ecclesiastical statistics that Anglia would "soon be all German in language, as already was the case along the Schlei, where one rarely hears Danish anymore, except among very old people, whereas the adults still speak Danish amongst themselves further north."[44] For the middle of the nineteenth century, P. K. Thorsen subsequently confirmed that Low German had turned into the preferred idiom of the younger generations of northern Anglia.[45]

Anglia also became the focus of a new kind of language policy, which already reflected the spirit of nationalism. Previous decades had brought occasional governmental attempts to steer linguistic developments. Yet even the most significant decree of that earlier period only adjusted the local language of court to the language of the church and school.[46] Whereas this measure gave a population that was completely socialized in Danish improved access to the legal system, the language ordinances of 1851 pursued more ambitious goals. In response to the Sleswig-Holstein secessionism of 1848-1850, the Danish government, led by the national liberals, attempted to turn back the linguistic clock in central Sleswig.

Danish was to become the language of daily and public life in a broad belt of land at the center of the duchy where it had been the dominant vernacular up to the late 1700s. Southernmost Anglia around the city of Schleswig and along the Schlei retained the existing regulations, whereas the remainder of Anglia and the high plains was declared bilingual. Within this region, Danish became the language of instruction, whereas German was taught as a subject. The churches were to use both languages, but the insistence on Danish confirmation classes indicated the long-term goals.

In already largely German-speaking Anglia, the language ordinances were bitterly opposed. The often historically trained Danish officials and activists were convinced that the population would revert to its earlier, and thus more authentic, cultural identity, once the legal framework was provided. Yet it soon became obvious that prenational linguistic trends could not so easily be reversed through national programs. Rather, the bulk of the population experienced the new measures as coercive. They had acquired the German language through the encompassing impact of modern education. Moreover, they already approached the language question from a national perspective themselves. Anglia had been strongly affected by the Sleswig-Holstein movement; a return to Danish was also rejected for political reasons.

Since Danish again lost its public function in central Sleswig after Denmark's military defeat in 1864, the language ordinances remained a brief interlude. It is possible that a more prolonged governmental effort may have succeeded. It is also possible, however, that governments no longer were in a position to unilaterally change linguistic preferences. One way or the other, the period of the language ordinances coincided with the end of significant Danish language use in Anglia.

Conditions were somewhat different on the sandy high plains of the interior called the geest. The South Jutland dialect persisted longer in this marginal region, which barely bordered on German-speaking districts until the language change in Anglia. German had long dominated as the idiom of church and education, although the northernmost communities had also used Danish at times. Like a slowly receding wedge, however, the Danish vernacular extended southward almost to the Schlei. In the mid 1800s, C. F. Allen still considered Viöl a purely Danish community, and he even insisted on the occasional occurrence of Danish further south in Olderup and Schwesing.[47]

Yet on the central plains, too, the use of South Jutland Danish was not based on national considerations. The local communities identified less ardently with the Sleswig-Holstein movement than their Anglian neighbors. Nonetheless, many centuries with German as the language of culture had tied the population to the south. The language ordinances of 1851 were widely rejected, even if some northern communities pragmatically availed themselves of Danish religious and cultural offerings.[48]

Therefore, the return of German in the local schools and churches after 1864 soon reinitiated the gradual decline of the Danish dialect. On the high plains, this decline reflected the marginalization of localized cultural forms in modern mass societies. Largely German-oriented, with a tradition of supplementing the Danish dialect with a German literary superstructure, the population resembled their Frisian neighbors to the west. There was little struggle between official German and Danish. Rather, the conflict involved the preservation of local tradition against the forces of homogenization emanating from the societal center.

In this clash between traditionalism and modernization, the South Jutland dialect shared the fate of North Frisian and increasingly also Low German. H. V. Clausen only recorded a moderate decline of South Jutland Danish on the geest in the second half of the nineteenth century. Yet J. G. C. Adler's simultaneous assessment that the dialect was receding toward a line connecting Flensburg and Tønder, defending only a small strip of land and the parish of Wiehe to the south of it, foreshadowed the further development.[49]

In the plebiscite of 1920, all Danish-speaking communities of zone 2 returned German majorities. In the Weimar Republic, the autochthonous Danish dialect could still be heard regularly in and around the parishes of Ladelund, Süderlügum, Humptrup, Braderup, and Aventoft.[50] This area also contained the largest number of genuine Danish speakers when the arrival of the East German refugees almost doubled the population and made compact Danish-speaking communities illusionary. This did not entail the immediate disappearance of the South Jutland dialect, as can be seen from Søren Ryge Petersen's study of Achtrup near Leck. In 1973, one quarter of the villagers still reported a good command of this idiom.[51] Since then, the decline of the local dialect has continued, however. In South Sleswig, Danish is now learned primarily in schools and institutions.[52]

Developments north of the modern-day border followed a somewhat different path. To be sure, this region, too, contained rural communities with conditions reminiscent of central Sleswig, in other words, with a Danish vernacular and an established German tradition in church and school. One such community was the parish of Bov to the north of Flensburg. In the community of Ubjerg near Tønder, the percentage of German speakers in the census of 1905 surpassed the share of Süderlügum and Humptrup further south.[53] Even if one treats individual self-assessments in politicized censuses with caution, they remain useful for the relative comparison of adjacent communities.

In many rural communities, however, the identification with the German language was politically motivated. Only rarely did it reflect the factual use of German in everyday life, in spite of the basic command of that language acquired in school. This command increased in the Prussian period, when German became a subject in Danish schools in 1871, the language of instruction during seven additional hours per week in 1878, and the sole language of instruction, except for subject of religion, in 1888.[54] Just like the Danish language ordinances of 1851, these linguistic decrees merely stiffened popular resistance and brought about few lasting changes. With the departure of German civil servants after World War I, at the latest, most rural communities of northern Sleswig became monolingually Danish again.

Linguistic conditions in urban North Sleswig were more complex. Although standard Danish was also represented in those communities, public life, including education, had long been predominantly German. The Danish surroundings and especially the continuous immigration from them reinforced the vernacular dominance of Danish, however. The language ordinances privileged Danish in church and school but were immediately rescinded in 1864.

The subsequent era up to World War I was not merely a return to the established practice of German dominance in the official and Danish in the everyday sphere. Haderslev, Aabenraa, and Sønderborg did revert to German school and mixed church language.[55] Yet in the urban communities, modernization also altered the demographic structure. The language use in education and public administration impacted urban professionals more than farmers. The new industries attracted laborers from other parts of the country. Together, these developments established German more broadly as a second vernacular.[56] This process went farthest in traditionally German-leaning Tønder, which was largely seen as a German-speaking town at the onset of the twentieth century.[57] More than in other North Sleswig towns, German also defended its position in Tønder during the interwar years, although it again lost its hegemony. In the decades since World War II, however, German has largely disappeared from everyday life in Tønder as well. [58] This development relied on assimilation as well as the demographic reversal, which entailed migration from central Denmark and the embedding of Danish elites.[59] Today, linguistic conditions largely mirror the political border.

Even though the central questions politically as well as culturally revolved around the German-Danish relationship, the presence of a third linguistic community should not be overlooked. For two reasons, Frisian played a less significant role. The limited number of Frisian speakers and the absence of a unified North Frisian written standard entailed that the Frisians during central historical periods were subsumed in the duchy's German element. Not until the twentieth century, when the Frisian language had already lost most of its domains, did alternative voices make themselves heard.

The special significance of the Frisians in early Sleswig history lay in their distinction from Danes. The south of Jutland was thus not a completely normal part of the Danish realm, even at a time when Lower Saxon, not to mention standard German, lacked any local basis. The early Frisian presence, which at that time still coincided with a significant Frisian element in the Roman-German empire, created cultural links between Sleswig and the heart of Europe.

This integration with the south was deepened when the Bible was not translated into North Frisian during the Reformation. German became the area's church and school language. It could be more than mere coincidence that the ecclesiastical language divide and subsequently the modern political border in essence connected the northern tip of the Frisian language area with the early Germanized city of Flensburg. Without the Frisian west coast, the linguistic enclave of Flensburg may have shared the fate of the urban communities further north.

Due to its integration into a German superstructure, modern North Frisian developed more along the lines of a dialect than of a distinct language. This functional limitation was even more pronounced than that of central Sleswig's Jutish dialect, which was at least sporadically reinforced by standard Danish. The relationship between German and Frisian, on the other hand, almost universally reflected a duality of language of culture and education on the one hand, regional vernacular on the other. This had to undermine the position of Frisian in an era when centralized linguistic standards began to dominate communication in the peripheries.

Frisian increasingly lost influence, both in regard to its number of speakers and in regard to its social functions. The numerical decline had several aspects. At first, entire districts were lost when Eiderstedt and adjacent areas in the south switched to Low German after 1600. Whereas approximately 50,000 Sleswigers spoke Frisian in the Middle Ages, this number had fallen to around 30,000 by 1840.[60]

Even more perilous than the language change in individual districts was the internal dissolution of the Frisian cultural sphere. The growing integration of North Frisia into a transregional economic exchange brought immigration and the touristic development of the coastline. The local language hierarchy meant that almost all Frisian speakers also developed an excellent command of Low German and sometimes High German, whereas most native speakers of Low German only learned the High German standard, not Frisian. The speakers of High German, whose numbers continually grew, rarely acquired more than a rudimentary knowledge of the regional vernaculars. This relegated Frisian to the private sphere. In the census of 1905, only 16,000 Sleswigers still listed Frisian as their native tongue.[61] They no longer inhabited a separate linguistic sphere, but shared it with approximately 1,000 Danish speakers and more than 20,000 German speakers.[62]

The relative as well as absolute decline of Frisian continued and was accelerated at the end of World War II by the previously mentioned arrival of Germans expelled from the east. No exact counts have been made, which has led to the establishment of a symbolic number of 10,000 active Frisian speakers and an additional 20,000 who understand the language. Nils Århammar, one of the leading experts in the field, considered an estimate of 6,000-7,000 Frisian speakers more realistic.[63] Within a total population of around 160,000 in the county of North Frisia at the end of the twentieth century, Frisian speakers have become a small minority. Frisian is still described as the dominant language on parts of the island of Föhr.[64]

Conclusion

Its transitional location at the interchange of central and northern Europe has given Sleswig a multifaceted linguistic history. Originally the home of a North Sea Germanic population that combined Scandinavian and continental influences, the region became Danish in the early Middle Ages. Its southwestern coast was inhabited by Frisians, however, and its southern margins lay barren. The Saxon settlement of the border region established the cultural triad of the later duchy. The close integration with neighboring Holstein triggered a further Germanization of the public sphere, whereas everyday language use, especially in the countryside, changed little.

When modernization expanded education and social interaction, the public sphere increased its impact on the private. As a consequence, German also established itself as the vernacular in those regions of central Sleswig in which it already prevailed in official use. This process was accelerated rather than decelerated by the Danish language ordinances of the mid 1800s, because nationally motivated language policies then encountered a population that also approached the language question from a political perspective. For the same reason, the subsequent Germanization drive in Prussian North Sleswig made little progress in rural communities. Its seeming success in urban centers, which partially resulted from immigration, did not persist beyond the incorporation of North Sleswig into Denmark.

By the postwar era, at the latest, political and linguistic boundaries had essentially merged. Within the minority populations on both sides of the borders, the linguistic alternatives are kept alive. Only to a limited extent do they still represent the factual medium of communication, however. Many only avail themselves of these languages within the confines of minority institutions. As will become clear in the following chapter, minority affiliation is rooted in personal decision rather than in language.

Notes

1. Jörg K. Hoensch, *Geschichte Böhmens: Von der slavischen Landnahme bis zur Gegenwart,* 3d ed. (Munich, 1997), 423.
2. The *Dani* were originally just one of the cultural groups that inhabited the later Denmark. As has frequently been the case, the name of one group subsequently extended to a larger entity.
3. See still Hans Valdemar Gregersen, *Slesvig og Holsten før 1830* (Copenhagen, 1981), 28.
4. Hans Frede Nielsen, *Guldhornsindskriften fra Gallehus* (Odense, 2002).
5. "Contra Langobardos paucitas nobilitat; plurimis ac valentissimis nationibus cincti non per obsequium, sed praeliis et periclitando tuti sunt. Reudigni deinde et Aviones et Angli et Varini et Eudoses et Suardones et Nuithones fluminibus aut silvis muniuntur." [Ludwig Doederlein, ed., *Taciti Germania* (Erlangen, 1850), 64.]
6. For one of the central early lines of argument, see Peder Lauridsen, "Vort folks sydgrænse," *Sønderjyske Årbøger* (1893): 28-50. National orientation and historical interpretation did not always coincide, however. Christian Paulsen, for example, still assigned early Jutland to the West Germanic sphere. See Christian Paulsen, "Bidrag til sprogets historie paa den jydske halvø, fornemlig i dens søndre del," in idem, *Samlede mindre skrifter* (Copenhagen, 1857), 1:114ff.
7. The evidence was provided by the Egyptian geographer Ptolemy and by bishop Adam of Bremen.
8. "Porro de Anglis, hoc est, de illa patria quae Angulus dicitur et ab eo tempore usque hodie manere desertus inter provincias Iutarum et Saxonom perhibetur..." [Beda, *Opera historica* (London, 1962), 1:70.]
9. Newer German scholarship has widely accepted this, as can be seen in the joint German-Danish recommendations for school books. See Karl-Ernst Jeismann, ed., *Zur Geschichte und Problematik der deutsch-dänischen Beziehungen von der Wikingerzeit bis zur Gegenwart* (Braunschweig, 1984), 13.
10. See Georg Waitz, *Schleswig-Holsteins Geschichte* (Göttingen, 1851), 1:7.

11. See, for example, Hans Valdemar Gregersen, *Slesvig og Holsten før 1830* (Copenhagen, 1981), 20f.
12. See Jacob Grimm, *Geschichte der deutschen Sprache*, 3d ed. (Leipzig, 1868), 513 and 581. In a letter to the Danish scholar Christian Rafn of 15 December 1848, Grimm expressed his position most clearly:

    Originally the peninsula was entirely German or Germanic (whichever term you prefer); the ancestors of the Jutes had the same origins as the Saxons and the Cimbrians. Eventually—I do not know exactly when—the Danes invaded, subjugated the Jutes, and advanced toward the Saxons all the way to the Eider...

    Just as Denmark and Sweden could not hold on to Livonia and Pomerania, Danish rule over the Germans in Sleswig-Holstein will not continue much longer. Even Jutland's trade is directed primarily toward the south.

    On the larger and smaller islands, Scandinavia should rule and flourish.

    [Ernst Schmidt, ed., *Briefwechsel der Brüder Grimm mit nordischen Gelehrten* (Berlin, 1885; reprint Walluf, 1974), 160.]
13. Kristen Jensen Lyngby, *Bidrag til en sønderjysk sproglære* (Copenhagen, 1858), 14-24. For the immediate rejection of Grimm's political conclusions, see Rafn's response of 13 February 1849 in Ernst Schmidt, ed., *Briefwechsel der Brüder Grimm mit nordischen Gelehrten* (Berlin, 1885; reprint Walluf, 1974), 164.
14. For the settlement of Sleswig, see, for example, August Sach, *Das Herzogtum Schleswig in seiner ethnographischen und nationalen Entwicklung*, 3 vols. (Halle, 1896-1907), and Karl Nielsen Bock, *Niederdeutsch auf dänischem Substrat* (Copenhagen, 1933).
15. Caspar Danckwerth, *Newe Landesbeschreibung der zwei Herzogthümer Schleswich und Holstein* (N. P., 1652), 54-55.
16. For a history of the Protestant Pietists of Christiansfeld, who are mainly known as Moravians in English and as Herrnhuter in German and Danish, see Anders Pontoppidan Thyssen, ed., *Herrnhuter-samfundet i Christiansfeld,* 2 vols. (Åbenrå, 1984).
17. Hans Valdemar Gregersen provides a list of noblemen who immigrated from Holstein between 1325 and 1350 on pages 70-72 of his study *Plattysk i Sønderjylland* (Odense, 1974).
18. Johann Friederich Hansen states in 1758: "The courts of Haderslev county usually hold trials in Danish. Therefore, the minutes and verdicts have to be translated into German when they are appealed to the higher court in Gottorp." [Johann Friedrich Hansen, *Staatsbeschreibung des Herzogthums Schleswig* (Hamburg, 1758), 8.] See also C. L. E. von Stemann, *Schleswigs Recht und Gerichtsverfassung im siebenzehnten Jahrhundert* (Schleswig, 1855), 19f., C. F. Allen, *Det danske sprogs historie i hertugdømmet Slesvig eller Sønderjylland* (Copenhagen, 1857), 1:214, and Hans Valdemar Gregersen, *Plattysk i Sønderjylland* (Odense, 1974), 275.
19. See Martin Rheinheimer, *Die Dorfordnungen im Herzogtum Schleswig: Dorf und Obrigkeit in der Frühen Neuzeit* (Stuttgart, 1999), 1:215-232.
20. For an in-depth discussion, see Einar Haugen, *The Scandinavian Languages* (London, 1976), 313-323. Haugen's theory is not undisputed, however, and other researchers have seen grammatical simplification as an inherent trait of Germanic language history.
21. August Sach, *Das Herzogtum Schleswig in seiner ethnographischen und nationalen Entwicklung* (Halle, 1907), 3:227; C. F. Allen, *Det danske sprogs historie i hertugdømmet Slesvig eller Sønderjylland* (Copenhagen, 1857), 1:235. See also Ulrich Petersen,

"Beschreibung der Stadt Schleswig," Landesarchiv Schleswig-Holstein, Abteilung 400.1, Nr. 512.

22. See Hans Valdemar Gregersen, *Plattysk i Sønderjylland* (Odense, 1974), 167f.
23. See Troels Fink, "Flensborgs borgerskab i det 15. aarhundrede," in *Til Knud Fabricius*, ed. Hans Fussing (Copenhagen, 1945), 13-29; Erich Hoffmann, *Die Herkunft des Bürgertums in den Städten des Herzogtums Schleswig* (Neumünster, 1953), 113-125.
24. This criticism was found among both Danes and Germans. The Dane Christiern Petersen complained in the 1500s: "What are we supposed to do with these books; we cannot understand them. They are in Flensburg Danish (because there one speaks Danish and German mixed together)." [Christiern Pedersen, *Danske Skrifter* IV (Copenhagen, 1854), 154.]

    Centuries later, August Sach still lists idiosyncrasies of Flensburg German that betray Danish influence. See August Sach, *Das Herzogtum Schleswig in seiner ethnographischen und nationalen Entwicklung* (Halle, 1907), 3:259. This sometimes overemphasized mixing of languages was more common in the colloquial speech of recent arrivals, however, than in the public and educational spheres.
25. For Tønder, see Anders Bjerrum, "Folkesproget i Tønder gennem tiderne," in *Tønder gennem tiderne*, ed. Mourits Mackeprang (Tønder, 1944), 2:440-464; and Ludwig Andresen, *Bürger- und Einwohnerbuch der Stadt Tondern* (Kiel, 1937).
26. "Children should not only not be educated in High German out of concern for the Danish language in this district. This should also be done out of concern for the Low German language as it is spoken in southern Anglia...

    Children who are used to speaking this language have great difficulties in learning High German, whereas they easily learn Danish." [C. F. Allen, *Det danske sprogs historie i hertugdømmet Slesvig eller Sønderjylland* (Copenhagen, 1857), 2:598 and 599.]

    And Peder Lauridsen stated in a similar vein: "One way or the other, the Anglian children who spoke Low German had to learn a new language in school—either High German or standard Danish. Yet in vocabulary and sentence structure the latter lay much closer to Anglian Low German than the difficult and elaborate High German." [Peder Lauridsen, "Vort folks sydgrænse," in *Danmark: Land og Folk*, ed. Daniel Bruun (Copenhagen, 1919), 2:4:108f.]
27. "At that time, one cannot expect that civil servants would have fully understood that the Jutish dialect represents a separate language in its relationship to standard Danish." [August Sach, *Das Herzogtum Schleswig in seiner ethnographischen und nationalen Entwicklung* (Halle, 1907), 3:277.]
28. Otto Mensing, "Das Plattdeutsche in Schleswig und die neue Bewegung," in *Schleswig-Holsteinisches Jahrbuch 1921*, ed. Ernst Sauermann (Hamburg, 1921), 78; August Sach, *Das Herzogtum Schleswig in seiner ethnographischen und nationalen Entwicklung* (Halle, 1907), 3:387f.
29. See the map in Hans Valdemar Gregersen, *Plattysk i Sønderjylland* (Odense, 1974), 181. See also Troels Fink, "Den kirkelige sproggrænse," *Sønderjyske Årbøger* (1964): 282.
30. See, for example, Walter Göbell, ed., *Die Schleswig-Holsteinische Kirchenordnung von 1543* (Neumünster, 1986), 54, 56, 346.
31. Hans Valdemar Gregersen, *Plattysk i Sønderjylland* (Odense, 1974), 291f.; P. K. Thorsen, *Afhandlinger og Breve* (Copenhagen, 1927), 1:10.
32. See, for example, Thomas Otto Achelis, "Deutsche und dänische Gottesdienste im Herzogtum Schleswig," *Schriften des Vereins für Schleswig-Holsteinische Kirchengeschichte,* 2d ser., 10 (1949): 86.

33. For the very negative assessment of Klotz's seventeenth-century role in the Danish nationalist tradition, see C. F. Allen, *Det danske sprogs historie i hertugdømmet Slesvig eller Sønderjylland* (Copenhagen, 1857), 1:108-124. On the German side, in contrast, August Sach argued that Klotz's language policy primarily affected Low German. See August Sach, *Das Herzogtum Schleswig in seiner ethnographischen und nationalen Entwicklung* (Halle, 1907), 3:367. See also Erich Hoffmann's portrayal of Klotz in Verein für Schleswig-Holsteinische Kirchengeschichte, ed., *Schleswig-Holsteinische Kirchengeschichte*, vol. 4, *Orthodoxie und Pietismus* (Neumünster, 1984), 95-112.
34. Troels Fink, "Den kirkelige sproggrænse," *Sønderjyske Årbøger* (1964): 281f.
35. The church ordinance of 1543 already provided that the pastor should "together with his sexton teach people the catechism." [Walter Göbell, ed., *Die Schleswig-Holsteinische Kirchenordnung von 1543* (Neumünster, 1986), 108.]
36. Gottfried Japsen has shown that Danish schools also frequently taught some subjects in German. This applied especially to mathematics, due to the duchies' separate units of measure. See Gottfried Japsen, *Det dansksprogede skolevesen i Sønderjylland indtil 1814* (Tønder, 1968), 202-204.
37. Gottfried Japsen, *Det dansksprogede skolevesen i Sønderjylland indtil 1814* (Tønder, 1968), 27ff.; 198.
38. In spite of its shortcomings, this instruction established rudimentary literacy in early modern Sleswig. See Gottfried Japsen, *Det dansksprogede skolevesen i Sønderjylland indtil 1814* (Tønder, 1968), 26.
39. See C. F. Allen, *Det danske sprogs historie i hertugdømmet Slesvig eller Sønderjylland* (Copenhagen, 1857), 1:104-108; and August Sach, *Das Herzogtum Schleswig in seiner ethnographischen und nationalen Entwicklung* (Halle, 1907), 3:364.
40. Martin Rheinheimer, *Die Dorfordnungen im Herzogtum Schleswig: Dorf und Obrigkeit in der Frühen Neuzeit* (Stuttgart, 1999), 1:219.
41. "He is a peasant; he speaks Danish," stated the townspeople in Flensburg according to P. K. Thorsen. See Peder Kristian Thorsen, *Afhandlinger og Breve* (Copenhagen, 1927), 1:179.
42. Hans Schultz Hansen discussed this bourgeoisization of wealthier Sleswig farmers in *Det sønderjyske landbrugs historie 1830-1993* (Aabenraa, 1994).
43. See C. F. Allen, *Det danske sprogs historie i hertugdømmet Slesvig eller Sønderjylland* (Copenhagen, 1857), 2:157-159.
44. Hans Nicolai Andreas Jensen, *Versuch einer kirchlichen Statistik des Herzogthums Schleswig* (Flensburg, 1840), 1:21.
45. See Peder Kristian Thorsen, *Afhandlinger og Breve* (Copenhagen, 1927), 1:175.
46. For the central passages of this language ordinance of 1840, see Institut für Regionale Forschung und Information and Institut for grænseregionsforskning, eds., *Der nationale Gegensatz/De nationale modsætninger, 1800-1864* (Flensburg, 1984), 79.
47. C. F. Allen, *Det danske sprogs historie i hertugdømmet Slesvig eller Sønderjylland* (Copenhagen, 1857), 2:384-387.
48. Hans Schultz Hansen, *Danskheden i Sydslesvig 1840-1918 som folkelig og national bevægelse* (Flensburg, 1918), 133f.
49. Clausen and Adler developed their thoughts in H. V. Clausen, "Folkesproget i Sønderjylland," *Sønderjyske Årbøger* (1892): 182-212 and (1893): 89-105; and (J.) G. (C.) Adler, "Die Volkssprache in dem Herzogthum Schleswig seit 1864," *Zeitschrift der Gesellschaft für Schleswig-Holstein-Lauenburgische Geschichte* 21 (1891): 1-135.
50. Paul Selk, *Die sprachlichen Verhältnisse im deutsch-dänischen Sprachgebiet südlich der Grenze* (Hamburg, 1986), 180.

51. Søren Ryge Petersen, *Dansk eller tysk? En undersøgelse af sprogforholdene i en flersproget sydslesvigsk kommune* 1973 (Flensburg, 1975), 50.
52. This development is also visible in Søren Ryge Petersen's study, which found that one quarter of all inhabitants knew South Jutland Danish in 1973, but merely a few percent of children under ten. See Søren Ryge Petersen, *Dansk eller tysk? En undersøgelse af sprogforholdene i en flersproget sydslesvigsk kommune* 1973 (Flensburg, 1975), 71f. Thus, the Danish spoken within the contemporary Danish minority is predominantly a standard Danish with German influences and not the South Jutland dialect.
53. Whereas 233 of Ubjerg's 420 inhabitants declared German their main language in 1905, only 307 of 807 did in Süderlügum and 133 of 547 in Humptrup. See J. G. C. Adler, "Die Volkssprache in dem vormaligen Herzogtum Schleswig auf Grund der Sprachenzählung vom 1. Dezember 1905," *Zeitschrift der Gesellschaft für Schleswig-Holsteinische Geschichte* 45 (1915): 64.
54. J. G. C. Adler, "Die Volkssprache in dem Herzogthum Schleswig seit 1864," *Zeitschrift der Gesellschaft für Schleswig-Holstein-Lauenburgische Geschichte* 21 (1891): 125-131.
55. August Sach, *Das Herzogtum Schleswig in seiner ethnographischen und nationalen Entwicklung* (Halle, 1907), 3:456.
56. The censuses of the era occasionally showed German majorities in the towns of northern Sleswig. The census of 1905 had the following distribution of Danish (listed first) and German: in Aabenraa, 3,489 versus 3,413; in Haderslev, 1,695 versus 1,174; in Sønderborg, 2,625 versus 4,089; and in Tønder, 1,117 versus 2,954. The rapid turnaround in the interwar years gives some credence to Danish criticisms of the census results; at the same time, a substantial German presence in the towns of northern Sleswig remains indisputable. For the numbers, see J. G. C. Adler, "Die Volkssprache in dem vormaligen Herzogtum Schleswig auf Grund der Sprachenzählung vom 1. Dezember 1905," *Zeitschrift der Gesellschaft für Schleswig-Holsteinische Geschichte* 45 (1915): 66f.
57. In regard to the late 1800s, see H. V. Clausen's Danish perspective: "Whereas the boys use Danish in the streets of Aabenraa, Haderslev, Sønderborg, Gråsten, etc., they often speak German in Tønder. Everywhere, the situation is worse among the girls." [H. V. Clausen, "Folkesproget i Sønderjylland, " *Sønderjyske Årbøger* (1893): 100.]
58. Within the confines of minority life, of course, there continues to exist a Germanophone sphere. History and geography also gave the Danish-speaking inhabitants of Tønder an above average familiarity with German. Therefore, 73 percent of the local populace stated as late as 1960 that they could communicate in German. See Kaare Svalastoga and Preben Wolf, eds., *En by ved grænsen* (Copenhagen, 1963), 160.
59. Svalastoga and Wolf showed in the 1960s that the German minority was noticeably overrepresented among the well-established Tønder families, whereas new arrivals continually diminished the minority's relative share in the overall population. See Kaare Svalastoga and Preben Wolf, eds., *En by ved grænsen* (Copenhagen, 1963), 53.
60. Claas Riecken, *Nordfriesische Sprachforschung im 19. Jahrhundert* (Bredstedt, 2001), 20f.
61. J. G. C. Adler, "Die Volkssprache in dem vormaligen Herzogtum Schleswig auf Grund der Sprachenzählung vom 1. Dezember 1905," *Zeitschrift der Gesellschaft für Schleswig-Holsteinische Geschichte* 45 (1915): 69.
62. J. G. C. Adler, "Die Volkssprache in dem vormaligen Herzogtum Schleswig auf Grund der Sprachenzählung vom 1. Dezember 1905," *Zeitschrift der Gesellschaft für Schleswig-Holsteinische Geschichte* 45 (1915): 68.
63. See also Horst Haider Munske, ed., *Handbuch des Friesischen* (Tübingen, 2001), 267.
64. Horst Haider Munske, ed., *Handbuch des Friesischen* (Tübingen, 2001), 267.

CHAPTER FOUR

A Tale of Three Communities

National Identification in Changing Times

When the modern concepts of nationalism and liberalism spread throughout Europe, they encountered different political and cultural environments. In polities that were rooted in one dominant culture, they transformed the nature of society but left its structures intact. In culturally composite territories such as Sleswig, by contrast, the new mode of thinking challenged the very existence of the body politic. On one level, it pitted the representatives of the old order against middle-class reformers. On another, the monarchic elites found themselves in the midst of a bitter feud between competing national movements, trying to hold together what liberal revolutionaries seemed to tear apart.

This chapter explores national identification in Sleswig by examining three cultural communities. It describes the changing public appearance of these communities at different points in time, but it also reveals diverse layers of affiliation within them. By focusing on the prewar Danish community in Prussian North Sleswig, the interwar German community in Denmark, and the postwar Danish community in Germany, the chapter examines the national dichotomy in different temporal and societal settings. Whereas the prewar Danish community of northern Sleswig constituted a local majority intent on preserving its cultural distinctiveness until territorial change seemed feasible, the other two communities had markedly fewer cultural characteristics to defend. Their distinctiveness originated primarily in their sense of self and only subsequently acquired cultural overtones. In fact, the requisite depth of these cultural elements remained hotly contested.

Different types of identity did not only set apart communities but also coexisted within them. Although this internal diversity complicates categorization, the individual groupings remained sufficiently distinguishable to suggest a typology based on the respective role of objective and subjective markers of identity. The continuous interplay of cultural distinctions and personal identifications constitutes the central subject of investigation in this chapter.

Before examining interlocking German and Danish identities, however, one has to reflect on the third indigenous community in Sleswig. The North Frisians added an important variable to the national equation, without fully functioning as a national community themselves. In the early Middle Ages, their presence set southern Jutland slightly apart from the rest of Scandinavia. Following the German colonization of southernmost Sleswig and the political integration of Sleswig and Holstein, the Frisians were drawn into the orbit of German literary culture. Frisian and German turned into parallel native languages with different domains. Since Frisian dominated colloquial communication, it assumed the role of a dialect, albeit based on functional rather than philological criteria.[1]

When national conceptions reached Sleswig, most Frisians merged into a broader German Sleswig-Holsteinism. Frisian cultural efforts focused on the preservation of local traditions, including language, but in a manner more reminiscent of corresponding efforts in the German heartland. Unlike their Danish neighbors to the north, the Frisians did not engage in national confrontation with the Prussian authorities. If frictions arose, they were rooted in Sleswig-Holsteinism and its desire for provincial autonomy. Only in the former royal enclaves on the islands of Föhr and Amrum did Danish sympathies persist into the Prussian era.[2]

At the time of the Sleswig plebiscite in 1920, alternative voices emerged. Most eloquent was Cornelius Petersen, a native of Eiderstedt, who urged his compatriots to break free of Prussia and seek autonomy within Denmark.[3] Overall, this Frisian nationalism with Danish sympathies remained isolated, and the vast majority voted to remain within Germany.[4] Yet the public debate about the postwar future of the region initiated an open split in the Frisian movement. The North Frisian Society continued its cultural preservation efforts under the roof of German patriotism and cooperated with the Sleswig-Holstein League, the leading German nationalist organization in the region. The newly founded Frisian-Sleswig Society, in contrast, formulated the tenets of autonomous Frisian nationhood.[5] In their eyes, Frisians were a self-contained people, not a German regional variety. They should establish this individuality in the linguistic and the political sphere. Since political independence seemed utopian, many nationalist Frisians set their hopes on a generous autonomy within Denmark.

In the interwar era, the nationalist wing remained a small minority.[6] When it strove for internationally recognized minority status for the North Frisians, the German-minded majority countered with a massive petition drive. In the Bohmstedt Declaration, 13,000 North Frisians proclaimed their attachment to Germany and rejected the label of national minority.[7] This conflict even occupied the European Congress of Nationalities, which after bitter controversies decided to reject the Frisian-Sleswig Society's application due to a yet insufficient level of cultural activism.[8]

Ironically, the opposing camps were not so far apart on the core questions of Frisian language and culture. The bitterness of the dispute derived from its association with the Danish-German conflict. Whereas the national Frisians saw Frisian autonomy secured most safely in affiliation with Denmark and Danish South Sleswigers, the majority considered this attitude a betrayal of Frisia's historical integration in a German cultural orbit. This interference of the larger border conflict continued into the postwar era, during which a distancing from German nationalism also convinced many Frisians to advocate unification with Denmark. The national Frisians became directly affiliated with the major organizations of the Danish minority and shared in their dramatic expansion. In the long run, however, this development primarily established Danish cultural expressions in areas where they had few historical precedents, without truly reinvigorating Frisian traditions. To the contrary, the influx of German refugees further undermined Frisian distinctiveness and especially the everyday use of the Frisian language. Thus, Frisian identity has been facing the danger of becoming folkloristic symbolism on the one hand, Danish sidekick on the other. On the positive side, the recent decades have brought increasing cooperation between the formerly hostile camps and the establishment of Frisian scholarly institutions.

The history of the North Frisians highlights the dilemma of ethnic groups that lack the human, cultural, and economic resources for independent nationhood. The small coastal community found itself squeezed between the evolving state societies of Germany and Denmark. Yet also members of the larger Danish and German communities have faced minority status at different points in time. Their experience is analyzed in the remainder of this chapter.

A Classic Minority: The Danish Community in Prussian North Sleswig

Danish nationalism in Sleswig had diverse roots and inspirations. Among merchants and artisans, especially in Flensburg, a traditionalist royalism predominated, coupled with an economic orientation toward central Denmark. Intellectuals such as Christian Paulsen and Christian Flor personified the middle-class national-liberalism so typical of nineteenth-century Europe. They were influenced by German romanticism as well as by the Danish reformer, bishop, and poet N. F. S. Grundtvig.[9] Last, but not least, there was a socially rooted opposition against the German-speaking elites among farmers and workers in North Sleswig. These independent strains coalesced in the Danish national movement.

National conflict also surfaced in the provincial assembly. In 1836, Nis Lorenzen demanded that Danish be made the language of public affairs wherever it was used in school. Although the initiative did not achieve immediate success, its aspirations became an integral part of the political debate. They were largely fulfilled in the royal language ordinance of 1840.

The language question transformed from a matter of practicality into a matter of principle. When Nis Lorenzen intermittently resorted to Danish in the diet, in which German served as the ordinary medium of discussion, it reflected his limited fluency in the latter. In 1842, by contrast, Peter Hiort Lorenzen insisted on using Danish although he was better versed at expressing himself politically in German. The Sleswig-Holsteiners, in turn, were only willing to accommodate Danish on a pragmatic basis. Language had become a national symbol.

Gradually, the new way of thinking spread to broader segments of the population. In 1838, Peter Christian Koch began to publish *Dannevirke*, the first Danish-language periodical in the duchy. In 1843, the Danish national movement began to assemble in large outdoor festivals at Skamlingsbanken. The second such meeting in 1844 already gathered more than 10,000 people from both Sleswig and the kingdom. The Danish folk colleges called *højskoler* represented a practically oriented as well as politically engaged new school type. They influenced young rural adults all over Denmark but became especially important for North Sleswig, where national activists founded the first Danish folk college in 1844.

By 1848, when the conflict between the leaders of the kingdom and the duchies erupted in open war, the national divide in Sleswig had become palpable. Whereas southern Sleswig and several northern towns supported the revolutionary Sleswig-Holstein government, most of the rural north remained hostile. Traditional royalism and modern nationalism coalesced into a sentiment of loyalty to Denmark. In pamphlets and petition drives, the diverging national camps formulated their agendas. Popular militias, German in the south, Danish in the north, further accentuated the rift.

The defeat of the uprising temporarily changed the character of the national conflict. The central government took a leading role, trying to promote Danish interests within the limits set by international agreements. Flensburg became the seat of regional administration in 1850. The customs border was moved from the Kongeå to the Eider in August 1850. The duchies switched to a common currency with the kingdom.

Many leading Sleswig-Holsteiners went into exile. Yet the national movement among Danish Sleswigers stagnated as well. The reorganized civil service took a decidedly national stance, which made popular activism less urgent. At the same time, many newly arrived officials from the kingdom brushed aside local sensitivities, which put a damper on the national enthusiasm of the general public.

The wars in 1864 and 1866 and the ensuing incorporation of Sleswig, as well as Holstein, into the kingdom of Prussia transformed the duchy. Communal and legal reforms modernized the new province of Schleswig-Holstein. Language legislation largely reverted to the period prior to 1848, which pleased the Germans and displeased the Danes. Both were united, however, in their opposition to raised taxes and the loss of provincial autonomy. The first elections to the North German parliament in 1867 showed a clear majority for anti-Prussian candidates.

Danish activists initially expected a swift redrawing of the border. They pinned their hopes on the Treaty of Prague, which concluded the war between Prussia and Austria in 1866. In article 5 of that agreement, Austria had transferred all its rights in the duchies to Prussia, but in such a manner "that the inhabitants of the northern districts of Sleswig should be ceded to Denmark, if they in a free vote had expressed a desire to be united with Denmark."[10] Considering Prussian rule a short-term affair, minority leaders advocated a hard line against the government. The so-called protest policy dominated. Danish deputies refused to take the requisite oath on the Prussian constitution, even if this entailed their exclusion from the chamber. Teachers and pastors lost their jobs due to equivalent gestures. The few who relented found themselves ostracized by their fellow Danes.

The community was weakened numerically as well. Public servants who had lost their livelihoods left for the kingdom. After the transfer of sovereignty, it was possible to opt for Danish citizenship. The mandatory three-year service in the military motivated many more to leave for Denmark or the United States. Emigration from North Sleswig was a multifaceted phenomenon, however. While its absolute numbers were substantial, they were only moderately higher than in German and Frisian South Sleswig. On a district level, the German-speaking west coast experienced especially high rates of emigration.[11] The prevalence of non-proprietors among the emigrants points to the social aspects of the phenomenon. By the late 1880s, emigration was declining again.[12]

When those who had opted for Denmark rejoined their families, their status became contested. The so-called optants could return to Sleswig as Danish subjects.[13] This enabled them to resume their private and professional lives but deprived them of the political rights reserved for citizens, such as suffrage. While there were 4,575 Danish citizens in North Sleswig in 1867, their number had grown to 25,000 in 1881.[14]

Tentative negotiations about an implementation of article 5 in the late 1860s brought no result. When Austria and Prussia bilaterally rescinded this stipulation in 1878, Danish hopes for an impending border revision were dashed. Although some Danish activists, led by the editors of *Flensborg Avis,* insisted on the continued validity of article 5, others resolved that the politics of demonstrative protest no longer sufficed. Whereas the former promoted a historical and constitutional approach, which would allow for the inclusion of Flensburg in Danish Sleswig, the latter preferred a cultural strategy that secured the solidly Danish-speaking districts further to the north.

◆ ◆ ◆

Due to the rural character of late-nineteenth-century North Sleswig, the future of the region was decided in the countryside. The majority of the working population was employed in agriculture, and the towns grew more slowly than in many other Danish and German regions. Independent farmers, owning 60 percent of the soil, held a central position. They were not only employers but also natural leaders of such cooperative ventures as dairies and credit unions.

The Danish national movement did not originate in rural Sleswig. At first, its tenets were promoted by urban intellectuals such as Christian Paulsen and Christian Flor.[15] Before long, however, North Sleswig's farmers turned into the backbone of the Danish movement. Whereas the towns were tightly contested politically, the Danes secured hegemony over much of the countryside.

The driving force behind the Danish national mobilization in Sleswig has been interpreted in different ways. The classic understanding, which found its early formulation in Peder Lauridsen's *Da Sønderjylland vaagnede*, put Danish activism into a direct interplay with its German counterpart.[16] The Danish population in Sleswig mobilized in response to the rise of Sleswig-Holsteinism and subsequently German nationalism. Every move on the German side triggered a countermove on the Danish. For the Prussian period, this basic interpretation had already surfaced in Mouritz Mackeprang's contemporary *Nordslesvig 1864-1909*.[17]

In the 1970s, Gottlieb Japsen presented an alternative view.[18] Whereas the Sleswig-Holstein movement was carried by the liberal bourgeoisie and had an elitist orientation, its Danish counterpart was based on the farming population of northern Sleswig. Its social and economic grievances found their expression in Danish nationalism. Since Japsen saw nationalism as a middle-class phenomenon, however, he assigned it to those innovative districts whose farmers had adopted middle-class values. It was the strength of Danish nationalism that it also contained a socioeconomic component and allied itself with the progressive traditions of the era.

In his study *Det nordslesvigske landbrug og den danske bevægelse 1880-1914*, Hans Schultz Hansen subsequently tried to assess the respective impact of economic and political factors on the inner consolidation of the Danish community in Sleswig.[19] Schultz Hansen described two central economic aspects. In contrast to Japsen, he saw the comparatively slow pace of socioeconomic change as an advantage for the Danish movement. Because independent farmers remained the leading social stratum, they were able to dominate the political climate. In the cities, Danish influence waned, but due to delayed urbanization, this potentially hazardous development did not shift the overall balance between Danish and German in northern Sleswig. In Schultz Hansen's eyes, the economy indirectly reinforced the minority, since the economic upswing in turn of the century Sleswig provided the Danish agricultural elite with the resources to pursue political and cultural activities. The motivation for this activism, however, lay in the Prussian strategy of assimilation.

What were the policies the Danish minority had to respond to? Bureaucratic attitudes varied according to environment. In the southern districts of Tønder and Aabenraa, Prussian administrators were confident of a slow but steady acculturation process. A substantial minority leaned toward the German side. The remainder was to be familiarized with German language and culture. In general, officials from those districts advocated gradual measures and warned against unnecessary provocations.

In the more pronouncedly Danish districts of Haderslev and Sønderborg, in contrast, the bureaucracy followed a stricter course. The national camps stood in sharp opposition. Developments along the eastern border, especially in Poznania, reverberated in Danish North Sleswig. The struggle was not completely one-sided, however, and some Danish activists felt confident enough to warn local Germans against counteracting Danish political ambitions, lest they risk economic retaliation.[20]

Lothar Blatt has examined the judicial experience of the Danish minority under Prussian rule.[21] Based especially on the judgments of the Prussian administrative court of appeals, he traced the restrictions the minority experienced as well as the protections it enjoyed. The Prussian administrative courts gave citizens recourse against decisions made by the public administration.

The court's record on Danish minority rights was mixed. It usually tolerated measures against those who had opted for Denmark but had remained in or returned to Sleswig. It also upheld the removal of Danish colors from private buildings and proscriptions against decorating military graves with Danish flags.[22] On the other hand, the court voided indiscriminate proscriptions against the so-called blue songbook, which contained songs deemed inflammatory by the local authorities.[23]

Another area of conflict was the eligibility to vote and to run for public office. Frequently, the disputes centered on the citizenship status of Danish residents and were interconnected with the optant question. The challenges worked both ways, however, and some lawsuits contested the local residence of potential German voters.

Many court cases revolved around the activities of Danish clubs and associations. The Prussian law of association granted all citizens the right to found such bodies, as long as they did not pursue unlawful goals. Local police incommoded Danish activities, but they could not suppress them. Thus, the authorities were able to classify Danish agricultural and savings associations as political, which subjected them to stricter surveillance. Beyond that, however, the higher courts were not willing to go. The rights explicitly granted to political associations applied to all of them, regardless of ethnic background.[24] In 1908, a new federal law of association created uniform and simplified regulations, which largely benefited the minority associations. It did, however, require that public assemblies be conducted in German, unless they formed a part of election campaigns or took place in districts in which at least 60 percent of the population spoke a minority language.[25] This burdensome stipulation triggered legal disputes about the public or private nature of political meetings.

Yet the courts only delineated the rules of engagement. The foremost battlegrounds were churches, schools, and electoral bodies. Since both Germans and Danes were predominantly Lutheran, the church was drawn into the language debate.[26] From a theological perspective, many pastors preferred a stronger role for the parishioners' native tongue. As public officials, they were bound to follow the government's guidelines.[27]

Most important were the schools, however, since they influenced the linguistic socialization of future generations. In 1864, the language laws largely reverted to the status of 1840, while providing the local population the opportunity to petition for additional instruction in German.[28] Starting in 1871, Danish schools had to offer German as a subject.[29] Whereas these initial measures assured the familiarity of German citizens with the country's official language, the language ordinances of 1878 exceeded this pragmatic goal and established German as the language of instruction in additional subjects.[30] In 1888, German was made the sole language of instruction in North Sleswig schools, with the exception of up to six hours of religious instruction.[31] Only in the lowest grades, Danish could be used as an auxiliary language for students who lacked any prior command of German. The authorities permitted neither voluntary language classes nor Danish private schools. Finally, the possibility to opt for German religious instruction reduced the number of students receiving instruction in Danish to approximately 50 percent by 1911.[32]

The Danish minority responded to these challenges by setting up large defense organizations. As the first of these groupings, the Language Association was founded in 1880.[33] It concentrated its efforts on distributing Danish books and periodicals. The North Sleswig School Association, established in 1892, strove to secure sufficient mother tongue instruction for Danish children.[34] Initially, it was open to all types of schooling, but as domestically based activities proved difficult, its focus shifted toward providing educational opportunities in Denmark.

Danish free churches and community centers added to the richness of cultural life. Lecture societies offered intellectual interchange in the mother tongue. The new editor Jens Jessen strengthened the position of *Flensborg Avis,* originally founded in 1869, as the public voice of the Danish minority. Additional Danish newspapers were launched around 1880. With the introduction of *Sønderjyske Årbøger* in 1889, Sleswig became the focus of a Danish scholarly journal as well.

Next to these cultural enterprises, the Danish minority also pursued the electoral route.[35] In the political arena, the field was divided in three, with the Sleswig-Holstein movement as a third factor next to Prussians and Danes. Initially, the Danes preferred the more remote Prussian opponent to the local Sleswig-Holsteiners. In the long run, the two German-oriented wings moved closer to each other, creating a more clear-cut Danish-German dichotomy. Only the rising Social Democratic movement attempted to bridge the national divide.

At the outset, Danish electoral efforts lacked a central organization and relied on local notables and newspapers. With the founding of the Electoral Association in 1888, the minority gained a modern political instrument.[36] In general, the minority maintained a solid position in the electoral arena. Although its overall vote for parliament declined from 27,488 votes in the strongly charged first elections of 1867 to 21,114 in 1871 and as little as 12,360 in 1887, it had rebounded to 17,289 by 1912.[37] Danes consistently held one of Sleswig's four seats in the federal German parliament, the Reichstag, and sometimes two.[38] In the Prussian diet, based on a less equitable suffrage than the federal parliament, the Danes also defended their bastions.[39]

Not all was well, however. Whereas the Danish movement consolidated its electoral base, its share of the overall vote declined. This development was most visible on the provincial level, where the political relevance of the minority continually eroded. A major contributing factor was North Sleswig's stagnant voter base, which in part resulted from emigration and the loss of citizenship. Yet the receding Danish share was also attributable to gains made by German and Social Democratic candidates, especially in urban communities. The province of Schleswig-Holstein formed one of the strongholds of the Social Democratic party. As early as 1874, the Social Democrats received over 30 percent of the parliamentary vote; in the last prewar elections in 1912, this number had risen to 40 percent.[41] The SPD also made inroads into the Danish vote, especially in Flensburg, where it surpassed it as early as 1886.[42] The Danes could rely on a rural base that showed little inclination to defect to the SPD. They had to be concerned about the urban vote, however, and when Denmark's Social Democrats contemplated supporting their sister party in North Sleswig, other political factions in Copenhagen intervened to prevent this.[43]

Table 1. Danish Vote in Schleswig-Holstein in Reichstag Elections, 1871-1912

Year	Total Valid Vote	Total Danish Vote	Percentage Danish Vote
1871	91,825	21,114	23.0
1874	141,354	19,856	14.0
1877	150,783	17,277	11.5
1878	149,320	16,145	10.8
1881	125,804	14,398	11.4
1884	137,755	14,447	10.5
1887	185,854	12,360	6.7
1890	191,874	13,672	7.1
1893	200,404	14,363	7.2
1898	210,232	15,439	7.3
1903	247,631	14,843	6.0
1907	291,162	15,425	5.3
1912	315,497	17,289	5.5

Source: Statistisches Landesamt Schleswig-Holstein, ed., *Beiträge zur historischen Statistik Schleswig-Holsteins* (Kiel, 1967), 72f.; Hans Meyersahm, *Die Vertretung der einzelnen Parteien in Schleswig-Holstein bei den Reichstagswahlen seit 1867* (Kiel, 1912), 4f.[40]

Table 2. Reichstag Elections in Flensburg in Select Years 1874-1898 (Absolute Numbers)

Year	1874	1884	1886	1890	1898
Danes	1400	1628	1024	590	485
Social Democrats	659	806	1726	2543	2934
German liberals/ conservatives	1406	1632	1883	2449	3341

Source: Franz von Jessen, ed., *Haandbog i det nordslesvigske spørgsmaals historie* (Copenhagen, 1901), 382.

Whereas Danish electoral strength receded moderately, the minority held its ground in another area. The important role of farm families in the national conflict triggered a desire to influence their national composition. Both official and private institutions attempted to expand German landholdings. The Danish side responded with its own defense organization and was able to stop and even reverse land losses. In the end, the competing efforts barely altered the national composition of North Sleswig's farming population.[44]

From 1890 onward, Danish defense organizations also faced a nongovernmental opponent. The German Association for Northern Sleswig was established to put German initiatives in North Sleswig on a broader foundation.[45] While it was backed and promoted by German officials, the bulk of its membership consisted of local Germans. The association attempted to match the popular activism of the Danish movement, since it considered it unwise to leave this task solely to public institutions. It grew to 10,000 members in 1908, 7,000 of whom lived in North Sleswig, including Flensburg. About 5,000 members were native-born North Sleswigers.[46]

The years between 1898 and 1903 have become engrained in Danish historical memory and its images. The tenure of provincial administrator Ernst Matthias von Köller (1898-1901) is associated with the strongest attempts at curtailing Danish activism. The measures taken included expanded deportations of Danish citizens, not least of all of agricultural laborers employed by activist farmers.[47] Although the original focus was on foreign citizens, the measures were subsequently also extended to groups of optants.[48] After widespread protests in both Denmark and Germany, these deportations were reduced again. The harassment of Danish associations continued, however.

During the period of increased pressure, the Danish community lost some ground numerically. Its support in national elections stagnated at 15,000 between 1898 and 1907, whereas the German vote expanded from less than 7,000 to over 9,000. Internally, on the other hand, the minority further consolidated its position. When the German authorities eased their restrictions again after 1903, the fundamentals of the national conflict had remained unchanged.

The last decade under German rule exhibited conflicting tendencies. Some long-term problems were alleviated. Most important among those was the status of optant families. In some North Sleswig districts, between 10 and 25 percent of the local residents did not hold German citizenship in the 1880s.[49] Early in the 1890s, about 6,000 to 7,000 optants, about a quarter of the overall number, were naturalized.[50] At the turn of the century, by contrast, the Prussian authorities chose a stricter course and even questioned the citizenship status of several hundred North Sleswigers who had opted for Denmark in the 1860s without taking up residence there.[51] They had generally been treated as German citizens thereafter but saw their status endangered now. As an expression of improved bilateral relations, Prussian and Danish officials finally agreed to resolve this perennial conflict. In 1907, the two states signed a convention, in which the Prussian government promised to naturalize the stateless children of optants, whereas the Danish side once more acknowledged the existing borders.

During that period, new moderate German voices made themselves heard. In 1909, a "North Sleswig Pastors' Association" and a "Peace Association" were founded, both advocating improved relations between the ethnic communities.[52] At the same time, the large activist associations among both Danes and Germans expanded their membership, and public policy every so often reverted to harsher measures.

It took another war to reopen the Sleswig question on an international level. During the conflict, the Danish Sleswigers shared the hardships experienced by their German fellow citizens. Although the loyal response of most Danish draftees improved interethnic relations, the heated wartime atmosphere also triggered such countervailing measures as the temporary detention of Danish activists and the ban on foreign languages in the military. With increased duration of the war, the number of Danes who evaded service rose, and German military setbacks generated hopes for a border revision. In October 1918, the North Sleswig deputy H. P. Hanssen raised the issue in the German parliament, and following a demarche of the Danish foreign secretary in late November, it was included in the negotiations at Versailles.[53]

During the final period of North Sleswig's Prussian interlude, the tables between Germans and Danes had been turned again. Favored by France's desire to weaken the defeated German enemy, Denmark largely shaped the rules and procedures of the plebiscites. The Danish public was split internally, however. A moderate wing supported the official governmental line of not overburdening the country with a large German minority, whereas a more radical wing wanted to secure as much of Sleswig as the Allies were willing to concede. When northern Sleswig voted for Denmark in February 1920 and central Sleswig for Germany the month after, moderate historian H. V. Clausen's line of separation between Danish and German Sleswig became the new border. The Danes of North Sleswig were no longer a national minority.

The Danish side had achieved a majority of 75 percent and prevailed throughout most of North Sleswig. It had been narrowly defeated in bigger towns such as Aabenraa and Sønderborg, however. More importantly, it had lost in border districts such as Tønder, Højer, and Tinglev, sometimes by large margins. In the future, it would be Denmark that had to develop policies for a local minority.

The Minority that Came out of Nowhere? The Origins of the German Community of North Sleswig

The history of the Danish population in nineteenth- and early twentieth-century North Sleswig presents a picture well-known from other European regions. A largely parochial and province-based cultural identity is gradually politicized. Although the initial catalysts are middle-class intellectuals, their concepts soon spread to larger segments of the population. The competition between two national movements leaves less and less room for neutral positions. Pressure triggers counterpressure. In the end, the community becomes coherent enough to withstand governmental efforts at assimilation. It loses less committed members, but its core remains intact.

The history of German North Sleswigers adds a less commonplace facet. When the Danish national movement began to take root in North Sleswig, it did not resonate in all segments of the population. The cities had long contained a substantial German element. Some of its members hailed from the southern half of the duchies or the German abroad. Others had been born in Danish-speaking regions but had been drawn into the German cultural sphere through higher education and professional advancement.

Not even in the more uniformly Danish-speaking rural districts did everyone share the goals and aspirations of the new movement. During the period of competing petition drives in the 1830s, pro-German texts also found support in North Sleswig.[54] In the following decade, the Slesvig-Holstein Patriotic Association included northern farmers who were culturally indistinguishable from their Danish-oriented neighbors.[55]

Various impulses coalesced in the forming of this population. Superior economic conditions in the duchies strengthened the regional identification of Sleswigers, who encountered their neighbors from the kingdom primarily as migrant agricultural workers. Since the customs border ran along the river Kongeå, the economic exchange tied North Sleswig in with the rest of the duchies. Thus, the Danish-speaking farmers had a practical interest in the German language, even if they found it cumbersome as the official medium of administration.

Language played a symbolic role as well. The idiom spoken by the spiritual and political elites enjoyed prestige beyond the circle of its native users. Moreover, there was a duality of colloquial and intellectual speech. Standard literary German assumed an important place in the minds of some who encountered it in schools and churches, even if they used Danish in everyday communication. With regard to the late 1800s, Lorenz Christensen also described the appeal of so important a cultural and political power as the newly founded German empire.[56]

Finally, one should not overlook the ties between rural and urban Sleswig. Among the more successful farmers, especially, there frequently existed familial bonds with the German-oriented middle class.[57] Younger sons of the better-situated farmers pursued an education or learned a trade that gained them employment in the cities. Craftsmen and professionals considered the daughters of prosperous freeholders attractive marital choices. The ensuing kinship circles acquainted rural families with the intellectual currents in the urban centers and exposed them to Sleswig-Holsteinism.

The special legal and social conditions in the duchies formed central markers of identity. Thus, the German orientation of rural North Sleswigers typically derived from a Sleswig regional identity.[58] This identity upheld the traditional order, in which the two duchies of Sleswig and Holstein formed an independent entity coexistent with the kingdom, albeit under the common roof of the composite monarchy. Both the new German Sleswig-Holsteinism in the south and the new Danish national movement in the north strove to supplant this traditional order. Those who remained attached to it found themselves in opposition to the locally prevailing faction. In Flensburg, many German speakers were loyal to the monarchy and supported the Danish cause. In some regions of northern Sleswig, Danish speakers upheld the duchy's autonomy and self-sufficiency and became the foundation of a German community.

In North Sleswig and Denmark proper, many felt provoked by Danish speakers who refused to identify with the Danish nation. Critics could only explain this conduct with character flaws.[59] Among Danes, that puzzling community became known as *hjemmetyskere*, the home or local Germans. The term denoted native North Sleswigers, usually with the South Jutland Danish dialect as their native tongue, in contrast to officials or immigrants from German majority regions. Although the designation was used unflatteringly in the beginning, it was embraced by the Germans themselves and gradually lost its negative connotations.[60]

During the Prussian period, the German-minded population throughout Sleswig enjoyed the benefits of majority affiliation. In June 1920, however, the northern half of the duchy joined Denmark. Most residents welcomed this development and enthusiastically greeted King Christian X when he rode over the border on horseback on July 10. To the German-oriented inhabitants, these developments were less gratifying. Judging by the results of the plebiscite, they were to comprise a quarter of the population. The actual numbers looked different. For one, 9,000 voters had their residence south of the new border, and unlike the 14,000 who had arrived from Denmark, virtually none of them was willing or able to return to the now Danish region. More ominous for the minority was the additional departure of local residents. Public officials saw no future for themselves in Denmark; neither did most German-minded teachers. Many workers and domestic servants joined the exodus.[61] Although some of them moved south of the border as well, farmers were most deeply rooted in the region and became overrepresented in the German community.[62] Urban areas experienced a disproportionately high emigration, with approximately 1,700 people, or close to a third of the overall population, leaving from Tønder alone in the course of the 1920s.[63]

Considering these setbacks, the Germans maintained their position surprisingly well. To be sure, they generally proved unable to preserve local dominance. By 1926, only Højer and Ubjerg had retained clear German majorities. In the cities, the drop was particularly steep; even in the remaining urban bastion of Tønder, the minority vote had fallen to 36.7 percent by 1932. This decline also led to the essential disappearance of German from public administration.[64]

As a regional electoral force, however, the minority held its ground. Its political representative, the Sleswig Party, managed to consolidate its relative share of the vote at around 15 percent. In absolute numbers, the minority party even expanded its support.

Table 3. Parliamentary Vote for Sleswig Party in North Sleswig, 1920-1939

Year	Votes	Percentage
1920	7505	14.4
1924	7715	13.5
1926	10422	15.6
1929	9787	14.3
1932	9868	13.3
1935	12617	15.5
1939	15016	15.9

Source: Jakob Petersen, *En kort oversigt over folketingsvalgene fra 1920-1935* (Aabenraa, 1939), 15; Aksel Lassen, *Valg mellem tysk og dansk* (Aabenraa, 1976), 374f.; Henrik Becker-Christensen, *Det tyske mindretal i Nordslesvig 1920-1932* (Aabenraa, 1990), 2:213.

Closer inspection shows that these numbers exclude some segments of the minority. At its core, the Sleswig Party was a middle-class movement that continued the traditions of the German conservative and centrist factions. Workers were underrepresented; many of them supported the Danish Social Democrats. Thus, the German community consisted of an activist nucleus plus outer circles of Social Democrats and nationally noncommittal church groups.

Many German initiatives were reminiscent of Danish prewar activism. The minority established or expanded libraries as well as educational, ecclesiastical, and electoral associations. It set up the credit association Vogelgesang to combat the ongoing loss of agricultural holdings.[65] It tried to sustain the existing German newspapers, even though it ultimately had to consolidate them into one regional medium, the *Nordschleswigsche Zeitung*, in 1929.

Among Danes, there were conflicting views about the appropriate treatment of the German community. Fearing continual interference from its powerful neighbor, the Danish government shunned explicit minority agreements with Germany. At heart, many Danish nationalists were convinced that the German minority would soon dissipate.[66] The large organizations formed to protect Danish North Sleswigers within a hostile foreign state did not disband, although some of their members suggested doing so. Instead, they concentrated on promoting Danish activities in the most German districts close to the border.[67]

The parties on the left advocated a more accommodating approach. The Social Democrats, in particular, attempted to bridge the political differences. In nationally mixed areas, they held party meetings and waged election campaigns in both languages. In the Herning agreement of 1928, they even promised to improve minority education in exchange for occasional tactical cooperation.[68] But there were limits to the tolerance of the Social Democrats as well, and overt German activism could lead to exclusion.[69]

Although some voices portrayed the German community as an ideological body without a claim to cultural privileges, Copenhagen afforded its new minority generous protections. Conflicts between majority and minority revolved not so much around the form of these safeguards but around their content. The differences were exemplified in the divergent views on minority education. The government was more willing to offer instruction in German than by Germans and wanted to assign German-speaking Danes a prominent role in the classrooms. The minority, on the other hand, was discontented with teachers who might know German but did not share its views and values.

Overall, between 11 and 15 percent of the local student body attended German schools.[70] The minority had a slow start in the early 1920s, when its previous educational facilities had been dismantled by the transfer of sovereignty. It gradually availed itself of the opportunities available in the Danish system and expanded its enrollment from approximately 3,000 in 1921 to a peak of over 4,000 in 1934, whereupon it slowly began to recede again. About a third of the students attended private schools, which were especially common in the more peripheral minority areas. They grew from 7 to 24 and expanded their enrollment from 145 to 915 students in the course of the 1920s.[71]

A similar development occurred within the state church. German parishioners did not merely want to attend occasional German services from Danish pastors but requested clergymen that were taken from their own ranks. The ensuing clashes surfaced in elections to the church councils. German lists were fairly successful at defending their urban representation. In the countryside, however, services disappeared as German-oriented pastors retired and were replaced by Danes.[72] Although it was permissible to employ an auxiliary pastor for German parishioners, much of the additional expense would have to be born by the congregation itself. Outside the four city parishes, which had separate German pastors, many gravitated toward a free-church solution with close ties to the synod in Schleswig-Holstein.

Whereas disagreements in cultural matters could potentially be solved, the fundamental political viewpoints were irreconcilable. The German minority was thoroughly disillusioned with the modalities of the plebiscite. To many Danes, the new border had fulfilled the most modest Danish demands imaginable. It had left half of the initially Danish duchy of Sleswig in German hands and even accommodated the change of opinion in the city of Flensburg, which had still provided a slight majority to the Danish candidate in the parliamentary elections of 1867. Consequently, the arguments within the Danish camp pitted those who accepted the new border against those who wanted it drawn further to the south.[73]

Most Germans perceived the course of events differently. Their historical interpretation viewed Sleswig as an independent polity; for centuries, it had no more been a part of Denmark proper than neighboring Holstein. They scorned neutral and noncombatant Denmark for turning a bilateral dispute over to the victorious Allies. Their most intense criticism, however, was reserved for the modalities of the plebiscite. Even moderate Germans were resentful that North Sleswig had voted as one, whereas adjacent Central Sleswig was assessed on a local basis. By placing overwhelmingly German border communities such as Tønder and Højer in the northern zone, these terms had in essence nullified their vote.[74] Thus, German North Sleswigers remained focused on a border revision and an encompassing cultural autonomy.

The German government, too, refused to accept the moral legitimacy of the border. Compared to the disputes along the eastern boundaries, however, the Sleswig question paled in significance. The German foreign ministry repeatedly expressed an interest in good relations with Scandinavia and did not become very active in Sleswig. Still, Danish authorities were attentive to any demand for border revision and monitored events in Czechoslovakia and Poland to be prepared for parallels at home.[75]

In the 1930s, the minority further consolidated its position, based in part on the economic difficulties faced by North Sleswig farmers and in part on an improved internal structure, which mobilized previously passive sympathizers. At the same time, its organizations increasingly came under National Socialist influence, as groupings that did not enjoy German support found it difficult to succeed. The interconnection with German politics even forced the minority to bow to pronouncements that conflicted with its own objectives, such as Hitler's public recognition of the German-Danish border in October 1939. This dependence became more ominous when German troops occupied Denmark in April 1940. German North Sleswigers were as surprised by the military assault as the rest of Denmark, but many soon expressed support for the invading troops. Subsequently, they were able to wrest far-reaching concessions from the Danish government, which tried to deflect a renewed debate about border revisions. At the same time, the minority faced growing demands from the German authorities, who expected all Germans, regardless of citizenship, to contribute to the war effort.

The issue that has overshadowed the wartime history of German North Sleswigers is their association with the German armed forces. Even prior to April 1940, small groups were recruited into the Waffen SS, the military's preferred unit for foreign citizens.[76] After the occupation of Denmark, recruitment was taken up in earnest. Minority leaders expressed concerns about the political and demographic implications, especially when the SS tried to assuage the foreign office by inducing the volunteers to apply for German citizenship. Moreover, the parallel attempt to recruit Danish National Socialists with images of Germanic brotherhood emphasized arguments that contradicted the minority's own aspirations.

Therefore, the combined number of recruitments did not exceed one thousand prior to the final phase of the war. Mounting fatalities on the eastern front triggered renewed attempts to tap the manpower of German minorities all over Europe. The recruitment drive of winter 1942 brought more volunteers in Denmark than all the previous drives combined. Even though minority officials succeeded at keeping many of them in Denmark by classifying them as irreplaceable, almost 500 new recruits were called up. Altogether, more than 2,000 North Sleswigers served directly in the German armed forces, most of them in the Waffen SS. While this number may seem high in a minority of approximately 30,000 people, it lay lower than in most of the other German minorities in Europe.[77] A third of them, 745 in all, did not survive.

In 1943, the minority also began to organize paramilitaries to be stationed in North Sleswig. These units served more than one purpose. On the one hand, they gave the minority access to an armed force composed of its own members. On the other, they promised to keep a larger segment of the male population in the area, as opposed to far-away theaters of war. The paramilitaries were bitterly resented by the Danish population, however, who considered itself their natural target.[78]

It is impossible to evaluate the behavior of the German minority in North Sleswig without examining the psychological environment in which it lived. Elaborate mystifications notwithstanding, political allegiances are also rooted in socialization and in a pragmatic appreciation of power relationships. It would be simplistic to conclude that German North Sleswigers only cooperated with the Third Reich due to these constrictions. In fact, many of them had subscribed to National Socialist ideas long before the arrival of German troops. For German North Sleswigers living in a Denmark occupied by Germany, however, contributing to the German war effort was not simply a question of personal choice. They could not be drafted in the legal sense applicable to German citizens, but their participation was expected within a multilayered system of voluntary and imposed loyalties.

Throughout this period, the traditional conservative elites in the minority kept losing influence. Younger forces affiliated with the NSDAP laid claim to leadership positions. The interwar establishment responded in different ways. Some leaders mimicked the newer, more militant political style. Others withdrew from the limelight and formed an internal opposition, which also expressed itself in the establishment of the Haderslev Circle in 1943.[79] This informal group wanted to redefine its relationship to the Danish state and recognize the international border. Although it became instrumental in the founding of the League of German North Sleswigers, the Haderslev Circle only represented a small section of the community.

With the German surrender in May 1945, the minority faced an existential crisis. To be sure, acts of physical violence remained the exception, unlike in many other parts of Europe.[80] Attacks on monuments and institutions were more widespread.[81] Although the resistance movement called for the expulsion of a substantial segment of the minority, sober voices prevailed, and deportations were limited to German citizens.[82]

The minority's organizational structure came tumbling down, however. Many German institutions such as libraries or the credit union Vogelgesang were confiscated.[83] German public education was officially abolished in 1946. Yet also the private schools came under pressure. There was general agreement on the Danish side that school buildings erected during the occupation should be confiscated. More controversial were demands to reimburse the Danish state for wartime subsidies made by the German government. After all, cross-border support for minority schools was commonplace on both sides, and the claim would in essence bankrupt the German schools. After long negotiations, the minority was able to repurchase 13 of its school buildings at favorable conditions. Slowly, German education was reestablished, and by 1956, 1,039 students participated in the now exclusively private minority school system. Compared to the 2,166 public and 1,686 private students of 1938, the decline was steep.[84]

The most severe consequences resulted from the judicial crackdown. Around 3,500 Germans were arrested by the Danish police and resistance movement. Nearly 3,000 ultimately were sentenced, predominantly for serving in German military and paramilitary formations. The largest number of sentences, almost 1,300, consisted of prison terms between one and two years; 837 sentences lay below, the remainder above this range.[85] Thus, a quarter of adult German males in North Sleswig found themselves on the margins of society. The legal measures against pro-German activity shook the minority to its core, as is visible not only in the high percentage of people affected, but also in their social profile. Whereas ethnic Danes punished for collaboration often came from more peripheral segments of Danish society, Germans represented a broad cross-section of the populace.[86]

By the time the legal process had run its course, the mood of the country had begun to change. By 1950, the last minority members sentenced for political offenses had been released.[87] The social and professional consequences lasted longer. As a group, however, the minority also benefited from the postwar retaliations. The detention in camps and prisons added a further layer of shared experiences to the lives of many German North Sleswigers and reinforced the divide between the national communities. Within a few years, many social and cultural associations were reestablished.[88] Once again, the German minority was able to recover.

Many Danes and a Few Germans, Too: New Concepts of Identity in Postwar Sleswig

At the end of World War II, fewer than 3,000 people were registered members of the Danish umbrella organization in South Sleswig.[89] By 1946, this number exceeded 10,000, and within a few years, it had multiplied to approximately 70,000. After 1950, membership dropped noticeably again, until it began to stabilize at somewhat below 20,000 several decades later.

This unusually large fluctuation represents one of the most noteworthy aspects of identity formation in Sleswig. The analysis of this shift in allegiance will form the centerpiece of this section. Before examining the postwar development, however, one has to revisit the historical background of Danish identity in the southern part of Sleswig.

By the time the national conflict arose, the southern half of Sleswig had become overwhelmingly German-speaking. As far as the official language in church and school is concerned, this applied everywhere. As the language of daily life, Frisian dominated along the west coast. The South Jutland dialect of Danish had recently given way to Low German in the district of Anglia between Schleswig and Flensburg, but it still survived in a slowly receding wedge on the central high plains.

After the uprising in the duchies had been suppressed in 1851, the Danish government tried to strengthen Danish identity in central Sleswig. Standard Danish achieved official status in areas where the South Jutland dialect had prevailed in living people's memory. Due to its limited duration and popular resistance, this policy accomplished little; it was rescinded as soon as Denmark had to cede the duchies in 1864.

In the first elections following incorporation into Prussia, Danish candidates were successful in the northern districts of Sleswig all the way to Flensburg. In and around this city, Danish candidates eked out a slight lead. In a small strip of land extending both to the east and to the west, the Danish vote remained a significant factor.

A few decades later, this electoral presence had receded substantially. Farther away from Flensburg, it had become almost insignificant. Even in the city, it had clearly become a minority phenomenon. In the last elections prior to World War I, the Danish vote both in Flensburg and in other former Danish bastions in South Sleswig had fallen to noticeably below 10 percent.[90]

Only a small share of the minority vote originated in the still Danish-speaking belt in the high plains. This area was thinly populated, and most of the local Danish speakers considered themselves Germans. Flensburg, on the other hand, had been predominantly German-speaking since the late Middle Ages. To retain a minimal presence in the city, the Danish language depended on migration from northern districts. Thus, most Danish speakers in South Sleswig identified themselves as Germans, whereas the majority of those who considered themselves Danes used German as their primary language.[91]

During the Danish era, many leading families in Flensburg harbored a patriotic affection for the composite monarchy, often reinforced by established trade relations. These historic leanings persisted into the early Prussian period but were eventually overtaken by the new political and especially economic realities. The German-speaking urban elite made its peace with the German empire. Flensburg became the center of many Danish cultural endeavors, not least of all as the headquarters of *Flensborg Avis*. Their main proponents, however, had to be recruited from other parts of Sleswig. In some ways, Flensburg housed the government of Danish Sleswig—but it resembled a government in exile.

When the German defeat in World War I reopened the Sleswig question, the plebiscite zone 2 in essence consisted of those mid-Sleswig communities that lay south of H. V. Clausen's line of separation between Danish and German predominance, but had displayed some form of Danish sympathies in the past. The election campaign mobilized more Danish support than preceding parliamentary elections. Nonetheless, all parishes returned German majorities, smaller ones in Flensburg and environs, larger ones in far-away rural districts with the exception of select island communities.

The outcome of the plebiscite came as a disappointment to Danish activists south of the new border. Most of them had conceived of their movement as an initiative to redraw the political boundary. Instead, they had to define themselves as a national minority. Flensburg remained the center of Danish activism. Outside this core city, the community was represented primarily in a thin belt stretching along the border and in slowly forming southern outposts in the towns of Schleswig and Tönning. Even there, however, the Danish-minded population formed only a small minority.[92]

One of the most interesting aspects of the modern Danish community in South Sleswig was already visible in the interwar years. Minority strength fluctuated, typically in tune with the fortunes of German society. In periods of crisis, support for Danish organizations increased. When the crisis had passed, membership declined again.

Even if this wave movement became more pronounced in postwar Germany, it can be traced throughout the interwar era as well. In the shadow of military defeat, twenty percent of the electorate chose Denmark in the 1920 plebiscite, far exceeding prewar support for Danish candidates. The subsequent decline was followed by new growth triggered by the hyperinflation of 1923. During Weimar's brief golden years, Danish activism receded, until the worldwide depression brought a slight upturn. If one continues this pattern, the economic consolidation in the mid 1930s must be seen as one factor in the renewed weakening of minority strength, even though the pressures of a one-party dictatorship form an additional variable that accounts for the greater extent of the decline.[93]

This volatility expressed itself in various quantifiable forms. In the rural areas of Flensburg county, Danish candidates received 279 votes in the parliamentary elections of 1921, 412 in May 1924, 151 in 1928, and 232 in November 1932.[94] Based on contemporary sources, the membership numbers of the Sleswig Association (DSF) in interwar Flensburg followed a similar outline.[95]

Table 4. Membership of Sleswig Association in Flensburg

late 1920	4,699
mid 1924	5,797
mid 1929	3,374
early 1933	3,493
early 1936	3,016
mid 1939	2,419
1944/1945	1,882

Source: Johan Peter Noack, *Det danske mindretal i Sydslesvig 1920-1947* (Aabenraa, 1989), 2:307.

The pattern of support reflects the nature of a national community that is not rooted primarily in language and culture.[96] The minority consciously appealed to majority members, for example through German-language newspapers. There were no difficult hurdles on the way into the minority, but it was just as easy to leave. The minority constantly exchanged members with the majority.

When Hitler came to power in 1933, Danish institutions faced a strong challenge. Some of their more peripheral members switched to the German side, which also profited from the economic upturn. The central government did not fundamentally change its policy toward the minority; foreign policy considerations and the interests of the German minority in Denmark advised against that. Local National Socialists, on the other hand, attempted to curtail Danish activism.[97]

Most of all, the Danes in South Sleswig faced indirect pressures. If they cooperated with other minorities in Germany, they ran the risk of being drawn into the acerbic German-Polish conflict.[98] Even more taxing were the challenges of a one-party state. How was the Danish minority to relate to demands that tied social and occupational benefits to participation in party-dominated institutions? Attitudes toward mass organizations like the German Labor Front or the Hitler Youth were hotly contested.

Toward the end of World War II, membership in Danish organizations had fallen to its lowest levels since the plebiscite. The official minority had been reduced to its innermost core. Yet at the same time, German society was approaching its total collapse.

In May 1945, a new chapter began in the history of the Danish community in South Sleswig. For a moment, it seemed that its days as a minority were over. The central Danish association expanded its membership from less than 3,000 in 1944 to almost 75,000 in 1948. In a number of communities, including Flensburg, Danish administrations assumed power.

This impressive outward strength masked some structural weaknesses, however. Almost all the new converts had been socialized as Germans; their national reorientation relied on a subjective decision that could be easily reversed. For many, a vote for Danish lists did not express a desire to join a Danish minority. Instead, they hoped for a border revision that would bring political and economic stability. Others supported the Danish movement to underscore their Frisian or even their local Sleswig-German identity, especially vis-à-vis the refugees expelled from provinces annexed by Poland and the Soviet Union.[99] The minority party experienced bitter rifts between a Danish and a regionalist wing.[100]

When it became clear that South Sleswig was going to remain German and the refugees were there to stay, support for the Danish movement waned. The consolidation of the West German economy furthered the reintegration of temporarily alienated German speakers into majority society. At the same time, the fading threat of border revisions reduced animosities on the German side. Therefore, the Danish minority was able to secure its legal status and its public representation in the 1950s.

The Danes in South Sleswig established an extensive institutional network. The largest Danish organization in South Sleswig is the South Sleswig Association (SSF), with around 14,000 members in 2002.[101] It aims to represent the interests of the Danish minority, to promote Danish culture and language, and to strengthen the ties between South Sleswig and Scandinavia. The SSF works together closely with the Association of National Frisians, which speaks for the Danish-oriented wing of the Frisian movement.

In the fields of religion and education, the minority can rely on a solid infrastructure as well. The Lutheran congregations of the Danish minority are organized in a private association; they cooperate closely with the Danish state church's international service. The Lutheran Church of Schleswig-Holstein provides the salaries for four pastors. The Danish school system is organized as a private association. The German government covers the expenses of these schools based on the requirements of comparable public schools. Since the private schools proved to be more expensive, the Danish government contributes the required additional funds. During the final decades of the twentieth century, more than 5,000 children attended Danish schools at any given time.

The minority can rely on a well-established daily newspaper. *Flensborg Avis* has a regular circulation of around 7,500 copies, one-third of which is distributed in Denmark. It is supported by the Danish government and by nongovernmental border associations. Although the paper includes German pages and inserts, its core section is Danish. In the early postwar decades, the minority also published *Südschleswigsche Heimatzeitung*, but this monolingually German paper eventually merged with *Flensborg Avis.*

The exact strength of the minority is impossible to establish. Postwar German censuses contain no information on either language or national orientation, since such inquiries are seen as incompatible with a voluntaristic definition of nationhood.[102] The minority itself has no comprehensive membership registry. Thus, researchers have depended on indirect measurements to evaluate the size of the minority. These different measurements do not necessarily develop in a parallel manner, however.

Active membership in a Danish organization could be one criterion. Next to the approximately 14,000 members of the South Sleswig Association in the early twenty-first century, the organizational network also includes around 13,000 members of affiliated societies. Many members of those affiliated societies have also joined the SSF, however, so that the two categories cannot simply be combined. Moreover, a number of social and athletic clubs also attract people who do not necessarily consider themselves Danes.

Another measure of minority strength is electoral support. In electoral politics, the Danish minority has been represented by the South Sleswig Electoral Association (SSW) since 1948.[103] In the interwar period, the minority was weak and attracted merely 1,500 to 7,000 votes.[104] In the late 1940s, by contrast, it gained unprecedented strength. This success culminated in the regional elections of 1947, in which it received 99,500 votes. This accounted for a third of the overall Sleswig vote and—deducting the refugees from eastern Germany—roughly half of the local vote. [105] By 1954, electoral support had decreased to 42,000 votes, which still represented 15 percent of the South Sleswig vote but less than the five percent necessary for representation in the Schleswig-Holstein diet. As part of intergovernmental attempts to pacify the border region, the SSW was exempted from the five percent hurdle in 1955. It has consistently been able to send at least one deputy to the diet ever since. While its support gradually shrank to approximately 20,000 votes in the 1970s, it has recently grown considerably again, based not least of all on successful appeals to German voters.

The electoral trends reinforce the ambiguity of minority affiliation in the German-Danish borderlands. In isolation, a vote for the SSW does not necessarily reflect national orientation. The electoral victory of 2000, in which the Danish vote increased from 38,285 to 60,286, did not originate in Sleswig. In fact, the SSW slightly declined in the official minority area. In contrast, it was able to attract approximately 25,000 votes in Holstein, which has never contained an indigenous Danish element. In order to ensure its protected status, the SSW refrained from fielding candidates and campaigning in Holstein. When a new election law nonetheless made it possible to support the minority party throughout the whole province, many German Holsteiners availed themselves of this opportunity.

In this respect, the postwar Danish minority was far more successful than its German counterpart in the north. Whereas the latter had previously outnumbered the former, the tables had been turned in the postwar years. By all measures, the German minority had become numerically weaker, and nowhere did this discrepancy surface more clearly than on the political stage. The Sleswig Party struggled to secure its core vote. It had little appeal to Danish voters and increasingly suffered from the assimilation of the younger generations.

Table 5. Votes for Sleswig Party in Parliamentary Elections, 1920-1971

Year	Votes	Year	Votes
1920	7505	1953(1)	8438
1924	7715	1953(2)	9721
1926	10422	1957	9202
1929	9787	1960	9058
1932	9868	1964	9274
1935	12617	1966	-
1939	15016	1968	6831
1947	7464	1971	6743
1950	6406		

Source: Statistisches Landesamt Schleswig-Holstein, ed., *Beiträge zur historischen Statistik Schleswig-Holsteins* (Kiel, 1967), 80; Gösta Toft, "Slesvigsk Parti 1945-2000," in *En europæisk model?*, ed. Jørgen Kühl (Aabenraa, 2002), 162. The minority filed independent candidates in 1947, 1950, and 1953(2) and did not contest the election of 1966.

Realizing that winning seats had become impossible, the Sleswig Party stopped filing its own candidates in 1971. Between 1973 and 1979, a German representative was elected on the list of a centrist Danish party, but after 1979, this cooperation was discontinued. The Sleswig Party still defended a gradually diminishing representation in the South Jutland regional and a number of local assemblies, but it ceased to be a factor on the national scene.

The South Sleswig minority, by contrast, may have experienced a stagnation in its cultural endeavors but has rebounded strongly in the political arena. Apart from the watershed election of 1947, different expressions of Danish activism in South Sleswig long developed similarly. Throughout much of the 1950s and 1960s, membership in the cultural South Sleswig Association slightly surpassed support at the voting booth. From the 1980s on, however, the curves began to diverge in favor of the electoral wing. By the end of the century, the SSW attracted twice the support of the SSF and even extended its reach into Holstein. The majority of SSW voters were no longer affiliated with the organized Danish minority.

Table 6. Comparative Support for the Danish Minority in Select Postwar Years

Year	Membership in SSF	Vote for minority party
1947	68,317	99,500
1958	35,091	34,136
1967	25,731	23,577
1979	21,425	22,291
1988	18,690	26,646
1996	16,654	38,285
2000	15,150	60,286

Source: Jørgen Kühl, ed., *En europæisk model?* (Aabenraa, 2002), 212.[106]

The concrete parameters of this sociolinguistic environment surface in Karen Margrethe Pedersen's two-volume *Dansk sprog i Sydslesvig.*[107] In the late 1990s, Pedersen conducted an investigation based on questionnaires and interviews among more than 200 students from Danish schools in South Sleswig.[108] The resulting study constitutes the most comprehensive analysis of linguistic practices and attitudes among this population in recent history.

What are the requirements for being accepted into Danish minority schools? Whereas students do not have to know Danish or be affiliated with the Danish minority prior to enrollment, they must subscribe to the school's mission, which emphasizes Danish language and culture. In kindergarten, German is used more extensively, because this period provides an opportunity for German-speaking children and parents to acquire a basic knowledge of Danish.[109] Almost all children who attend Danish kindergartens go on to Danish primary schools, whereas only two thirds of German kindergarteners in Denmark proceed to minority schools.[110]

Approximately one quarter of the students' parents had not grown up in either South Sleswig or Denmark. Most of those parents hailed from other parts of Germany; a few were born abroad. More than half of the students had parents who themselves had been educated in German schools; approximately 20 percent of the parents had attended Danish schools in South Sleswig. A German background was more common in those regions of South Sleswig that are far removed from the minority's traditional centers. In the border districts, about 40 percent of the parents had attended German schools; further south, this number lay at around 60 percent. During a heated debate about the nature of Danish minority schools in 1996, the principal of Niebüll's Danish school estimated that only 30 percent of students came from a true minority background. Another 30 percent of parents viewed the institutions as language centers. The remaining 40 percent preferred their teaching philosophy.[111] Whereas other discussants questioned the concrete numbers, they confirmed (and deplored) the basic pattern.[112]

Consequently, most students had learned German as their first language. For about 10 percent of them, the childhood language was Danish; another five percent reported Danish in combination with German. Of these relatively few students, the majority had parents from Denmark proper. The status of Danish as the actual home language was therefore largely tied to roots in Denmark. For the bulk of the students, Danish constituted primarily an institutional language, that is, a language that is learned and practiced within the framework of the organized minority. Even in their interaction with schoolmates during breaks, three quarters of the students preferred German. High school students reported a more frequent use of Danish. This shows the decisive influence of education and marks a striking difference to otherwise comparable regions, where children learn the minority language at home and the majority language in school.

Almost half of the high school students considered themselves mainly Danish or equally German and Danish. The younger children, in contrast, saw themselves more as Germans than as Danes, even though a strong third identified equally with both. Only 14 percent of grade-schoolers defined themselves as predominantly Danish, and this again included a sizeable segment with parents from Denmark proper. Pedersen surmised that "this German identity may be an expression of the fact that the children at that age continue to be more influenced by their parents' German background than by the cultural and linguistic norms and values they have encountered in kindergarten and school."[113]

On one level, the linguistic environment in North Sleswig minority schools resembles its southern counterpart. In 1982, the German school in Tinglev defined the home language of its students as follows: 14.8 percent used German (half of them were children of teachers from Germany); 62.2 percent spoke South Jutland Danish; 17.5 reported speaking both languages, depending on the situational context; 1.6 percent spoke standard Danish.[114]

Most children spoke South Jutland's Danish dialect until they started in kindergarten. They had heard German on television, however, because the family would often watch German programs. They considered the dialect their mother tongue and tended to use it in non-official situations, but mixed in more German phrases than their Danish peers.

Up to this point, the environments largely coincide. Due to the image differential between matters German and Danish in both postwar societies, however, German minority schools attract noticeably fewer children from regular majority families than do Danish ones. The intimate German kindergartens and schools are attractive for parents interested in close teacher-student contact, and some Danish parents indeed send their children to German kindergartens. Subsequently, however, these Danish children often switch to regular Danish schools.[115]

Like their Danish counterparts in South Sleswig, the students in North Sleswig's German schools tend to describe the majority language as their mother tongue. Unlike the former, however, they primarily come from families who grew up within the minority. The objective linguistic conditions are similar; the subjective identity background is not.

The findings from Tinglev school correspond to the broader parameters of German minority life in late twentieth-century North Sleswig. In the 1970s, the Danish researchers Jørgen Elklit, Johan Peter Noack, and Ole Tonsgaard conducted an interview survey among North Sleswigers to establish the nature of national sentiment and intergroup relations in the region. Again, the connection between the use of German as a primary language and a sense of German nationality was not as strong as in many other political settings. Sixty-one percent of German-oriented North Sleswigers listed Danish as the language of their home; 28 percent indicated German.[116] Yet language was not insignificant. The postwar decades showed a linguistic assimilation to Danish as well as a corresponding switch to Danish self-identification. While native competency of German was not a prerequisite for a German national consciousness, the increasing use of Danish had contributed to the gradual erosion in the number of minority members.

Since the social distance between the national communities in North Sleswig is not very pronounced, there is considerable movement between them. The strongest such movement in postwar North Sleswig occurred from German to indifferent. Low social distance also entailed high rates of intermarriage. Three quarters of nationally mixed homes identified themselves as Danes, and children from mixed marriages attended Danish schools to a large degree.[117]

As a consequence, the German minority in North Sleswig has been on the defensive throughout the postwar era and has been more concerned about retaining its own members than about expanding into the majority population. It is important to bear in mind, however, that the identity pattern described for North Sleswig can also be found in the south. It might even exist in similar numbers. In South Sleswig, this subjective but intergenerational community is complemented by an additional subgroup, whose ties to the minority's core culture are more tentative. The postwar German minority has not been able to attract a corresponding element. This resulted from the contrasting image of the two minorities, but also from the different sense of self among the two majority populations. Whereas a sizable number of German citizens were interested in finding an alternative to a national identity they perceived as cumbersome, few Danes displayed corresponding sentiments. The German minority in postwar Denmark did not have a pool of potential new members to recruit from.

Whereas the German minority faced a decline in numbers and the accompanying fear of marginalization, the more successful Danish minority had to pay a different price. Numerical expansion came at the expense of cultural integration, and the ensuing debate about the respective significance of quantity and quality has followed the minority throughout the postwar decades. Everyone could agree on attracting new members and assisting them in their acculturation. Yet the reality often looked different. Many postwar newcomers never became fluent enough in Danish to participate in Danish-based activities. Whereas the younger generations acquired linguistic competence in school, the fluctuation in membership kept the internal divide alive. On a regular basis, the controversy about the role of German within the Danish minority erupted anew.

In the fall of 1996, this debate found a forum on the pages of *Flensborg Avis*.[118] When parents at the Danish school in Niebüll demanded an increased use of German at parent-teacher meetings, an emotional and sometimes acerbic debate about the nature and purpose of the Danish minority took shape.[119] The lines were sharply drawn. Whereas some minority members advocated a pragmatic approach and argued that fluency in Danish was no prerequisite for Danish sympathies, others emphasized the connection between language and identity and decried the use of minority schools for nationally indifferent language training and educational experimentation.

A number of contributions took up core aspects of Danish identity in South Sleswig. Heinrich Schultz, the president of the SSF, demanded a sharper profile for the minority. Otherwise, it might be assimilated to the majority population, not due to external pressure, but due to its own indifference. Schulz emphasized that minority organizations did not exist merely to satisfy individual needs and desires.[120]

Janne Marcussen, the former chair of the Danish school association, added that the Danish government would not be willing to fund minority schools if they were turning into language centers for Germans. Minority schools should not enroll recent arrivals from other parts of Germany but focus on students from minority families. He felt that identification with the minority and achievement of Danish language competency were inseparable. One cannot be Danish in German.[121]

Rolf Küssner, director of a Danish daycare institution in Husum, pointed at another downside of the minority's numerical advances. The increasing progressivism of the German middle class had brought a new type of German-speaking parents into contact with the Danish minority schools. These parents were looking for alternative pedagogical approaches and multicultural environments for their children but strictly rejected any focus on national identity. Küssner warned against letting these parents turn the Danish educational facilities into another form of Waldorf schools.[122]

Albert Gregersen, a long-time member of the Danish minority, recalled the linguistic situation in the postwar era. In the early years, meetings had to be held in German because hardly anyone knew Danish. When the following generation had internalized Danish in school, many institutions could finally abandon this practice. Gregersen considered parents who want to send their children to minority schools without being willing to learn Danish themselves more of a burden than an asset. The minority should focus on its true supporters instead of catering to peripheral sympathizers.[123]

Other members of the minority viewed the situation in a different light. Parents and teachers from marginal minority areas expressed concern about the future of minority institutions without the intake of German speakers.[124] Ingrid Thomsen from the city of Schleswig pointed out that members recruited into the successful local rowing club ignored other aspects of Danish minority life.[125] Lene Bastiansen from the outskirts of Flensburg did not believe that German-speaking parents lacked an interest in learning Danish. For many of them it simply proved a severe challenge to learn a foreign language, especially as adults. Bastiansen considered bilingual meetings the natural solution in a border region.[126]

In a two-part opinion piece, teacher Fidde Schultz stressed the heterogeneity of South Sleswig's Danish community. When Danish orientation reemerged in postwar Sleswig, it was not able to revert the linguistic realities to the 1700s. Thus, German, Danish, and sometimes also Frisian components coexist within most minority members. The future of the minority lies in this multicultural diversity.[127]

Some contributors attempted to carve out a middle way. From her own experience at the Danish high school in Flensburg, Elena Strehlow recalled many students from German-speaking homes—with all the consequences that implied. Could the minority afford to lose such students as a consequence of strict linguistic demands? Many of them proved solid supporters of the minority later in life. They became assets. Yet this process involved a constant accommodation with German-speaking parents.[128] Albert Gabriel Jensen, one of the many activists from Denmark who work as teachers in South Sleswig minority schools, conceded that language and national orientation do not necessarily coincide. He insisted, however, that language and culture are tied together and that the desire to be Danish ought to be accompanied by a desire to learn the language.[129]

Toward the end of the months-long public debate, college student Mirco Fischer tried to wrap up the different threads by focusing on the goals and purpose of the Danish minority. Should it recruit extensively in the German majority, at the risk of diluting the cultural essence of the minority, or should it focus primarily on defining its core profile? While prioritizing quality over quantity, Fischer located the essence of the minority in a value system. As long as the minority takes care of these values, it will continue to exist. At the same time, it remains open to new members who share these values.[130]

These intermediate positions resembled the pragmatic approach forwarded by the long-time parliamentary leader of the minority, Karl Otto Meyer. The minority depends on new members, because it is drained by outmigration and social amalgamation. Therefore, it has to accommodate new supporters without sufficient familiarity with Danish language and culture. On the other hand, these new recruits must strive to acquire this familiarity within a reasonable time frame. With those words, Meyer came close to formulating a core message to which most contributors could subscribe.[131]

Conclusion

The historical experience of three minorities at different points in time highlights the diverse paths of identity formation in the German-Danish borderlands. In the early nineteenth century, the Danish-speaking peasantry of northern Sleswig slowly politicized its ethnolinguistic distinctions. This process was inspired by a vanguard of middle-class intellectuals, but it also grounded in cultural and social realities. It resembled the nationalization of small ethnies all over Europe.[132] Rooted in a combination of objective and subjective factors, it proved resilient to governmental pressure. Its final result was the modern Danish majority population of South Jutland.

Next to this idealtypical politicization of ethnicity, there also emerges an alternative route to national identity. Although it also bolstered Danish identity in Flensburg, it was most significant in northern Sleswig, where it engendered a German community that widely spoke the local Danish dialect in everyday life. This population anchored its identity to a larger extent in its established political and economic integration with the German south of the duchies than in its linguistic origins. Identity formation was complex and subjective, but it created a lasting intergenerational community.

In German South Sleswig, a comparable community took shape in the twentieth century. Drawing on established institutions but galvanized by the plebiscite campaign, Danish and German speakers especially in Flensburg merged into a small but resilient community of Danish South Sleswigers. This interwar minority even survived the tribulations of the National Socialist era and provided the foundations of Danish life at the conclusion of World War II. In the following years, however, it was eclipsed by a rapidly growing community called new Danes. Although some of the latter assimilated with the traditional minority, others retained a more tentative affiliation.

Paradoxically, the relationship of many German-speaking South Sleswigers to the Danish minority was shaped both by their discomfort with German national identity and by their rootedness in German social and cultural reality. Their alienation from German national identity led people without Danish family ties to gravitate toward the Danish minority. The Danish minority constituted a viable local alternative; together with the co-opted national Frisians, the only legally established one. Estrangement from the German national tradition was only one side of the coin, however. The other side expressed itself in the difficulty of assimilating the German newcomers linguistically into a Danish mainstream. Many German speakers proved unable or unwilling to fully adapt Danish cultural codes. They still considered themselves normal members of the Danish minority, however. They wanted to enjoy the pragmatic advantages of living as Germans in a German society while sharing in the emotional warmth of being Danish.

The different expressions of Danish and German identity continue to exist today. They separate communities, but they also coexist within one and the same. This multifaceted sense of identity is a distinct characteristic of the German-Danish borderlands. It will be examined on an individual basis in the following chapter.

Notes

1. Thomas Steensen, *Die friesische Bewegung in Nordfriesland im 19. und 20. Jahrhundert* (Neumünster, 1986), 35f.
2. On western Föhr, the Danish candidate trounced his German counterparts in the elections of 1867. See Aksel Lassen, *Valg mellem tysk og dansk* (Aabenraa, 1976), 54f.
3. See the discussion of Petersen in Chapter 5.
4. Again, Danish votes emerged on the islands, especially on Föhr, even though they remained clearly in the minority there as well. See Aksel Lassen, *Valg mellem tysk og dansk* (Aabenraa, 1976), 194.
5. For select documents from the founding years of the Frisian-Sleswig Association, see Thomas Steensen, *Die friesische Bewegung in Nordfriesland im 19. und 20. Jahrhundert* (Neumünster, 1986), 2:80-89.
6. The Prussian government was concerned about its activity, however. Interestingly, it also feared the spread of Frisian nationalism to East Frisia. See Prussian Minister of the Interior to Regierungspräsident [Chief Administrator] in Schleswig, 25 June 1929, Landesarchiv Schleswig-Holstein, Abteilung 309, Nr. 35252.
7. The text of the petition was as follows:

   > We North Frisians are German-minded. For centuries, we have felt tied to Sleswig-Holstein and German culture. Within the framework of this culture, we want to preserve our regional character. We want to see our language cultivated in the schools and churches of the Frisian language area. We reject being viewed as a national minority.

   See Nordfriesischer Verein für Heimatkunde und Heimatliebe, ed., *13.000 Nordfriesen an den Minderheitenkongreß in Genf* (Husum, 1926).
8. Thomas Steensen, *Die friesische Bewegung in Nordfriesland im 19. und 20. Jahrhundert* (Neumünster, 1986), 1:271.
9. The enormous significance of Nikolaj Frederik Severin Grundtvig for Danish religious, cultural, and political life is reflected in a plethora of Danish literature. For an English-language introduction to Grundtvig and his writings, see Arthur Macdonald Allchin, *N. F. S. Grundtvig: An Introduction to his Life and Work* (Århus, 1997); Christian Thodberg and Anders Pontoppidan Thyssen, eds., *N.F.S. Grundtvig, Tradition and Renewal: Grundtvig's Vision of Man and People, Education and the Church, in Relation to World Issues Today* (Copenhagen, 1983); and Niels Lyhne Jensen, ed., *A Grundtvig Anthology: Selections from the Writings* (Cambridge, 2000).

10. Franz von Jessen, ed., *Haandbog i det nordslesvigske spørgsmaals historie* (Copenhagen, 1901), 270.
11. See Paul-Heinz Pauseback, *Übersee-Auswanderer aus Schleswig-Holstein* (Husum, 2000), 67.
12. For a brief discussion of the emigration from Sleswig, see Hans Schultz Hansen, *Det nordslesvigske landbrug og den danske bevægelse 1880-1914* (Aabenraa, 1985), 25-27.
13. The term "optant" refers to a person who had received the right to opt for one of two or more citizenships, usually as a consequence of border changes. The term was best known in English in the interwar era.
14. Oswald Hauser, *Preußische Staatsräson und nationaler Gedanke* (Neumünster, 1960), 47.
15. Christian Paulsen will be examined more closely in the following chapter. For an introduction to Flor, see Jens Peter Ægidius, *Christian Flor: Pædagogen, politikeren, folkeoplyseren* (Odense, 1994).
16. Peder Lauridsen, *Da Sønderjylland vaagnede*, 8 vols. (Copenhagen, 1909-22).
17. M. Mackeprang, *Nordslesvig 1864-1909* (Copenhagen, 1910).
18. See especially Gottlieb Japsen, "Betragtninger over den danske bevægelse i Nordslesvig," *Sønderjyske Årbøger* (1973): 63-75.
19. Hans Schultz Hansen, *Det nordslesvigske landbrug og den danske bevægelse 1880-1914* (Aabenraa, 1985).
20. See M. Mackeprang, *Nordslesvig 1864-1909* (Copenhagen, 1910), 105f.
21. Lothar Blatt, *Die rechtliche Behandlung der dänischen Minderheit in Schleswig-Holstein von 1866 bis 1914* (Husum, 1980).
22. A number of documents on judicial proceedings against the use of Danish colors are collected in Landesarchiv Schleswig-Holstein, Abteilung 301, Nr. 2384. The wider discussion about appropriate flag use did not only involve the Danish colors, but also the blue-white-red of the Sleswig-Holstein movement. [Landesarchiv Schleswig-Holstein, Abteilung 301, Nr. 5654.]
23. Lothar Blatt, *Die rechtliche Behandlung der dänischen Minderheit in Schleswig-Holstein von 1866 bis 1914* (Husum, 1980), 84-86. The court considered individual songs incendiary, however. The publishers decided to leave the incriminated pages blank so that individuals could add the missing texts themselves.
24. Lothar Blatt, *Die rechtliche Behandlung der dänischen Minderheit in Schleswig-Holstein von 1866 bis 1914* (Husum, 1980), 43.
25. For discussions of the 1908 law of association, see Lothar Blatt, *Die rechtliche Behandlung der dänischen Minderheit in Schleswig-Holstein von 1866 bis 1914* (Husum, 1980), 79-84, and M. Mackeprang, *Nordslesvig 1864-1909* (Copenhagen, 1910), 272f.
26. For an overview, see Lars N. Henningsen, "Lutherske kirker mellem dansk og tysk," *Sønderjyske Årbøger* (2004): 133-170.
27. See M. Mackeprang, *Nordslesvig 1864-1909* (Copenhagen, 1910), 191-193; Oswald Hauser, *Preußische Staatsräson und nationaler Gedanke* (Neumünster, 1960), 128-130. In an exchange of letters with Sleswig clergy, the Prussian minister of church and education made it clear that pastors had to refrain from activities that could be seen as hostile toward the state. [Von Trott zu Solz to the Royal Consistory in Kiel, 25 April 1910, Landesarchiv Schleswig-Holstein, Abteilung 301, Nr. 2310.] The fact that the authorities also kept tabs on the national orientation of individual pastors can be seen in Landesarchiv Schleswig-Holstein, Abteilung 301, Nr. 2308.
28. Oswald Hauser, *Preußische Staatsräson und nationaler Gedanke* (Neumünster, 1960), 64f.

29. *Amtsblatt der königlichen Regierung zu Schleswig* 41/1871.
30. "Instruktion für die Ertheilung des deutschen Unterrichts in den nordschleswigschen Volksschulen vom 9. März 1878." Published in *Beilage zum Amtsblatt der königlichen Regierung zu Schleswig* 11/1878, 71ff.
31. "Anweisung für den Unterricht in den nordschleswigschen Volksschulen." Published in *Amtsblatt der königlichen Regierung zu Schleswig* 60/1888.
32. Lorenz Rerup, *Slesvig og Holsten efter 1830* (Copenhagen, 1982), 282.
33. The original name of the association was "Foreningen til det danske Sprogs Bevarelse i Nordslesvig," which translates to Association for the Preservation of the Danish Language in North Sleswig. Before long, however, it became known by the shorter designation of Language Association. For a summary of its first 50 years of activities, see Jakob Petersen, "Sprogforeningens Udvikling gennem 50 Aar," in *Aarsberetning 1929-30*, ed. Sprogforeningen (Aabenraa, 1930), 5-52.
34. For an inside perspective of the school association, see Anders Lebeck, *Tyve Aars Elever: Den nordslesvigske Skoleforenings Virksomhed fra 1894-1913* (Haderslev, 1914).
35. For insights into electoral life in Prussian Schleswig-Holstein, see the materials in Landesarchiv Schleswig-Holstein, Abteilung 301, Nr. 809.
36. The Electoral Association for North Sleswig (Vælgerforeningen for Nordslesvig) was founded by H. P. Hanssen, who became member of parliament and leading representative of the Danish North Sleswigers in the last part of the Prussian period.
37. Statistisches Landesamt Schleswig-Holstein, ed., *Beiträge zur historischen Statistik Schleswig-Holsteins* (Kiel, 1967), 72f.; Hans Meyersahm, *Die Vertretung der einzelnen Parteien in Schleswig-Holstein bei den Reichstagswahlen seit 1867* (Kiel, 1912), 4f.; Otto Brandt, *Geschichte Schleswig-Holsteins*, 8th ed. (Kiel, 1981), 312-315. For the most comprehensive quantitative examination of elections in Sleswig from a Danish perspective, see Aksel Lassen, *Valg mellem tysk og dansk* (Aabenraa, 1976). The differences in electoral support are also interconnected with the changing numbers of eligible voters caused by the optant question.
38. Two Danish candidates were elected to the North German parliament in 1867 and again to the federal German parliament in 1881.
39. The Prussian authorities followed the minority's electoral progress even on the local level, as visible in the records collected in Landesarchiv Schleswig-Holstein, Abteilung 301, Nr. 2390.
40. The sources display some differences in regard to the overall Danish vote in select years, but they are too small to be of significance other than in 1871, where the official statistics of Statistisches Landesamt Schleswig-Holstein, ed., *Beiträge zur historischen Statistik Schleswig-Holsteins* (Kiel, 1967) seem to have left out the Danish vote south of the 1920 border and have been corrected accordingly.
41. For election results, see Hans Meyersahm, *Die Vertretung der einzelnen Parteien in Schleswig-Holstein bei den Reichstagswahlen seit 1867* (Kiel, 1912), 4f. For an introduction to working-class politics in Schleswig-Holstein, see Rainer Paetau and Holger Rüdel, eds., *Arbeiter und Arbeiterbewegung in Schleswig-Holstein* (Neumünster, 1987).
42. The 1886 vote was a special ballot in the electoral district that included the city of Flensburg.
43. M. Mackeprang, *Nordslesvig 1864-1909* (Copenhagen, 1910), 264.
44. The Danes founded the "Association of October 5, 1898" in 1898 and Landeværnet (Land Guard) in 1913. The foremost studies of the rural conflict and its associations are Hans Schultz Hansen, *Det nordslesvigske landbrug og den danske bevægelse 1880-1914*

(Aabenraa, 1985), and idem, *"Dansk jord på danske hænder": Foreningen Landeværnet og den nationale jordkamp i Sønderjylland 1927-2002* (Aabenraa, 2002).

45. In its bylaws, the association listed a wide array of activities through which it wanted to promote German ethnicity in North Sleswig. ["Satzungen des Deutschen Vereins für das nördliche Schleswig," Landesarchiv Schleswig-Holstein, Abteilung 301, Nr. 2326.]
46. For an in-depth examination of the German Association for Northern Sleswig, see Gottlieb Japsen, *Den fejlslagne germanisering* (Aabenraa, 1983).
47. Thus, Peter Vestergaard had to leave Germany within three days because "his employer is a fanatical Danish agitator." [Oberpräsidium Schleswig, "Nachweisung über verfügte Ausweisungen," 2 November 1898, Landesarchiv Schleswig-Holstein, Abteilung 301, Nr. 2437.]
48. According to Erich Hoffmann, approximately 1,000 natives of Denmark and approximately 60 optants and their descendants were deported. See Olaf Klose and Erich Hoffmann, eds., *Geschichte Schleswig-Holsteins*, vol 8:2, *Das Nationalitätenproblem in Schleswig*, by Erich Hoffmann (Neumünster, 1995), 268.
49. M. Mackeprang, *Nordslesvig 1864-1909* (Copenhagen, 1910), 161.
50. This number includes family members of the original optants. A statistical overview compiled by the Prussian administration in Schleswig-Holstein in 1898 listed that 377 former optants plus 1,322 family members had been naturalized during the preceding three years, whereas 50 applications had been rejected. [Regierungs-Präsident zu Schleswig, "Übersicht der in den Jahren 1895, 1896, und 1897 in den 5 nordschleswigschen Kreisen stattgefundenen Naturalisationen früherer dänischer Optanten...," 22 January 1898, Landesarchiv Schleswig-Holstein, Abteilung 301, Nr. 2962.] Individual cases are collected in Landesarchiv Schleswig-Holstein, Abteilung 301, Nr. 2961-2963.
51. This group consisted of people who had themselves opted for Denmark or whose fathers had done so.
52. In a central passage of the bylaws, the proponents of the Peace Association emphasized that they wanted to respect Danish ethnicity in North Sleswig while rejecting attempts to turn the Danish population against the Germans. ["Satzungsentwurf des 'Friedensvereins'," *Apenrader Tageblatt,* 27 November 1909, Landesarchiv Schleswig-Holstein, Abteilung 301, Nr. 2385.]

    Again, as in the case of the Danish associations, the original official designations were more elaborate than the popular ones. Thus, the full name of the Peace Association was "Verein für deutsche Friedensarbeit in der Nordmark" (Association for German Peace Efforts in the Northern Marches).

    Due to the increasingly voluntaristic nature of postwar minority affiliation in Sleswig, local discourse emphasizes their status as not ethnic but national minorities. In English, however, it will also be warranted to refer to the Danes of prewar Prussia as an ethnic community.
53. For Hanssen's experiences at the end of the war, see especially H. P. Hanssen, *Fra krigstiden* (Copenhagen, 1924), 2:217-411.
54. For some of these petitions, see Jürgen Rohweder, *Sprache und Nationalität* (Glückstadt, 1976), 151f.
55. For the Sleswig-Holstein Patriotic Association, see Hans Schultz Hansen, *Hjemmetyskheden i Nordslesvig 1840-1867* (Aabenraa, 2005), 1:281-296.
56. Lorenz Christensen, "Hjemmetyskheds-Problemet," *Sønderjyske Årbøger* (1929): 242-246.

57. For a discussion of the phenomenon, see Erich Hoffmann, "Die Entstehung des nordschleswigschen Deutschtums," *Schriften der Heimatkundlichen Arbeitsgemeinschaft für Nordschleswig* 51 (1985): 12f.
58. For a personal perspective, see also the interview with the German North Sleswiger Harro Marquardsen in H. E. Sørensen, *Mellem dansk og tysk* (Skærbæk, 1987), 83-98.
59. See Lorenz Christensen, "Hjemmetyskheds-Problemet," *Sønderjyske Årbøger* (1929): 225f. Even a moderate Danish nationalist such as H. V. Clausen ascribed this national orientation to, apart from family tradition, pretentiousness, stupidity, and cowardice. See H. V. Clausen, "Nordslesvig 1863-93: Den nationale Stilling pa Landet," *Sønderjyske Årbøger* (1894): 69. Clausen reportedly regretted this disparaging verdict later in life.
60. For a discussion of the origins of the term, see Hans Schultz Hansen, *Hjemmetyskheden i Nordslesvig 1840-1867* (Aabenraa, 2005), 1:17-24; and Erich Hoffmann, "Die Entstehung des nordschleswigschen Deutschtums," *Schriften der Heimatkundlichen Arbeitsgemeinschaft für Nordschleswig* 51 (1985): 6.
61. Henrik Becker-Christensen, *Det tyske mindretal i Nordslesvig 1920-1932* (Aabenraa, 1990), 2:43.
62. For an in-depth examination of this social composition in the postwar era, see Gösta Toft, *Die bäuerliche Struktur der deutschen Volksgruppe in Nordschleswig* (Flensburg, 1982).
63. Henrik Becker-Christensen, *Det tyske mindretal i Nordslesvig 1920-1932* (Aabenraa, 1990), 1:41f.
64. It was more than a symbolic act when the minutes of the Tønder city council became monolingually Danish in 1937.
65. The Danish side countered with its own farm association called Landeværnet. For the latter, see Hans Schultz Hansen, *"Dansk jord på danske hænder": Foreningen Landeværnet og den nationale jordkamp i Sønderjylland 1927-2002* (Aabenraa, 2002).
66. See, for example, H. V. Clausen, *Før afgørelsen* (Copenhagen, 1918), 33.
67. For the discussions and decisions of the Danish mass organizations, see Kim Salomon, *Konflikt i grænseland* (Copenhagen, 1980), 79-85.
68. For the details of the agreement, see Henrik Becker-Christensen, *Det tyske mindretal i Nordslesvig 1920-1932* (Aabenraa, 1990), 2:234-237.
69. See Kim Salomon, *Konflikt i grænseland* (Copenhagen, 1980), 54.
70. For the numbers on school attendance, see Henrik Becker-Christensen, *Det tyske mindretal i Nordslesvig 1920-1932* (Aabenraa, 1990), 1:207-219.
71. Kim Salomon, *Konflikt i grænseland* (Copenhagen, 1980), 65.
72. For an analysis of the developments on parish level, see Henrik Becker-Christensen, *Det tyske mindretal i Nordslesvig 1920-1932* (Aabenraa, 1990), 1:225ff.
73. For an in-depth investigation of interwar Danish activism in favor of an eventual border change, see Axel Johnsen, *Dannevirkemænd og Ejderfolk: Den grænsepolitiske opposition i Danmark 1920-1940* (Flensburg, 2005).
74. Both sides had numerous additional complaints, revolving not least of all around the criteria for suffrage. These aspects, however, were less universally accepted even within the respective national communities or would not have changed the eventual location of the border.
75. See, for example, Henrik Becker-Christensen, *Det tyske mindretal i Nordslesvig 1920-1932* (Aabenraa, 1990), 2:125.
76. Due to the international legal implications of foreign citizens in the regular armed forces, the German leadership widely used the nominally volunteer Waffen SS for this

purpose. For a closer look at the function and composition of the Waffen SS, see Bernd Wegner, *Hitlers politische Soldaten* (Paderborn, 1982).

77. Johan Peter Noack, *Det tyske mindretal i Nordslesvig under besættelsen* (Copenhagen, 1975), 14f. For the role of German minorities in the Waffen SS, see also Robert Herzog, *Die Volksdeutschen in der Waffen-SS* (Tübingen, 1955).
78. For a recent examination of North Sleswig during World War II, see Hans Schultz Hansen and Henrik Skov Kristensen, eds., *Sønderjylland under krig og besættelse 1940-1945* (Aabenraa, 2003).
79. Frank Lubowitz, "Det tyske mindretals organisationer," in *En europæisk model?,* ed. Jørgen Kühl (Aabenraa, 2002), 119-123.
80. The most serious incident occurred in 1948, when a young woman was killed by a random shot fired at the hotel in which a German theater group was playing. See Ernst Siegfried Hansen, *Disteln am Wege* (Bielefeld, 1957), 247-251.
81. See Ernst Siegfried Hansen, *Disteln am Wege* (Bielefeld, 1957), 98-103.
82. Ditlev Tamm, *Retsopgøret efter besættelsen* (Copenhagen, 1984), 413 and 418f.
83. Jürgen Zeh, *Die deutsche Sprachgemeinschaft in Nordschleswig* (Stuttgart, 1982), 124.
84. Jürgen Zeh, *Die deutsche Sprachgemeinschaft in Nordschleswig* (Stuttgart, 1982), 136.
85. Ernst Siegfried Hansen, *Disteln am Wege* (Bielefeld, 1957), 268. For an in-depth analysis of the legal measures in individual districts, see Sabina Lorek, *Rechtsabrechnung—Retsopgør: Politische Säuberung nach dem Zweiten Weltkrieg in Nordschleswig* (Neumünster, 1998).
86. For statistical material on the social composition of different groups sentenced for collaboration, see Karl O. Christiansen, *Landssvigerkriminaliteten i sociologisk belysning* (Copenhagen, 1955), and idem, *Mandlige landssvigere i Danmark under besættelsen* (Copenhagen, 1950).
87. Ditlev Tamm, *Retsopgøret efter besættelsen* (Copenhagen, 1984), 431.
88. For a recent look at the minority during the early postwar years, see Jan Hyldal Christensen, "'Die neue Entwicklung in Dänemark hat begonnen': Det tyske mindretal i Nordslesvig 1945-47," *Sønderjyske Årbøger* (2004): 87-132.
89. The principal Danish minority organization in Germany was called Sleswig Association (Den slesvigske Forening/DSF) from 1920-1946 and South Sleswig Association (Sydslesvigsk Forening/SSF) from that year on. In 1948, a separate electoral wing was founded. It received the designation South Sleswig Electoral Association (Sydslesvigsk Vælgerforening) and is widely known by the German acronym SSW.
90. See Hans Schultz Hansen, *Danskheden i Sydslesvig 1840-1918* (Flensburg, 1990), 306-309.
91. Paul Selk estimated that around 92 percent of school children in Flensburg were German-speaking at the beginning of the twentieth century, and this number rose slowly throughout the interwar era. By 1935, the percentage of pupils with solely Danish as their mother tongue had fallen to one percent. Paul Selk, *Die sprachlichen Verhältnisse im deutsch-dänischen Sprachgebiet südlich der Grenze* (Hamburg, 1986), 146f.
92. A good overview of Danish activities in interwar South Sleswig and the German response can be found in Landesarchiv Schleswig-Holstein, Abteilung 309, Nr. 35244. See also Axel Johnsen, *Dannevirkemænd og Ejderfolk: Den grænsepolitiske opposition i Danmark 1920-1940* (Flensburg, 2005).
93. Not all parameters developed identically, however, and in the mid 1930s, both the founding of new and the expansion of existing minority schools still resulted in a small

growth in student enrollment. See Axel Johnsen, *Dannevirkemænd og Ejderfolk: Den grænsepolitiske opposition i Danmark 1920-1940* (Flensburg, 2005), 401.

94. Johan Peter Noack, *Det danske mindretal i Sydslesvig 1920-1945* (Aabenraa, 1989), 2:378.

95. Johan Peter Noack's own analysis based on surviving membership cards reaches somewhat different numbers. Except for the lower numbers for the year 1924, they mirror the trend that speaks from the contemporary numbers. See Johan Peter Noack, *Det danske mindretal i Sydslesvig 1920-1945* (Aabenraa, 1989), 2:304-325.

96. For the contemporary self-definition of the minority, see Dänisches General-Sekretariat, *Wo stehen wir* (Flensburg, n. d.), Landesarchiv Schleswig-Holstein, Abteilung 309, Nr. 35244.

97. For recent descriptions of Danish life in National Socialist Germany, see Martin Klatt, "Die dänische Minderheit—Ausgrenzung eines Bevölkerungsteils," in *Ausgebürgert. Ausgegrenzt. Ausgesondert: Opfer politischer und rassischer Verfolgung in Flensburg 1933-1945*, ed. Broder Schwensen, Gerhard Paul, and Peter Wulf (Flensburg, 1998), 62-88; Lars N. Henningsen, "Kulturelles Leben der dänischen Minderheit," in *Zwischen Konsens und Kritik*, ed. Broder Schwensen, Gerhard Paul, and Peter Wulf (Flensburg, 1999), 239-268; and René Rasmussen, "'Man lernt zu denken und zu schweigen'," in ibid., 269-307.

98. This cooperation was built on an established tradition and frequently entailed the representation of all minority groups by the numerically dominant Polish minority. See, for example, the memorandum submitted by the League of Poles in Germany to the Prussian Secretary of the Interior in 1924. ["Denkschrift der polnischen Minderheit in Deutschland," 12 August 1924, Landesarchiv Schleswig-Holstein, Abteilung 309, Nr. 35302.]

99. For an in-depth investigation of the relationship between the refugees and the Danish movement, see Martin Klatt, *Flygtningene og Sydslesvigs danske bevægelse 1945-1955* (Flensburg, 2001). See also Manfred Jessen-Klingenberg, *Standpunkte zur neueren Geschichte Schleswig-Holsteins* (Malente, 1998), 145-158.

100. For an investigation of Danish electoral politics in postwar Sleswig, see Lars N. Henningsen, Martin Klatt, and Jørgen Kühl, eds., *SSW: Dansksindet politik i Sydslesvig, 1945-1998* (Flensburg, 1998).

   Motions to use Low German to increase the appeal of Danish activities already surfaced in the interwar era, as can be seen in the police report of a meeting of Danish youth leaders in 1927. ["Bericht," 25 January 1927, Landesarchiv Schleswig-Holstein, Abteilung 309, Nr. 35284.]

101. The official numbers were 13,904 members plus 619 members of the Association of National Frisians. See Heinrich Schultz, "Vi mistede 376 trofaste medlemmer," *Sydslesvigsk Årbog* (2002): 15; Jørgen Kühl, ed., *En europæisk model?* (Aabenraa, 2002), 212.

102. The same holds true on the Danish side of the border. For a discussion of the much-quoted principle that anyone who wants to can be a minority member, see Jørgen Kühl and Marc Weiler, eds., *Minority Policy in Action: The Bonn-Copenhagen Declarations in a European Context 1955-2005* (Flensburg and Aabenraa, 2005), 19. The conclusion that public institutions should refrain from establishing the size of the minority is not an intrinsic consequence of voluntarism, however. As can be seen on the page cited above, it is not necessarily shared by international experts, either.

103. Prior to 1948, there was no separation of cultural and electoral politics, so that the Sleswig Association and subsequently the South Sleswig Association also served as electoral vehicles.

104. Franz von Jessen, *Haandbog i det slesvigske spørgsmaals historie 1900-1937* (Copenhagen, 1938), 3:523. The numbers refer to votes cast in South Sleswig.
105. Many researchers have translated the 33 percent overall share of Danish votes in South Sleswig into a majority of the local vote, that is, without the refugees from other German regions. Although Gerhard Isbary, *Problemgebiete im Spiegel politischer Wahlen am Beispiel Schleswig* (Bad Godesberg, 1960) confirmed this calculation based on separate ballots for locals and refugees in the rural region of Eiderstedt, the underlying assumption that refugees did not support Danish candidates is too one-dimensional. The results in Flensburg, which provided a third of all Danish votes, underscore this problem, because they would entail that the local population voted Danish almost in its entirety. While not impossible, this presupposition would require more concrete evidence to be universally accepted. Such notes of caution do not change the fact, however, that approximately half of the local population seems to have supported the Danish party in 1947.
106. The vote in 2000 included about 25,000 votes in Holstein.
107. Karen Margrethe Pedersen, *Dansk sprog i Sydslesvig*, 2 vols. (Aabenraa, 2000).
108. The main group consisted of 127 students from 11 of the 50 minority schools. An additional group of 88 high school students only answered the questionnaire. See Karen Margrethe Pedersen, *Dansk sprog i Sydslesvig* (Aabenraa, 2000), 1:30f. For documentation of the subsequent paragraphs, see ibid., 48-49, 53, 54, 57-58, 64, 90, 92-93, 119, 126-127, 132, 141, 159.
109. The Danish School Association for South Sleswig (Dansk Skoleforening for Sydslesvig) resolved in 1997:

    Article 4 (1): In South Slesvig's Danish kindergartens, the children are prepared for entering Danish schools. The kindergartens are charged with teaching the children to understand and speak Danish so that they become familiar with Danish and can be taught in Danish at school.

    See Karen Margrethe Pedersen, *Dansk sprog i Sydslesvig* (Aabenraa, 2000), 1:135.
110. Bent Søndergaard, *Fra tysk børnehave til tysk eller dansk skole—myte og realitet* (Aabenraa, 1988), 2ff.
111. "Danske skoler bliver brugt som sprogskoler," *Flensborg Avis*, 13 September 1996.
112. "Sprog og kultur hænger uløseligt sammen," *Flensborg Avis*, 17 September 1996. For further interesting insights into the self-perception of Danish high school students in Flensburg, see Lars N. Henningsen, ed., *Bonn-Erklæringen og de unge: Elevberetninger fra Duborg-Skolen 2005* (Flensburg, 2005).
113. Karen Margrethe Pedersen, *Dansk sprog i Sydslesvig* (Aabenraa, 2000), 1:170. The age in question is 12 to 13.
114. Michael Byram, *Minority Education and Ethnic Survival* (Clevedon, England, 1986), 41.
115. For a discussion of the reasons for this divergence, see Bent Søndergaard, *Fra tysk børnehave til tysk eller dansk skole—myte og realitet* (Aabenraa, 1988). Søndergaard argues that Danish parents are concerned that their children would be excluded from the Danish mainstream if they attended minority schools. Moreover, attending German schools is perceived as more unpatriotic than attending German kindergartens. Since the appearance of Søndergaard's study, however, this pattern has slowly begun to change, and the share of students from majority families has increased.
116. Jørgen Elklit, Johan Peter Noack, and Ole Tonsgaard, *Nationalt tilhørsforhold i Nordslesvig* (Århus, 1978), 91.

117. For the data in this paragraph, see ibid, 84-85, 87, 89, and 114. For a recent analysis of nationally noncommittal Sleswigers, see Kristian Jepsen Steg, "De Blakkede: National indifference og neutralitet i Nordslesvig 1890-1940," *Sønderjyske Årbøger* (2004): 67-86.
118. Earlier examples of this discussion surface in several of the editorials of *Flensborg Avis* in Else Prahl et al., eds., *Karl Otto Meyer og Flensborg Avis* (Flensburg, 1988).
119. It may be seen as an interesting reflection of identity concepts in Sleswig that the most outspoken parent was a recent arrival from Britain, who had decided to enroll his children in the Danish school. See "Danske skoler bliver brugt som sprogskoler," *Flensborg Avis,* 13 September 1996.
120. "Mindretallet er for løst i fugerne," *Flensborg Avis*, 9 September 1996, and "Beklager manglende agtpågivenhed m.h.t. rødderne i mindretallet," *Flensborg Avis*, 12 September 1996.
121. "Ingen dansk støtte til rene sprogskoler," and "Sprog og kultur hænger uløseligt sammen," *Flensborg Avis*, 17 September 1996.
122. "Åbenhed og konsekvens," *Flensborg Avis*, 17 and 18 September 1996.
123. "Den forkerte skole," *Flensborg Avis*, 21 September 1996.
124. "Gensidige sproglige hensyn," and "Tysk rekruttering nødvendig for de danske skoler," *Flensborg Avis*, 27 September 1996.
125. "Fest og rødvin efterlyses," *Flensborg Avis*, 9 September 1996.
126. "'De kan da bare lære dansk'," *Flensborg Avis*, 25 September 1996.
127. "'Så dansk som muligt…'," *Flensborg Avis*, 18 and 19 September 1996.
128. "En overfladisk diskussion," *Flensborg Avis*, 23 September 1996.
129. "Sprog og sindelag," *Flensborg Avis*, 14 October 1996.
130. Among these values, Fischer listed humanity, solidarity, democracy, and social justice. See "Hvad er målet for mindretallet?" *Flensborg Avis*, 6 and 7 December 1996.
131. "Sprogdebatten," *Flensborg Avis*, 19 September 1996.
132. A classic interpretation of this process is provided by Miroslav Hroch, *Social Preconditions of National Revival in Europe* (Cambridge, England, 1985).

CHAPTER FIVE

Identity on a Personal Level

Sleswig Biographies during the Age of Nationalism

Social identities represent a group phenomenon, but they are also lived and experienced on a personal level. This makes the dividing line between individual and collective identities less rigid. The line is further blurred in environments that permit a personal choice of group attachment. In earlier periods, many of these affiliations were predetermined. Modern societies with their focus on individualism have expanded autonomous self-definition.

This chapter explores the response of individual Sleswigers to the challenge of nationalism during the last two centuries. Together, they cover a broad selection of Sleswig society. They include people born in the late 1700s as well as people alive today, people from different walks of life, and people with differing national allegiances. Yet although the chapter examines intellectual life histories, it strives to provide more than abstract biographies. Instead, it uses concrete life experiences to empiricize the concept of subjective nationality in border regions.

In Sleswig, too, the most common path of identity formation followed the gradual politicization of cultural attributes, especially language. For a Sleswig-Holstein activist in the Danish composite monarchy such as Wilhelm Beseler and a Danish-minded deputy to the German Reichstag such as H. P. Hanssen, identification with their linguistic community proved powerful enough to withstand the ideological influence of the political center.[1] Following the division of Sleswig in 1920, in turn, a clear majority on both sides of the new border was socialized fairly unproblematically into its respective nation-state.

Yet a substantial number of people chose a different course. As a consequence, the chapter explores biographies at the national crossroads. The individuals examined were linked to more than one cultural community. They made choices that were influenced by their public and private socialization and their emancipation from it. Although the life stories also display a process, which ranges from the gradual transformation of prenational conceptions under the influence of social and economic modernization in the early 1800s all the way to the increasing questioning of national concepts in the period following World War II, this progression is not linear and leaves room for alternative self-definitions. The analysis reveals the different types of self-identification available to the inhabitants of nineteenth- and twentieth-century Sleswig.

Sober Rationalist in an Age of Passion: Nicolaus Falck

(Niels) Nicolaus Falck was born in 1784 in Emmerlev in western Sleswig, slightly to the north of the current German-Danish border.[2] The district has always been predominantly Danish-speaking. Falck's father was a fairly typical representative of the local farming tradition, albeit with a sojourn as a sea captain, which might explain his decision to afford his son a higher education. This education led Nicolaus Falck away from his social origins, although he always retained an appreciation of Sleswig peasant culture.

Following training at the Haderslev grammar school, Falck began the study of theology and philosophy in Kiel, which he completed with a doctoral dissertation titled "De historiae inter Graecos origine et natura" in 1808.[3] He subsequently undertook graduate study in law, passed his exams in Gottorf, and began his juridical career in the civil service. Falck found employment at the Sleswig-Holstein chancellery in Copenhagen, where he was thoroughly integrated into local society and established numerous contacts with the Danish intellectual and political elite. He preserved these connections all his life, even when the tone of German-Danish exchanges within the composite monarchy had become strident.

In 1814, Falck was called to the University of Kiel, which was to be the center of his professional career for the remainder of his life. As a professor of law in Kiel, he identified so strongly with the land of his birth and its academic institution that he rejected more lucrative offers from universities all over Germany. He was held in high esteem among his colleagues and honored with membership in the Danish academy of sciences as well as the presidency of the Society for the History of Sleswig and Holstein. In addition to his scholarly endeavors, he also pursued politics, serving in the assemblies of both duchies. He reached the height of his public career between 1838 and 1844, when he was called to preside over the Sleswig estates. Falck died in 1850, in the midst of a war that pitted liberal revolution against royal government and at the same time marked a struggle for the national future of the duchies.

Falck's personal and philosophical development was strongly influenced by the bonds he established early in life. He developed a long-time friendship with the Holstein aristocrat Adam von Moltke, at whose house he served as a private tutor in 1808. In the short-lived intellectual bloom that followed the Napoleonic Wars, he associated with the proponents of the *Kieler Blätter*, highly spirited young men, many of whom would later shape the political debate. These few years may have been the most political period of Falck's life, notwithstanding his greater public visibility in subsequent decades.

Falck did not truly share his friends' passion for practical politics, however. After the Karlsbad Decrees had curtailed the liberal movement, especially at the universities, Falck withdrew from the public activism that had surrounded the *Kieler Blätter* and focused on his academic career. Falck saw himself primarily as a scholar, not a politician. Moreover, he remained more closely bound to the existing social order than many of his colleagues. Although widely associated with the liberal movement, Falck never fully ascribed to many of its tenets, and the new brand of radical liberalism that arose in the 1830s remained alien to him.

Moderation also characterized Falck's position on the emerging national conflict. Whereas men like Friedrich Dahlmann and Adam von Moltke placed the duchies' autonomy in a yet ill-defined context of German nationhood, Falck remained tied to the Danish realm. Sleswig and Holstein enjoyed historical rights as the united German duchies, but as such they formed a part of the composite monarchy, personified by the king in Copenhagen.

Falck's attachment to the Danish realm was especially pronounced in his younger years. He underscored in 1819 that the duchies of Sleswig and Holstein were his most immediate fatherland. Yet he also clarified that this left room for a broader definition that included the entire monarchy.[4] Later in life, Falck would have defined his relationship to Denmark more pragmatically, but he never advocated a German nation-state. His ultimate allegiance belonged to the dynastic polity, compared to which the autonomy of cultural groups remained secondary.

Falck was raised as a Danish speaker and always retained a thorough knowledge of this language. German dominated higher education in the duchies, however, and became Falck's primary language. He also used it in his correspondence with Danes, even if he matter-of-factly accepted Danish replies. Although this preference could not elude politicization in a period of linguistic strife, Falck seems to have followed traditional custom rather than taking a political stance.

Falck's German-oriented bilingualism surfaced at a decisive moment in his political career. As president of the Sleswig estates, he was confronted in 1842 with the demonstrative use of Danish by the Danish-minded but German-speaking representative Peter Hiort Lorenzen. Falck attempted to deflect the issue through a pragmatic approach. He refused to serve as a translator for a deputy that in fact spoke better German than Danish, while conceding that representatives who did not master German were entitled to use Danish in the otherwise German-speaking assembly. Although the furor of the Sleswig-Holstein faction forced Falck to curtail the further use of Danish, his initial reaction confirmed both his pragmatism and his bilingualism.

If he never ascribed to the tenets of nationalism, German or otherwise, why did Falck become so important for the development of a Sleswig-Holstein movement that ultimately resulted in the incorporation of the duchies into the German empire? To answer this question, one has to appreciate the dual nature of both Sleswig-Holsteinism and its Danish counterpart. On the Danish side, a time-honored emphasis on preserving the undivided composite monarchy coexisted with the nascent Danish ethnonationalism that eventually supplanted it. By the same token, a historicist focus on the autonomy of Sleswig and Holstein within the composite monarchy preceded and merged with efforts to create a German nation-state that included these duchies.

Falck made the legal case for independent Sleswig-Holstein statehood. He argued that Sleswig, although originally a Danish province, had established an autonomous political existence by the late Middle Ages. It had preserved this separate status ever since, notwithstanding the constitutional changes that occurred in the subsequent centuries. According to Falck, not even the oath of allegiance taken by the Sleswig estates in 1721 led to the full reintegration of the duchy into the Danish kingdom. Instead, the events following the Great Northern War, in which the Swedish protector of the dukes of Gottorp was defeated, only resulted in the administrative stratification of royal and ducal Sleswig.[5]

Thus, Falck supplied the formal judicial argument for the Sleswig-Holstein movement. While historians such as Friedrich Dahlmann had examined the constitutional development of the duchies and coined the central concepts and phrases, jurists such as Falck molded historical sources into contemporary legal instruments. Falck saw the privileges exercised by the Sleswig and Holstein aristocracies as derived from underlying provincial or state rights. The estates only safeguarded these privileges, but they belonged to the body politic in general.[6] Falck provided the instrument for transferring the special rights historically exercised by the Sleswig and Holstein estates, represented largely by the nobility, to the new Sleswig-Holstein popular movement. To Falck, a political body derived its legitimacy not from popular will or from cultural coherence, but from its authentic constitutional legacy. This legacy does not necessarily reflect the legal status quo, but the chain of legal tradition unbroken by unilateral and unconstitutional change.

Falck always remained a man of accommodation and conciliation. While he made the legal case for Sleswig-Holsteinism, he did not orchestrate its practical application in the struggle for the future of the duchies. In fact, when younger Sleswig-Holsteiners such as Uwe Jens Lornsen began to apply Falck's teachings about historical law and constitutional development, Falck had already lost his belief in their applicability. Only his confrontation with a new, modern form of Danish activism in the years leading up to the war of 1848-1850 motivated him to reassert his classic constitutional opinion.

◆ ◆ ◆

Nicolaus Falck played a complex role in the political landscape of early nineteenth-century Denmark. Through his legal analyses, he provided crucial arguments for Sleswig-Holsteinism, a movement that ultimately stressed the German character of the two duchies and their separateness from the Danish kingdom. There can be no doubt, moreover, that Falck personally considered himself a German, at least in a cultural sense. It would nonetheless be misleading to characterize Falck as a German nationalist. While he had no understanding for the demands of Danish activists such as Christian Flor, his own concept of Sleswig-Holstein did not reflect the German ethnonationalism that began to take root among his one-time allies.

Just as precarious as his national stance was his position on political and constitutional matters, in which traditional rights and prerogatives merged with moderate early nineteenth-century liberalism. Although Falck associated freely with democratic reformers, he remained skeptical about unfettered popular sovereignty. He insisted that the majority could also be unreasonable and had visibly distanced himself from the liberals by the 1840s. Falck's distrust of mass politics was if not triggered then at least reinforced by the competing language petitions that stirred up Sleswig burghers and farmers in the 1830s.

Nicolaus Falck's national development reflects the time in which he lived. In many ways, his transformation from Danish farm boy to German university professor echoed the established cultural process in a society in which a substantial part of the peasantry was Danish-speaking, whereas most of the elite, be it rural-aristocratic or urban-educated, identified with the German cultural sphere. Moreover, Falck's brand of Germanness remained strongly tied to traditional patterns. It represented a Sleswig-Holsteinism rooted in the composite monarchy; a German identity affiliated with the Danish crown and without hostility toward Danish local traditions. It was a moderate, centrist position, which enabled him to retain good relations with the intellectual elites in both the kingdom and the duchies and to play a prominent public role throughout his life. At the same time, it was a political stance that was past its prime and rapidly losing ground to the new tendencies of popular representation and national mobilization. Even though his legal *ouevre* has become associated with the new era of nationalism, Falck represented the Sleswig of old more than the Sleswig to come.

A Flensburger's Journey to the Danish Nation: Christian Paulsen

Christian Paulsen was born in 1798 in the city of Flensburg.[7] His family belonged to the local merchant patriciate that dominated social and political life. Like most members of this social group, Paulsen's parents were patriotic citizens of the Danish composite monarchy, but culturally and linguistically German. Christian Paulsen, therefore, grew up as a German speaker and never developed a fully equivalent command of the Danish language.

In 1809, Paulsen enrolled in the distinguished Salzmann grammar school in the Thuringian village of Schnepfenthal. For more than a decade, he attended German secondary schools and universities, until he took up supplementary studies at the University of Copenhagen in 1821. During his stay in the German heartland, Paulsen came under the influence of the fraternity movement. He even participated in the famous Wartburg festival of 1817, which marked the climax of post-Napoleonic student activism in favor of political liberalism and German unification.

In view of this upbringing, Paulsen's contemporaries frequently marveled at his embrace of Danish nationalism. Paulsen himself, looking back on his life during the tumultuous events of 1848, speculated that his family history and the dynastic patriotism of his hometown must have drawn him to Denmark.[8] Many contemporaries who shared this cultural background developed a different sense of identity, however, so that Paulsen's retrospective reasoning might be more reflective of his own need for explanation. Paulsen also suspected that his schooling in the German heartland might have given him a greater appreciation of Danish culture, because he considered the educational system of Sleswig to be more critical of Denmark.[9]

While the divergence between cultural socialization and national orientation puzzled his contemporaries and sometimes even himself, Paulsen's personal sense of belonging developed more consistently. On an emotional level, Paulsen's self-identification as a Dane took root early, even if the exact meaning of this identification changed over time and became more consciously political in later life. As a student in Göttingen, he noted Denmark as his country of origin, whereas most of his fellow Sleswigers preferred to list Sleswig or even Holstein.[10] He associated with Danish speakers and began his lifelong debates with compatriots who defined themselves as Germans.[11]

After his return to the duchies in 1819, Paulsen prepared for further studies in Denmark proper. He arrived in Copenhagen in December 1821, and the subsequent four and a half years in the capital completed his integration into the Danish political and cultural sphere. Paulsen desired to secure his Danishness by extending it to the linguistic sphere and noted in his diary: "I have stated so often lately that—already being Danish at heart—I would also become Danish in speech. I want to make this true by recording my biographic comments in my dear Danish language."[12] He continued to write his diary in Danish, even though much of his social and professional life subsequently reverted to German.

Paulsen graduated with a doctorate of law from the University of Copenhagen in 1824. He envisioned an academic career there but received a call to the University of Kiel in 1825. Instead of moving his life from the border to the capital, Paulsen assumed a Danish mission right at that border. As professor of Danish and Sleswig-Holstein law at the duchies' German-language university, Paulsen became a central figure in the Danish national movement in Sleswig.

Although the ideological content of Paulsen's nationalism developed gradually, its central elements surfaced early. In an 1823 speech to fellow students in Copenhagen, Paulsen expressed his love for Denmark and emphasized Sleswig's Danish traditions.[13] To underline his point, Paulsen consciously called himself a *sønderjyde*, a South Jutlander, utilizing a designation that had been widely replaced by the more German-sounding term Sleswiger.[14] *Sønderjyde* emphasized the medieval Danish roots of the duchy and the connection to the remainder of Jutland. Paulsen was instrumental in the popularization of this historical designation within the Danish-speaking population of Sleswig and is therefore regularly referred to as "the first South Jutlander."[15]

During his initial years in Kiel, Paulsen quietly pursued his national goals by familiarizing his students with Scandinavian legal history and its relevance for the duchies' jurisprudence.[16] His encounter with the budding Sleswig-Holstein movement, personified not least of all by Uwe Jens Lornsen, redirected him toward a more explicitly political stance. In 1830, Lornsen, a promising young official from North Frisia, published a pamphlet titled *Ueber das Verfassungswerk in Schleswigholstein* [The Constitutional Issue in Sleswig-Holstein]."[17] In this brief piece, Lornsen suggested political reforms based on the Norwegian example. In addition to political liberalization, however, Lornsen also desired the transfer of the duchies' central administration from Copenhagen to Kiel and the transformation of the composite monarchy into a union between two political entities of equal status.

In response to such demands to treat Sleswig and Holstein as one, ultimately German, polity, Paulsen published his first major political treatise in 1832.[18] In his diary, he explicitly defined the study as a balancing counterweight to an exaggerated Germanness, which aimed at severing Sleswig completely from Denmark.[19] In spite of this objective, which consequently made it one of the classics of the Danish national movement in Sleswig, the study was sober and moderate enough to be appreciated by many German-oriented Sleswigers.[20]

In "Ethnic and Constitutional Conditions in the Duchy of Sleswig," as the title of the study could be freely translated, Paulsen develops his solution to the national conflict in Sleswig. He underscores that the duchy continues to be a Danish possession, even if it no longer forms a constituent part of the Danish kingdom. He sees its legal status as fundamentally different from that of neighboring Holstein, which is only connected with Denmark through the person of its ruler. As a consequence, Paulsen also advocates separate estates for the two duchies.[21]

In spite of his extensive use of constitutional arguments, Paulsen puts most emphasis on Sleswig's ethnolinguistic composition. He accentuates the duchy's Danish origins and the continuing majority status of Danish as the local vernacular.[22] Deeply influenced by Herder and German romanticism, Paulsen ascribes an innate spiritual value to language, to be understood as a native tongue passed down from generation to generation. He considers such a language sanctified and a true expression of individual identity.[23] The suppression and loss of one's native tongue does not only lead to numerous practical complications, which Paulsen diligently lists; even more important is the accompanying spiritual and cultural impoverishment.[24]

Paulsen wants to secure or reestablish standard Danish as the language of public life in those parts of Sleswig where it has survived as the vernacular.[25] In northern districts, where it already constitutes the language of church and school, it should also become the language of jurisdiction and administration. Further south, where the South Jutland dialect only exists as a domestic language, standard Danish should be gradually introduced into schools and churches, so that the local dialect speakers would become familiar with the cultural treasures available in their mother tongue. Both German and Danish Sleswigers would profit from being familiar with both national languages, however.

In his conclusion, Paulsen implicitly rejects the very concept of Sleswig-Holstein. Sleswig is not one of the German duchies, inseparably intertwined with Holstein. Instead, Sleswig's character as a bicultural territory would emerge fully as soon as the duchy was freed from its affiliation with Holstein. Its true calling is to be an intermediary, a bridge between Holstein and Denmark, between German and Danish.

Paulsen's 1832 study catapulted him into the political limelight and made him a standard bearer of the Danish movement in Sleswig. Nonetheless, it can not yet be taken as a full expression of later Danish nationalism, or Eiderdanism. To the Eiderdane movement, Sleswig was a Danish territory in its entirety. Its political and ethnic roots were Danish, regardless of subsequent German influences. German and Frisian could continue to exist as minority languages, but within a Danish context. Holstein, on the other hand, was free to decide its own fate.

In 1832, Paulsen had not yet reached this view of Sleswig history and promoted a truly bicultural solution, which he considered best suited for preserving the Danish composite monarchy. Yet the growing acrimony between the national factions began to impact Paulsen, too. By arguing in 1836 that Sleswig and parts of Holstein were tied more closely to the Danish royal dynasty than many of his colleagues had allowed for, he was drawn into the unfolding dispute about the dynastic line of succession in the duchies.[26] Paulsen's conviction that the Danish law of succession had been extended to Sleswig and parts of Holstein in 1721 challenged one of the major legal arguments of the Sleswig-Holsteiners. He came to be seen as an integral part of the Danish movement in Sleswig and as a close ally of such activists as Christian Flor and Peter Christian Koch, although his own ideological background did not fully correspond to the popular Grundtvigian nationalism of the latter.

In 1837, Paulsen followed the advice of fellow activists to publish his fundamental views on Sleswig's cultural conditions in Danish.[27] Although it contains many of the arguments previously published in German, the new treatise is more expressly political. Paulsen had become more involved in the political struggle, and he had a different audience to relate to. Whereas his prior work was directed at the largely German-speaking educated classes, the new contribution aimed at mobilizing a broader segment of Danish speakers, especially in North Sleswig. Paulsen's public role expanded further when he participated in the launching of *Dannevirke,* the first Danish-language periodical in Sleswig.[28] The newspaper evolved into a central forum for Danish activism in Sleswig.

The visibility Paulsen acquired through those political activities created a backlash in German circles and undermined his position at the university. Not only the relationship to his German-oriented colleagues suffered; enrollment in his classes dropped noticeably, too, as students began to avoid the controversial lecturer.[29] After Christian Flor had left Kiel to head Rødding folk college in 1845, Paulsen felt even more isolated in an unreceptive environment.

The revolution of 1848 and the accompanying military conflict between Germans and Danes transformed Paulsen's position. When Kiel fell to the Sleswig-Holstein forces, Paulsen departed for Copenhagen. He participated actively in both political and academic pursuits to restore royal control over the duchies and contributed to the *Antislesvigholstenske Fragmenter*, which members of Copenhagen University published in response to academic Sleswig-Holsteinism. In a short piece titled "Om Slesvigs indre forbindelse med Danmark" [About Sleswig's Internal Affiliation with Denmark], Paulsen further accentuated his argument that Sleswig continued to be a Danish fiefdom that was affiliated with Denmark in a real, not just a personal union.[30] Since Holstein continued to be a German fiefdom, the relationship between the two duchies had to have a more peripheral nature. By 1848, Paulsen had thus assumed the Eiderdane position, which ultimately entailed a dividing line that left Holstein on the German side, whereas all of Sleswig fell into the Danish political sphere.

Toward the end of his life, Christian Paulsen no longer saw the true calling of Sleswig in being a bridge between Germany and Scandinavia. Paulsen's thinking increasingly reflected the principles of the Danish national movement, although he retained a stronger focus on constitutional aspects than many of his more populist comrades.

Subsequent to the defeat of Sleswig-Holsteinism, Paulsen permanently returned to the duchies in 1851. Instead of reclaiming his academic position in Kiel, he assumed political and administrative duties in Flensburg. He died in his native city in 1854.

Erratic Rebel and Sleswiger for Life: Cornelius Petersen

Having examined two cases that revealed how modern national identities first took root in Sleswig, this chapter continues with a very different life story. The farmer and politician Cornelius Petersen (1882-1935) followed a path that brought him into both contact and conflict with all the ethnic groups that inhabited his homeland. For a short period in the interwar era, he became one of the most visible and controversial personalities in Sleswig.[31]

Petersen was born in the district of Eiderstedt in the southwestern corner of Sleswig. This prosperous coastal region had originally been Frisian but took on Low German speech in the 1600s. Petersen grew up with Low German as his mother tongue and High German as his language of education and culture. He learned Frisian and Danish later in life, after he had acquired a farm in the Danish-speaking outskirts of Tønder in 1904.

Petersen's father was a schoolteacher and local historian, who perceived himself as a Frisian in a regional sense but as a German in a national one. His mother hailed from a well-established Eiderstedt farming dynasty.[32] Thus, Petersen was raised in a home that was linguistically and politically German, if in a distinctly Sleswigian sense that accommodated local Frisian and Danish traditions. Petersen's maternal great-grandfather, Peter Hamkens, even had to go into exile because of his Sleswig-Holstein activism. Initially, Cornelius Petersen showed no signs of following a different path.

Petersen prepared himself for his chosen career as a farmer, first on a relative's homestead in North Frisia and subsequently at a German agricultural school in Holstein. His integration into German Sleswig society faced its first challenge when he purchased land in a predominantly Danish-speaking environment. His long-established aversion to the Prussian bureaucracy brought him into contact with Danish associations, who shared the same antagonist. Although Petersen remained active within the German political sphere, he could also be observed as a guest at Danish meetings and celebrations.

Before World War I, Petersen's political activities occurred on the side of conciliatory German centrism. He supported the German progressives, the left wing of German liberalism, as well as pastor Johannes Schmidt-Wodder's peace society, which attempted to improve interethnic relations in Sleswig. The patriotic exuberance of the early war years left Petersen untouched, and he remained skeptical of the war and the likelihood of victory.

Germany's defeat changed the political landscape in Sleswig. Initially, Petersen continued to support the German left liberals, now reorganized as the German Democratic Party. Yet the prospect of Danish sovereignty over North Sleswig drew him closer to the Danish side, as did his displeasure with the leftist components of the German revolution. Petersen did not want southern Sleswig detached from the north, and he envisioned a promising future for Frisian and German Sleswigers under lenient Danish governance. In addition, he easily transferred his dislike of non-local bureaucrats onto the non-local Marxist activists whom he considered the driving force behind the new republican order.

Petersen became an important voice in the struggle for the hearts and souls of the border population. Although he frequently embraced the Frisian tradition, Petersen also called himself a German Sleswiger. The emphasis lay on Sleswiger, and he argued that all indigenous Sleswigers north of the old ethnic divide along Dannevirke and Schlei were more closely tied to Scandinavia than to Germany. This assessment was interconnected with his rejection of centralized government and the state, both of which he identified with a loss of local self-government.

In several pamphlets, Petersen developed his vision for Sleswig and especially North Frisia. He adopted the Danish historical imagery that emphasized the non-German roots of the inhabitants of Sleswig. Prussian political tradition was based on the assimilation of numerous subject identities from Sleswig all the way to the eastern shore of the Baltic Sea. The defeat of Germany had granted the indigenous Danish, Frisian, and Low German speakers of Sleswig an opportunity to develop freely under a generous Danish roof. Denmark would accord them local autonomy, as it had in the past.

In his brochure *Die friesische Bewegung*, Petersen expressed his identification with the Frisian tradition.[33] Again, Prussian colonialism is conceptualized as the enemy, but it is put into a larger context that incorporates royal and aristocratic expansionism in general. Foreshadowing his place within the agrarian protest movement of the 1920s, Petersen defines the yeoman republicanism of Frisians, Dithmarshers, and medieval Saxons as an alternative vision to lordship and dominance, be it Frankish, Prussian, or Danish.

In Petersen's view, external domination had only changed appearance over the centuries. Whereas foreign rulers had suppressed the indigenous peasant population through military force and religious conversion in the past, they turned to education and bureaucracy in the modern era. The damage wrought by pastors and teachers was especially serious, because it also transformed the sense of self of many Frisians. They began to identify with foreign traditions and to look down on their own, which had been disparaged as provincial and anachronistic.

Petersen argued that the leading families were the first to change, because they measured themselves by the standards of an alien upper class. This is why his wealthy home district of Eiderstedt had surrendered the Frisian language. He depicted a development in which parents raised their children in a foreign tongue in order to improve their chances in society at large. With this semivoluntary final step, they completed a long process of colonialization and self-colonialization.

The plebiscites of 1920 brought half of Sleswig, including Petersen's adopted home district, under Danish rule, but they left the other half, including his native North Frisia, on the German side of the border. This outcome did not reflect Petersen's preferences, and by 1922, he showed first signs of dissatisfaction. His vision remained an idealized peasant republic, which he saw represented in historic Eiderstedt. In a tightly knit society of clans and small communities, local government would dominate. Peasant liberty had been suppressed by feudalism, yet feudalism's decline had not brought the return of ancient liberties, but a parliamentary system that retained bureaucratic and centralized rule.

In his aversion to external domination, Petersen drew heavily on the imagery of racial coherence and purity vis-à-vis alien intrusion. His emphasis on local decision-making went hand in hand with a rejection of parliamentary politics. Petersen's peasant republic was not a society of equals; it was a society in which the leading families enjoyed an elevated stature, while at the same time carrying special obligations toward the *res publica* and its weakest members.

The economic crisis in North Sleswig's agriculture deepened Petersen's frustration. In the mid 1920s, he launched *Bondens Selvstyre* (The Farmer's Self-Rule), which became the voice of radical agrarian protest in southwestern Denmark.[34] Petersen proved a skillful agitator and organized large-scale protest meetings, whose sweeping attacks on federal institutions triggered considerable interest and concern in the Copenhagen media. When the self-rule movement only mustered little over 2,000 votes in the parliamentary elections of 1926, however, its élan was broken.

In the following years, Petersen suffered both financial and personal setbacks and even had to temporarily commit himself to a psychiatric hospital. He spent his final years outside of the political limelight, only to surface briefly when he expressed sympathies for National Socialism. In tune with his national development, he associated with the Danish wing of the movement and not its counterpart in the German minority. Thus, it was fellow North Sleswiger and subsequent wartime collaborator Frits Clausen who bid farewell to Petersen at his funeral in 1935.

◆ ◆ ◆

Cornelius Petersen seems to have undergone a perplexing sequence of changes and conversions. He was raised a German and began his political career within the German mainstream, not within the Danish minority movement. In the aftermath of World War I, he made a name for himself both as a supporter of Danish rule in Sleswig and a promoter of an autonomous Frisian nationalism. In the interwar era, he founded a movement opposed to the central government in Copenhagen and championed the removal of customs barriers along the German-Danish border. At the end of his life, he sympathized with a party that represented the most radical strain of Danish nationalism and at the same time established close ties to the government in Berlin.

Ideologically, the company he kept seemed to change just as drastically. Before World War I, Petersen was associated with the Peace Association and the German progressives. In interwar Denmark, Petersen embraced the activist rightism of the agrarian protest movement and, to a certain degree, Danish National Socialism. At the same time, Petersen served as a spiritual godfather to the Frisian nationalist movement in Germany, which encountered sharp hostility from the German right.

Yet in spite of these apparent contradictions, Cornelius Petersen's worldview displayed considerable consistency. His guiding light was an idealized Frisian peasant republic, in which Frisian did not constitute an ethnolinguistic category but symbolized the yeoman tradition of southwestern Jutland. Petersen's sense of self derived from tradition and kinship; it juxtaposed an organic local community and a repressive state apparatus. Thus, his concept of identity was strictly opposed to state nationalism. Although his special wrath was reserved for the Prusso-German political legacy, Danish nationalism was not much closer to his heart. Petersen was a regionalist, a Sleswiger who was socialized as a German, supported political integration into Denmark, and most commonly referred to himself as a Frisian.

This premodern cultural identity coincided with his political agenda. His rejection of external domination, the educated elites, and urban society accompanied him throughout his lifetime. When he encountered these forces in the form of Prussian aristocrats and bureaucrats, he supported their democratic critics. When he encountered them in the shape of liberal or social democratic parliamentarians from Copenhagen, he started his conservative peasant rebellion. And the force and fanaticism that had endeared him to the Danish establishment when it had inspired his attacks on the imperial bureaucracy found a distant echo in the oppositional clamor of Frits Clausen's small National Socialist movement.

Cornelius Petersen was a difficult and idiosyncratic personality, who was not beyond merging idealistic and material interests. It would be simplistic to portray him as the embodiment of the third Sleswig, a Sleswig beyond German and Danish. Yet while he may not have been its most typical representative, Petersen lived and imagined this third Sleswig more than most others. He dwelt in all its cultural spheres and idealized its historical legacy. Ultimately, he even learned to speak all its languages, both separately and, as many observers commented, mixed together in a uniquely Sleswigian mélange.

Therefore, Petersen's erratic biography cannot be understood outside its Sleswigian context. He represented a border population with ties to several cultural communities. These communities were not divided by fundamental barriers of lifestyle, religion, or appearance. They even shared some of their historical symbolism. As a consequence, it seemed easier to pass from one community to the other and feasible to embrace more than one at the same time. Cornelius Petersen bewildered the core groups of German and Danish nationalism, because his Sleswig identity remained genuinely outside the framework of either. He was German, Danish, and Frisian, but he was all these things in his own way, which did not correspond to the manner in which nationally-minded Germans and Danes defined this identity. It was only fitting that his grand funeral in the churchyard of Møgeltønder gathered mourners from almost all segments of Sleswig society.

When South Sleswig Turned Upside Down: Life Stories from the Early Postwar Years

The biographies of Nicolaus Falck, Christian Paulsen, and Cornelius Petersen have shown that cultural identities in Sleswig were shaped by diverse influences. The final result of this process did not always reflect its sociocultural origins. Falck and Paulsen did choose sides, however, and they upheld their decisions throughout the remainder of their lives. Cornelius Petersen, in turn, consistently placed his regional identity above all others.

In periods of crisis, especially, personal identity formation in Sleswig could be more volatile. At no time did this volatility surface more dramatically than at the end of World War II. In the immediate postwar years, affiliation with the Danish minority in South Sleswig expanded from a few thousand to approximately one hundred thousand. A large percentage of the local populace changed its national orientation, at least temporarily.

What motivated so momentous a transformation? There have been many attempts to answer this question, also in parts of this study. It is intriguing, however, to look at the rationales given by individuals who themselves partook in or at least came into contact with this development. A compilation of testimonies published in 2003 offers a glimpse at individual motivations seen from a subjective and retrospective angle.[35] Twenty-seven Sleswigers, born between 1925 and 1950, describe how they or their parents experienced the passage from German to Danish identity. Many of them had no prior association with Danish traditions; more than a few had roots in parts of Germany that were far removed from the German-Danish borderlands. Why did they want to become Danes?

All the informants agree on some basic parameters. Germany lay in ruins. National Socialism had resulted in a catastrophe. There was a shortage of everything, and those essential supplies available had to be shared with the many refugees who had been expelled from Germany's eastern provinces.

Within these broad parameters, individual motivations varied. Some informants remember previous sympathies with Danish society.[36] Many list ideological reasons and juxtapose an authoritarian and National Socialist Germany with a liberal and democratic Denmark.[37] Others concede that they simply desired a better future within Denmark.[38]

The cultural background was more uniformly German, although there were exceptions. Wilhelm Klüver was born in 1929 in the village of Achtrup close to the border.[39] Achtrup lay on the small strip of land in the high plains where the South Jutland dialect extended into politically German territory even beyond World War I. Yet in spite of this cultural predisposition, he did not consciously identify himself as a Dane before the great reorientation in 1945. He does not think he *became* a Dane in 1945, but he became *aware* of being one at that time. Membership in Danish associations and visits to Denmark subsequently reinforced this awareness.

Few people had such concrete ties to the Danish community. More common were experiences like Ingrid Thomsen's.[40] Born in the city of Schleswig in 1929, she grew up in a completely German environment. In 1945, her stepfather joined the Danish minority. Ingrid herself was disillusioned with Germany and ready for new ideals, which she expected to find in Denmark. It was a spiritual and ideological conversion more than a cultural one, although her experiences with Danish schools and host families deepened her familiarity with the latter aspect as well.

For some, the national reorientation had profound implications. Günther Rahn was born in 1935 in the southern town of Friedrichstadt, close to Holstein and without a genuine Danish cultural tradition.[41] After the war, his parents affiliated with the minority and sent most of their children to Danish schools. The oldest one had already finished his education, however, and never switched to the Danish side. For the other siblings, their parents' postwar decision had lifelong consequences. One brother and one sister joined spouses in Denmark. Another sister moved there on her own. The last sister taught at a Danish school in Flensburg. Günther Rahn himself married a native Dane and became a councilman for the Danish minority party in his hometown.

For others, their Danish affiliation remained more tentative. Günther Gottschalk was born in 1950 to an eastern German refugee father and a local German-speaking mother.[42] Alone among the informants, Gottschalk openly concedes that his parents joined the minority to benefit from Danish food aid. He attended Danish minority schools, but more than anything else, his yearly visits with Danish host families established an emotional tie to Denmark. His adult life took place in a German environment, and he married a German speaker from the Hamburg region. Nonetheless, he retained a sentimental attachment to things Danish, colored primarily by memories of his childhood vacations. When he was able to afford it, he realized his dream of residing in a Danish-style cottage, in which he experienced life as though in a Danish vacation home.

Almost all informants report that they have retained their Danish orientation. At the same time, it frequently became less central to their daily routine, especially for those who moved to other parts of Germany.

How should we approach these personal recollections? They are sources, not analyses, and they are colored by time and personal perceptions. The reader has to distill relevant information from the autobiographical descriptions. In order to achieve this, one also has to read the texts against the grain.

Many informants address the material incentives for joining the minority. Most of all, this concerned care packages earmarked for the Danish minority in South Sleswig. Yet all except one maintain that economic considerations only influenced other families, not their own. This might reflect the fact that the interviewees, who generally have retained their Danish ties, constituted a more convinced core group, for whom material aspects were less significant. In other cases, it might just reflect a human tendency to view and present oneself in a positive light.

Similar questions surface in regard to ideological issues. Almost all informants indicate some form of oppositional sentiment during the war—even if they or their parents belonged to National Socialist organizations. Such retroactive self-images were commonplace in postwar Germany. Are they more authentic among postwar minority members?

In this context, one of the informants is especially interesting. Gerhard Ernst was born in Flensburg in 1931.[43] Although his mother hailed from Dessau in central Germany, the family joined the organized minority in the early 1930s. Gerhard Ernst attended Danish kindergarten and school under National Socialism, when few people wanted to be affiliated with the minority.

In May 1945, all this changed. Formerly hostile Germans streamed into Danish schools and associations. Ernst describes the puzzlement and resentment among the old-style Danish students when their schools changed character and were dominated by people who knew little of Danish life. These traditional minority members shared some of the skepticism that German society had toward the cultural conversion of so many.

The leaders of the minority took a more pragmatic stance. If the Danish community wanted to be politically relevant or even achieve a border revision, it needed to integrate former Germans. It was faced with a choice between size and depth. It chose size, hoping depth would develop in the course of time. This decision had a lasting impact on the nature of Danishness in southern Sleswig.

The autobiographical sketches illuminate important aspects of identity transformation. They demonstrate that many components coalesce in shaping a personal sense of self. They remind us that national consciousness is neither predetermined nor unalterable.

These personal recollections also document the genesis of a new Danish minority in southern Sleswig. Although it could build on earlier structures, the minority was soon defined by the newcomers. The postwar minority would be much stronger numerically, but it would be a different kind of minority. For most members of the postwar Danish community in Germany, Danish never turned into the language of daily life. It was a language learned in kindergarten and school that was used within the walls of organized Danishness and on visits to Denmark.

The numerical expansion of a minority within a foreign state is unusual. More typical is the opposite development. Minorities all over the world struggle to retain their identity against the assimilatory tendencies emanating from modern mass societies. Minorities are more likely to lose people to than gain them from the majority.

Postwar South Sleswig was different. Tens of thousands converted to the minority, and even though some of them ultimately reversed this step, many others did not. It was truly a conversion, however, a step rooted more in mind than in matter. It might have been easy to feel like a Dane, but it proved to be much harder to live as one. There was general agreement that one did not need to speak Danish to join the minority. But did one subsequently have to learn it? And how devoted and successful did one have to be?

Questions of this nature were the price that the minority had to pay for its numerical success. Most minority members have been willing to do so. In the peaceful and cooperative atmosphere that has developed in the borderland, the Danish minority can accommodate different layers of identification. The history of postwar Sleswig has taught new lessons about the nature of social identity—and it has raised new questions.

Crossing Borders in Divided Sleswig: Siegfried Matlok

The national reorientation of 1945 substantially enlarged the Danish minority in Germany, but it also reverberated in the lives of many individuals. Not all of them had made this decision for themselves. A new generation of Sleswigers was born into families who had taken the step from German to Danish self-identification. Many of them grew naturally into this new minority. Others were torn between their German-speaking homes and neighborhoods on the one hand and their Danish-oriented schools and associations on the other.

Siegfried Matlok was born on 5 June 1945 in Flensburg.[44] He had little contact with his father and was shaped by his maternal family. His grandfather used to work as a customs official in northern Sleswig and relocated to Flensburg following the border change in 1920. Together with his wife, he raised 10 children.

Like many other German-speaking South Sleswigers, the Matloks were caught up in the national reorientation following World War II. Some family members joined the Danish minority; others remained German. Siegfried Matlok's mother enrolled her two sons in Danish schools. The cultural and linguistic environment remained German, however, both at home and in the neighborhood.

After graduating from the Danish school system in Flensburg, Matlok aspired to become a journalist. When a Danish paper made him painfully aware of his linguistic limitations, he began to write for the minority's German-language publication. In 1964, however, he surprisingly transferred to *Der Nordschleswiger*, the daily newspaper of the German minority in Denmark. He was increasingly integrated into the institutional life of the minority, especially after assuming the paper's editorship in 1973. In the following decades, Matlok became one of the most visible representatives of the German community in Denmark. His brother, by contrast, remained active in the Danish minority in Germany.

◆ ◆ ◆

How does a person from so composite a background define his identity? This question demands a subjective assessment, which reflects Siegfried Matlok's personal sense of self. In his own eyes, Matlok had never been a conscious member of the Danish minority. He experienced his family environment as German and felt particularly close to his grandfather, with whom he regularly discussed history and politics. At home they spoke German, and the older generation never learned much Danish. His mother may have voted Danish in local elections, but she did not try to shape his national orientation.

Matlok ascribes his mother's decision to send her children to Danish schools to economic considerations. Nonetheless, he looks at this experience positively and emphasizes that it has enabled him to understand both communities and both sides of the historical conflict. Without his early familiarization with Danish culture and language, he could not have fulfilled his role as spokesperson for the German minority in Denmark, which he defines as being a bridge builder.

Yet how does Matlok perceive his passage from Danish to German minority institutions? To him, this step marked the logical completion of an inner journey that had begun much earlier. Throughout his youth, he perceived a powerful group pressure to distance himself from Germans and German society. When his talent as a soccer player was discovered, he was urged to play only for Danish clubs. When Germany won the world championship in this sport in 1954, he was dissuaded from sharing in this victory. The Germans were Nazis and could not be supported. Similar reactions accompanied the reappearance of German soldiers in 1955. Matlok felt alienated by this hostility toward things German.

Matlok also recalls bitter feuds within his family, which had become evenly split between Germans and Danes. In these discussions, the Danish members assumed an aura of moral superiority. By becoming Danish, they had proven to be democrats and antifascists, regardless of their actions and experiences during the war. Those who had remained German, by contrast, had failed to learn the lessons of history.

Matlok depicts an early disaffection with the Danish minority as an institution, mitigated by a continued appreciation of Danish social and intellectual life. Ironically, it was his marriage to a Dane that ultimately induced him to accept a position at the German paper in Aabenraa. His second wife, with whom he has two children, is Danish as well. He describes his home environment as bicultural and bilingual, although with a preponderance of Danish.

The life story of Siegfried Matlok illuminates national identity at the margins. On one level, he exemplifies the idiosyncrasies of this environment. He was born into a German-speaking family but sent to a Danish school. His grandparents had moved south when their place of residence became Danish, but many of their children became Danish-minded in 1945. He started his career at a Danish publication in Germany but continued it at a German one in Denmark. He moved to Denmark to join a Danish wife and a German newspaper. His children attended a

German school and grew up in a predominantly Danish-speaking household. His brother remained in Germany—and a Dane.

Although many of these features reflect the flexibility of identity along the border, they also contain countervailing aspects. Matlok was socialized in consciously Danish schools, but his linguistic background and his family history proved equally influential. Symbolic barriers that separated Danes from Germans, such as historical conflicts and sporting events, confused an adolescent who experienced the projected German Other as part of his self. Torn between conflicting subjective identity markers, he was drawn toward the camp that he experienced as more open to dual identifications.

Next to these subjective influences, one encounters palpable objective factors. Following his education at Danish minority schools in Germany, Matlok embarked on a career within the Danish sphere. Yet in his chosen field of journalism, he soon experienced the substantive limitations of his Danishness. His linguistic competence was sufficient to be a Dane within the predominantly German-speaking minority milieu of South Sleswig. But it did not suffice to compete with native Danish speakers in the open marketplace. Matlok shared in the experience of many Danish South Sleswigers—and German North Sleswigers.

Matlok's radical response has remained the exception. His brother Jürgen (or Jørgen) stayed within the protected confines of specifically South Sleswigian Danishness and found his calling in the minority school system.[45] Siegfried Matlok switched from the institutional life of Danish South Sleswig to its German counterpart in the north. To many, this seemed an extraordinary step.

Upon closer inspection, the change may have been smaller than it appears. On both sides of the border, people have moved in and out of their national communities, without raising eyebrows. Yet the passage between majority and minority on either side of the border objectively crosses a wider gulf than the passage between the two minorities. The gap between the latter is atmospheric more than substantive. By practical standards, these two communities lie closer to each other than any other ones, since they both combine Danish and German elements. By crossing the substantively small but psychologically deep barrier between the two minorities, Siegfried Matlok added another facet to the composite nature of border identities.

Conclusion

In a scholarly analysis that focuses on data and numbers, the individual human experience can easily fade into the background. Personal biographies offer a glimpse into the historic border environment from the perspective of the individuals who lived in it. They illuminate how individual Sleswigers responded to the challenge of national integration in a transnational environment. And they show the course of identity formation in this border region.

Nicolaus Falck and Christian Paulsen were born almost contemporaneously, but the modifier "almost" has significance in more than a purely temporal sense. These two scholars had much in common. They shared a moderate political disposition and an old-style liberalism that rejected radical upheaval. In spite of their divergent national identifications, their practical policy suggestions remained compatible initially. Ultimately, however, Paulsen was influenced more deeply by the new national conceptions than Falck. The 14 years that lay between the two had transformed public thinking. They drifted farther and farther apart. By 1848, their respective understandings of Sleswig's political and cultural future had become irreconcilable.

In a different manner, this multiple integration was shared by Cornelius Petersen. In his case, however, multiplicity was not so much rooted in the crossing of borders but in an alternative sense of belonging. In many ways, Petersen remained a prenational Sleswiger. His allegiance belonged to an idealized peasant republic, to a yeoman society with roots much older than the modern nation-state. He most often called this concept Frisian, but it was Frisian in an allegorical more than in a concrete cultural meaning. It was a comprehensive Sleswig identity that could accommodate all indigenous groups. At the same time, it was so anachronistic in its social and economic tenets that it was impossible to unite people around it.

The new Danes of 1945 reflect a later stage of development. Their reorientation marked a rebellion against the national framework into which they had been socialized. It was a conscious attempt to reshape one's cultural core. The volatility that grew from this divergence of objective and subjective conditions found its most visible expression in the life story of Siegfried Matlok. Socialized by German relatives and Danish teachers, he had to cross borders to find himself. In the course of this process, his biography became interwoven with the majority and minority communities on both sides of the border.

The experiences examined in this chapter reveal the diversity of subjective identity formation. All the individuals studied made choices about their national belonging. Yet the nature and motivation of these choices varied considerably. Experiencing the initial rise of national movements, Falck and Poulsen resolved to prioritize one of the two cultural traditions that had accompanied them since childhood. Confronted with the demands of nation-states at the zenith of their mass appeal, Cornelius Petersen invoked several national traditions but ultimately rejected them all in favor of an idealized home district. Living in an era more critical of nationalism in general and its German expressions in particular, the new Danes of 1945 embraced a national alternative whose cultural codes they did not fully master. In his own life, Siegfried Matlock faced the challenges that arose from this partial incongruence of culture and sense of self.

These examples of Sleswigian life stories have added individual components to the question of identity formation in the German-Danish borderlands. Thus, they have complemented the macrodata examined in the chapters before. Yet how does Sleswig fit into the larger picture of identity formation in zones of transition? How unique are its parameters? To receive an answer to this type of question, one has to undertake an analysis of other European border regions. This comparative examination forms the central aspect of the subsequent chapter.

Notes

1. For Beseler, see Gesellschaft für Schleswig-Holsteinische Geschichte und Verein für Lübeckische Geschichte und Altertumskunde, eds., *Biographisches Lexikon für Schleswig-Holstein und Lübeck* (Neumünster, 1987), 8:43-46; and Svend Cedergreen Bech, *Dansk biografisk leksikon*, 3d ed. (Copenhagen, 1979), 2:60f. The intellectual development of H. P. Hanssen can be followed in his autobiography *Et tilbageblik,* 4 vols. (Copenhagen, 1928-1934).
2. The use and spelling of Falck's first and middle name has varied, which can also be seen in the references. In the main text and the bibliography, he will consistently be referred to as Nicolaus Falck.
3. "About the origin and nature of history among the Greeks."
4. Nicolaus Falck, *Sammlungen zur nähern Kunde des Vaterlandes in historischer, statistischer und staatswirthschaftlicher Hinsicht* 1 (Altona, 1819), XI.
5. As Falck argued in 1842:

   > As the facts irrefutably show, the events described above concern exclusively the ducal part of the duchy of Sleswig. The royal part of the duchy was not affected in its constitutional affairs and has not been affected since. It is, furthermore, plain to see that the king did not resolve to unite the seized ducal portion with the kingdom of Denmark, but with the royal part of the duchy. In his role as duke, he brought the whole duchy under his control, without altering its constitutional relations with either the kingdom of Denmark or the duchy of Holstein.

   Nicolaus Falck, *Die historischen Landes-Rechte in Schleswig und Holstein urkundlich* (Kiel, 1842), 14.
6. Niels Nicolaus Falck, "Kurzer Inbegriff der schleswig-holsteinischen Landesprivilegien," *Kieler Blätter* 3 (1816): 159.
7. For an introduction to Paulsen, see H. N. Clausen, *Slesvigeren Christian Ditlef Paulsens livshistorie i omrids* (Copenhagen, 1857); Johann Runge, *Christian Paulsens politische Entwicklung* (Neumünster, 1969); and his own central writings, such as Christian Paulsen, *Ueber Volksthümlichkeit und Staatsrecht des Herzogthums Schleswig*, in *Samlede mindre skrifter* (Copenhagen, 1857), 2: 355-429. See also Knud Fabricius and Johannes Lomholt-Thomsen, eds., *Flensborgeren, Professor Christian Paulsens dagbøger* (Copenhagen, 1946).
8. Christian Paulsen, *Samlede mindre skrifter* (Copenhagen, 1857), 1:694f.

9. See H. N. Clausen, *Slesvigeren Christian Ditlef Paulsens livshistorie i omrids* (Copenhagen, 1857), 6; Christian Paulsen, *Samlede mindre skrifter* (Copenhagen, 1857), 1:695.
10. Johann Runge, *Christian Paulsens politische Entwicklung* (Neumünster, 1969), 33f.
11. H. N. Clausen, *Slesvigeren Christian Ditlef Paulsens livshistorie i omrids* (Copenhagen, 1857), 5.
12. Knud Fabricius and Johannes Lomholt-Thomsen, eds., *Flensborgeren, Professor Christian Paulsens dagbøger* (Copenhagen, 1946), 81f.
13. Christian Paulsen, *Om Retsvidenskaben*, in *Samlede mindre skrifter* (Copenhagen, 1857), 1:6.
14. Christian Paulsen, *Om Retsvidenskaben*, in *Samlede mindre skrifter* (Copenhagen, 1857), 1:6.
15. See still Lorenz Rerup, *Slesvig og Holsten efter 1830* (Copenhagen, 1982), 44.
16. Paulsen stated retrospectively in 1848:

    > When I was called to the University of Kiel as professor in Danish as well as Sleswig-Holstein law, I dared to hope that I could transplant Danish jurisprudence there, so that the duchies could in this respect, too, form a bridge between German and Danish scholarship. This hope seemed to be fulfilled in the first period, from 1826 to 1831.

    Christian Paulsen, *Indledningsforedrag*, in *Samlede mindre skrifter* (Copenhagen, 1857), 1:695.
17. Uwe Jens Lornsen, *Ueber das Verfassungswerk in Schleswigholstein* (Kiel, 1830). One may note that Lornsen and other supporters of the Sleswig-Holstein movement frequently combined the names of the duchies into one word.
18. Christian Paulsen, *Ueber Volksthümlichkeit und Staatsrecht des Herzogthums Schleswig*, in *Samlede mindre skrifter* (Copenhagen, 1857), 2:355-429.
19. Knud Fabricius and Johannes Lomholt-Thomsen, eds., *Flensborgeren, Professor Christian Paulsens dagbøger* (Copenhagen, 1946), 182. Paulsen's desire to respond to Lornsen is visible in the introduction to the study; see Christian Paulsen, *Ueber Volksthümlichkeit und Staatsrecht des Herzogthums Schleswig*, in *Samlede mindre skrifter* (Copenhagen, 1857), 2:358.
20. See Paulsen's own assessment in Knud Fabricius and Johannes Lomholt-Thomsen, eds., *Flensborgeren, Professor Christian Paulsens dagbøger* (Copenhagen, 1946), 184f.
21. Christian Paulsen, *Ueber Volksthümlichkeit und Staatsrecht des Herzogthums Schleswig*, in *Samlede mindre skrifter* (Copenhagen, 1857), 2:418-426. Paulsen allows for the possibility of an additional united assembly of both estates, however.
22. In contrast to later generations of Danish nationalists, however, Paulsen still presumed an originally West Germanic population in premedieval Jutland. See Christian Paulsen, *Ueber Volksthümlichkeit und Staatsrecht des Herzogthums Schleswig*, in *Samlede mindre skrifter* (Copenhagen, 1857), 2:362 and 367.
23. Christian Paulsen, *Ueber Volksthümlichkeit und Staatsrecht des Herzogthums Schleswig*, in *Samlede mindre skrifter* (Copenhagen, 1857), 2:388f.
24. Christian Paulsen, *Ueber Volksthümlichkeit und Staatsrecht des Herzogthums Schleswig*, in *Samlede mindre skrifter* (Copenhagen, 1857), 2:399-401.
25. Christian Paulsen, *Ueber Volksthümlichkeit und Staatsrecht des Herzogthums Schleswig*, in *Samlede mindre skrifter* (Copenhagen, 1857), 2:402-418.
26. Christian Paulsen, *Für Dänemark und für Holstein*, in *Samlede mindre skrifter* (Copenhagen, 1857), 2:445-479.

27. Christian Paulsen, *Det danske sprog i hertugdømmet Slesvig*, in *Samlede mindre skrifter* (Copenhagen, 1857), 1:138-185. For the origins of the piece, see Knud Fabricius and Johannes Lomholt-Thomsen, eds., *Flensborgeren, Professor Christian Paulsens dagbøger* (Copenhagen, 1946), 255f.
28. Knud Fabricius and Johannes Lomholt-Thomsen, eds., *Flensborgeren, Professor Christian Paulsens dagbøger* (Copenhagen, 1946), 272f.
29. Knud Fabricius and Johannes Lomholt-Thomsen, eds., *Flensborgeren, Professor Christian Paulsens dagbøger* (Copenhagen, 1946), 256.
30. Christian Paulsen, "Om Slesvigs indre forbindelse med Danmark," in *Antislesvigholstenske Fragmenter 6,* ed. A. F. Krieger (Copenhagen, 1848), 1-8.
31. The information on Petersen is taken from the materials gathered about him in Landesarchiv Schleswig-Holstein, Abt. 309, Nr. 35311, as well as from *Dansk Biografisk Leksikon*; Svend Thorsen, *Delt efter anskuelser: Den politiske partidannelses forløb i Sønderjylland efter genforeningen i 1920* (Copenhagen, 1970), 100-107; Hans Beyer, "Der Friese Cornelius Petersen und 'Bondens Selvstyre': Ein dänisches Beispiel zur Problematik der Landvolkbewegung zwischen beiden Weltkriegen," *Zeitschrift für Agrargeschichte und Agrarsoziologie* 10 (1962): 212-230; M. Lorenzen, "Cornelius Petersen," *Grænsevagten* 17 (1935): 287-290; Sönnich Volquardsen, "Initiator im Verborgenen: Cornelius Petersen und der Friesisch-schleswigsche Verein," *Nordfriesland* 103/104 (1993): 30-32; Hans Schultz Hansen, *Det sønderjyske landbrugs historie 1830-1993* (Aabenraa, 1994), 222-234; and Petersen's own writings. Most accessible among the latter are: *Das schleswigsche Volk* (Flensburg, 1919); *Det slesvigske spørgsmaal og det slesvigske folk* (Copenhagen, 1919); *Entgegnung auf Herrn Julius Momsens Erwiderung* (Flensburg, 1919); *Uve Jens Lornsen Däne?* (Tønder, 1920); *Die friesische Bewegung* (Tønder, 1920); and *Parlamentarismens Sammenbrud* (Copenhagen, 1922).
32. German-oriented Frisians rejected Petersen's claims to representing Frisian sentiment, because his Danish orientation was shared by few and his paternal grandparents had been Danish-speaking North Sleswigers. See Karl Alnor, *Handbuch zur schleswigschen Frage* 3 (Neumünster, 1938), 1515f.
33. Cornelius Petersen, *Die friesische Bewegung* (Tønder, 1920).
34. Petersen subsequently changed the title of the publication to the more inclusive *Folkets Selvstyre* (The People's Self-Rule).
35. Lars N. Henningsen, ed., *Da Sydslesvig gik af lave: Erindringer fra sindelagsskiftets år* (Flensburg, 2003).
36. See, for example, ibid., 99-101.
37. See, for example, ibid., 56f.
38. See, for example, ibid., 179, 111.
39. For Klüver, see ibid., 251-256.
40. For Thomsen, see ibid., 76-86.
41. For Rahn, see ibid., 232-239.
42. For Gottschalk, see ibid., 214-221.
43. For Ernst, see ibid., 257-266.
44. Most of the information in this section is based on an interview with Siegfried Matlok on 27 May 2004 in Aabenraa. Additional information on Matlok and his views can be found in his entry in the biographical handbook *Kraks Blå Bog 2007/2008* (2007): 758f., and in his essays "Von den Schatten der Vergangenheit verfolgt," *Grenzfriedenshefte* 1978/1 (1978): 18-26, and "Dänemark zwischen Skepsis und Hoffnung," *Grenzfriedenshefte* 1979/2 (1979): 73-83, as well as in his numerous editorials in *Der Nordschleswiger*.

45. Offering another small glimpse at the symbolism of national identification, Matlok's brother was baptized Jürgen, but as a member of the Danish minority preferred the Danish form of his first name.

CHAPTER SIX

Where the Self Meets the Other

A Comparative Approach to Transitional Identities

In this study of identity formation and identity change in the German-Danish borderlands, the potential malleability and ambiguity of Sleswig identity has become apparent. Such distinct findings beg the question whether they represent a Sleswig idiosyncrasy, a regional exception that merely confirms the universal national rule, or point to a larger phenomenon. If history wants to function as more than a fact-finding mission for the subsequent interpretation by social scientists, it is imperative that historical works address and attempt to answer such theoretical questions as well.

Comparisons among Central European borderlands are complicated by the fact that the end of World War II brought the most comprehensive transformation of European settlement patterns in modern history. Following the conferences of Yalta and particularly Potsdam, the western border of Poland was moved far into politically and ethnically German territory.[1] Only a small segment of the indigenous population was allowed to remain in the now Polish territories; the remainder had to resettle in the new, smaller Germany. Replacing the removed German population, approximately five million Poles settled in Silesia, Pomerania, eastern Brandenburg, and southern East Prussia (the northern third of East Prussia with its capital, Königsberg/Kaliningrad, was annexed by the Soviet Union). The largest contingent—about three million—arrived from central Poland; at least one and a half million were refugees from the eastern Polish territories that had been incorporated into the Soviet Union; the remainder came from abroad.[2] By 1950, these five million new residents had joined the one million autochthonous inhabitants who had been permitted to remain in these regions, usually because the Polish government had classified them as ethnic Poles.

Since comparable events transformed the contact zone between German Central Europe and its eastern neighbors from the Alps to the Baltic Sea, the analysis of this cultural environment must focus on the period prior to 1945. For this purpose, we will examine pre-1945 border environments stretching from the

Klaipėda region of contemporary Lithuania to the South Styrian hill country in today's Republic of Slovenia. The selection of cases derives from personal research interests; many more could be added. In his prize-winning dissertation, Christopher Fischer showed that Alsatians frequently turned to regionalism to express their dissatisfaction with German or French governments.[3] Stephen Harp documented the sustained efforts by successive French and German school administrations to adapt young Alsatians to mainstream society.[4] Robert Minnich observed that many villagers of Ugovizza in northeastern Italy tended to employ their Slovenian dialect in everyday speech, identify with predominantly German-speaking Carinthia on an emotional level, and accept their integration into the Italian state.[5] Gary Cohen proposed that the German-speaking upper strata of Prague society only transformed themselves into self-conscious Germans in response to the social and political challenges posed by their Czech-speaking compatriots.[6] Jeremy King found that many citizens of České Budějovice/Budweis long refused to commit themselves to Czech or German nationhood.[7] And based on his examination of German-Czech, German-Slovenian, and German-Italian zones of transition in late Habsburg Austria, Pieter Judson held that frontier identities and linguistic borders were the result of nationalist agitation rather than their source.[8]

This chapter explores how the arrival of nationalism impacted culturally composite regions with ties to more than one emerging nation-state. It examines what motivated peripheral populations to identify with one national community or another, or to refuse to do so. The territories examined faced highly divergent political histories; all the more significant are the many similarities in their national experience.

Polish-speaking Germans, German-born Poles: Shifting Identities in Silesia, Masuria, and Poznania

Historical relations between Germans and Poles are widely seen as tense and confrontational. Considerably less is known about the many peaceful interactions between these two peoples. Along the German-Polish language divide from southern Silesia to eastern Masuria, there traditionally extended a zone of ethnic contact and passage, which could be situated in historically German (e.g., Upper Silesia) or Polish (e.g., the Poznań region) territory. Ethnic interaction could occur in different forms. In many towns and villages, Germans and Poles lived side by side, and numerous families straddled the ethnic divide. In some instances, the fluidity of national identity resulted from a process of homogenization, in which isolated linguistic splinters were assimilated into their larger environment. Yet there also existed a more enduring aspect of ambivalence, which expressed itself in transitional populations with ties to both larger communities.

The Cassubians along the lower Vistula exemplify such a Slavic-speaking population shaped by long-term interaction with both Poles and Germans. The Cassubians are the remnants of the historic West Slavic people called Pomeranians, who were largely Germanized after their duchy was incorporated into the Holy Roman Empire during the Middle Ages. Alternately under German and Polish rule, some Cassubians adopted a Polish or a German identity, but others insisted on remaining uniquely Cassubian. At the beginning of the twentieth century, between 100,000 and 200,000 Cassubians populated the districts surrounding the important Baltic port city of Danzig/Gdańsk, and their descendants continue to live there today, even though the removal of the German population in the aftermath of World War II and the subsequent influx of ethnic Poles has led to their accelerated assimilation into Polish culture.[9]

Even more interesting for the question of fluid identities than the interdependent but distinct ethnicity of the Cassubians are the intermediary identities that used to typify the cultural landscape of Upper Silesia and the southeastern quadrant of East Prussia. In these territories, German and Polish speakers lived alongside each other for centuries under German, or German-dominated transnational, governance. While the two settings resembled each other, there were also visible differences, which modified the otherwise similar response of the local populations to the challenges of modern political nationalism. This allows us to weigh the relative importance of individual social and cultural characteristics in the formation of national identity.

The village of Gwozdzice/Gwosdczütz lies in the Opole/Oppeln district of Upper Silesia. In Silesia, Germanic-speaking populations had been supplanted by Slavic speakers in the early Middle Ages. By the twelfth century, new German settlers began to move into the region. After Silesia had been incorporated into the Holy Roman Empire in the early 1300s, much of Silesia became monolingually German. Upper Silesia, the southeastern part of the province, remained predominantly Polish-speaking, though. After World War I, the Allies allowed the local population to decide its political future. The area was divided after 707,554 Upper Silesians had voted for Germany and 478,820 for Poland. Gwosdczütz remained in Germany until 1945, at which time the Allies awarded most of Silesia to Poland.

In the mid 1920s, a clear majority of 71.5 percent in the community of Rogau/Rogow, to which Gwosdczütz belongs, declared Polish *and* German as their native languages; 15.66 percent indicated Polish and 12.82 German.[10] An examination of the Gwosdczütz war memorials of World War I and II reveals more than 75 percent Slavic surnames, which in the fairly stable European surname environment confirms the substantial Slavic contribution to the local ethnogenesis. Yet in the 1921 plebiscite, 87.2 percent of the population of Rogau voted for Germany. The population of Rogau predominantly bore Slavic last names, was bilingual, and defined itself politically as German, which indicates that a large percentage of the declared Germans in this traditional border region had Slavic family ties.[11]

Upper Silesia demonstrated that a substantial number of Slavophones in this part of East Central Europe identified with the German political sphere, but it also showed that this orientation was not shared by all Slavic speakers under German rule. Although Silesia had not been Polish since the Middle Ages, the Polish national movement made substantial inroads. Forty percent of the overall electorate in the plebiscite zone, and thus a majority of the Slavophones, did opt for Polish political control. In Upper Silesia, sentiments were divided, and the rift cut through villages and families. In East Prussia, by contrast, national identity was more uniform, yet no less interesting to the researcher.

Beginning in the fourteenth and expanding in the fifteenth century, the Teutonic Knights who ruled the later East Prussia allowed settlers from the neighboring Polish territory of Masovia into their southeastern borderlands. These Masovian settlers melted together with the local Balto-Prussian and German inhabitants and became the dominant population in a region subsequently named Masuria after them.[12] The Masurians came to share the political destiny and the Lutheran faith of their German-speaking neighbors, but long retained their Slavic speech; not until the nineteenth century did a growing number of Masurians give up their ancestral dialect in favor of German.

Even those Masurians who retained the dialect were nearly impossible to reach by the Polish national movement, as was consistently demonstrated by their Prussian-conservative voting pattern. Throughout most of the Wilhelmine era, the governmental district of Gumbinnen, which included the bulk of Masuria and Prussian Lithuania, had one of the most conservative electoral records of the country.[13] From 1878 to 1907, Conservative candidates consistently won between 55 and 80 percent of the vote; only in 1912 did National Liberal competition push the Conservative share somewhat below the 50 percent mark.[14] Polish-oriented candidates only reached the 10 percent mark with the approximately 6,000 votes gained by the ambiguously named Masurian People's Party in 1898; their support dwindled to 4,699 votes in 1903 and to 1,451 in 1907 and recovered slightly to 2,698 of approximately 70,000 votes in the last prewar elections of 1912.[15]

In classic Masurian election districts, the results tended to be even more pronounced. With its 97 percent Protestant and over 55 percent Slavophone population, the electoral district of Oletzko-Lyck-Johannisburg constituted one of those archetypical Masurian districts.[16] Apart from 1877, when it went to a Liberal, the seat was always won by a Conservative in the first round, and usually by large majorities.[17] For Polish candidates, the district was hopeless, as can be seen in the election results of 1903 and 1907.

Table 7. Election Results in the Electoral District of Oletzko-Lyck-Johannisburg in 1903 and 1907

Party Affiliation	Percentage of Vote in 1903	1907
Conservative	89.0	94.6
Social Democratic	6.3	2.9
Liberal	3.9	3.8
Polish	0.7	0.2

Source: Kaiserliches Statistisches Amt, ed., *Statistik der Reichstagswahlen von 1907* (Berlin, 1907), 4f.

The Masurians retained their political orientation in the face of the German defeat of 1918. In the district of Sensburg (now Mrągowo), German speakers amounted to less than half of the population at the beginning of the twentieth century. In the census of 1900, 20,447 inhabitants of the district declared German their mother tongue, whereas 14,704 listed Masurian, 9,784 Polish, and 3,010 a combination of German and one of the two Slavic idioms.[18] Of an overall population of 48,403, 42 percent listed German alone as their native tongue. As a consequence, the Polish government claimed Sensburg and other Masurian districts for its reemerged state at the Versailles peace conference. When the Allies decided to arrange an internationally monitored plebiscite, they were surprised to find that in a predominantly Slavic-speaking district such as Sensburg, a mere 25 votes were cast for Poland as opposed to 34,334 in favor of continuous inclusion in Germany.[19]

The results in Sensburg were echoed in the overall outcome of the 1920 plebiscite, in which 363,209 votes were cast for German East Prussia versus 7,980 for Poland. If one examines these numbers more closely, one finds that most of the Polish vote did not originate in Masuria but in the Catholic region of Warmia (Ermland), whose southern tip contained a consciously Polish segment of the population. Of the not quite 8,000 votes in favor of Poland, 6,002, that is, three quarters, accrued in the Warmian plebiscite districts, where they amounted to 6.7 percent of the overall tally of 89,482. In Protestant Masuria, by contrast, the 1984 Polish votes represented a mere 0.7 percent of the total. Their largely Slavophone origins notwithstanding, the Masurians clearly identified with the German political sphere.

During the same period, cultural and political sentiments developed quite differently in another sector of the German-Polish borderlands. In the early 1700s, the city of Poznań in western Poland, which had suffered gravely from the ravages of the Great Northern War and the epidemics that ensued, invited

German Catholic farmers to colonize its rural outskirts. Since many of the early settlers, of whom the Poznanians expected a rejuvenation and modernization of their ailing farm economy, hailed from communities in the vicinity of Bamberg in Franconia, the Polish inhabitants began to address these German Catholic farmers generically as "Bambergers." The arrivals from the west thrived in their new environment and became a familiar facet of Poznanian life.

As a consequence of Poland's dismemberment in the late 1700s, the Poznań area was incorporated into the kingdom of Prussia. At that time, the immigration of the Bambergers was only a few generations removed, and their communities had remained German in customs and speech. For another half century, this basic cultural environment was preserved, but then a surprising development took shape. Under the influence of their Polish priests and neighbors, the Catholic Bambergers were drawn into the Polish national sphere. The equation of Polish and Catholic, which formed a central aspect of contemporary Polish national ideology, put into question the Germanness of the Bambergers, who indeed encountered Germans primarily as Protestants in this part of Europe. The Bambergers began to support Polish candidates in the highly ethnicized elections of Poznania and increasingly defined themselves as Poles. As can be seen from the language statistics in two Poznanian communities, the cultural parameters of the Bamberger settlements were fundamentally transformed.[20]

Table 8. Linguistic Affiliation in Two Poznanian Communities in 1861 and 1880

	1861		1880	
	German	Polish	German	Polish
Dębiec/Demsen	219	22	56	273
Luboń/Luban	175	25	9	246

Source: Max Bär, *Die "Bamberger" bei Posen* (Posen, 1882), 74.

At a time when their region formed a part of Prussia, many of the Catholic German settlers in the vicinity of Poznań became Poles. They were assimilated by their Polish coreligionists although they were governed by Germans. As many contemporary sources from the early settlement period document, the Bambergers had openly identified themselves as Germans when the Masurian population still centered largely on itself. One hundred years later the sociopsychological environments had changed considerably.[21] In Central Europe's borderlands, it was not uncommon to encounter people whose group identification did not correlate to that of their parents or even to their own linguistic background.

The People Between: Prussian Lithuania and an Old Wife's Tale

Lena Grigoleit was born in 1910 in the village of Bittehnen not far from the regional center of Tilsit in northern East Prussia.[22] Like most inhabitants of her area, she was Protestant and had ties to both German and Lithuanian culture. At the beginning of the twentieth century, just over half the community's inhabitants declared Lithuanian their mother tongue, and the percentages had been higher in previous decades.[23] The Grigoleits were bilingual, with the grandparents more attached to their Lithuanian heritage and the parents increasingly integrated into the wider German societal sphere.

Located on the north shore of the river Nyeman/Memel/Nemunas, East Prussia's Bittehnen became Lithuania's Bitėnai in 1923. A number of Catholic Lithuanians from Lithuania proper moved into the area, but in general, life continued as before, since the international Memel Convention of 1924 had guaranteed the indigenous population basic cultural rights.[24] Lena Grigoleit's marriage to one of the Catholic newcomers tied her more closely to Lithuanian society than was common among her peers. This caused hardships during World War II, when the area was reattached to Germany, but proved helpful thereafter, when most of the local families fled or were deported from Bittehnen. Beginning in the mid 1950s, another wave of emigration to Germany took further autochthons, including all of Lena's remaining fellow Bittehners and a number of her family members, to a Germany that had become far removed from the river Memel and its historic German-Lithuanian coexistence.[25] Lena Grigoleit, now Kondratavičiene, remained the only local Little Lithuanian in Bitėnai. She developed into a window to the past for the new settlers and a vestige of home to the old Bittehners, who were able to visit the area more freely after the collapse of Communism. She died in the provincial capital of Klaipėda in 1995.

Lena Grigoleit's biography offers us a glimpse into the historic border environment from the perspective of the individuals who lived in it. Her life story was unique, but her cultural background was not. At about the same time as Masovian Poles migrated to the southeastern sector of the later East Prussia, Lithuanian settlement expanded in the underdeveloped woodlands of the northeast.[26] The long historical association and intermarriage with Germans and the religious divide created by Reformation and Counterreformation separated the new settlers from their colinguals in the Grand Duchy, but they long preserved their unique Prusso-Lithuanian identity. During the time of increased Russian cultural pressure in the Grand Duchy, Prussian Lithuania even became a cultural beacon for the budding Lithuanian national movement on the other side of the border. Throughout the 1800s, however, the impact of modernization, mass education, and occupational mobility drew the Prussian Lithuanians ever closer into the German cultural sphere, and by 1900, no more than 100,000 East Prussians declared their mother tongue to be Lithuanian.[27]

In the districts to the north of the river Nyeman, the Lithuanian language had stood its ground the best. The 25,000 Lithuanian speakers in the district of Memel amounted to 43 percent of the local population in 1900; the 24,000 Lithuanian speakers of the district of Heydekrug even constituted a majority of 57 percent.[28] Altogether, the 140,000 East Prussians who lived to the north of the river were divided about equally between German and Lithuanian speakers on the eve of World War I.[29] This strong Lithuanian presence induced the Allies to separate the area from Germany after the war and to put up only token resistance when Lithuania annexed it in 1923.[30] Since the region had not formed an administrative unit but contained the former East Prussian district of Memel as well as parts of the districts of Heydekrug, Niederung, Tilsit, and Ragnit, there was no established name for it. In the interwar period, it came to be known as Memel territory in English (Memelland in German), whereas the Lithuanians tended to call it the Klaipėda region (Klaipėdos kraštas) or Little Lithuania (Mažoji Lietuva) as opposed to the Greater Lithuania represented by the former Grand Duchy.[31]

To the outside observer, the national dilemma in the Memel territory might arise from the presence of two comparably sized linguistic groups and the ensuing difficulty in assigning the region to either of the larger national communities. Upon closer inspection, however, the issue becomes more complex. On the one hand, the rural inhabitants of the area undoubtedly were of predominantly Lithuanian descent. This basic fact can be seen in the larger share of Lithuanian surnames and in the historical dominance of Lithuanian as the language of the rural population. In the eyes of Greater Lithuanian nationalists, this proved the Lithuanian character of the region.

Next to such arguments that resolve the national impasse of the Memel territory in favor of the Lithuanian side, however, there were potentially more significant ones that pointed in the opposite direction. Among the local population, there never arose much enthusiasm for the Lithuanian national movement, and Lithuanian parties gained only limited support in the parliamentary elections. In 1898, the Lithuanians won their first seat in a run-off election due to an alliance with the Liberals; on their own, they never managed to win a seat even in the most Lithuanian-speaking electoral districts.[32] The difference between the German-Lithuanian electoral landscape in northern East Prussia and its German-Polish equivalent in Poznania was palpable.

Based on the census of 1900, the electoral district Posen Two, consisting in essence of the Poznanian political districts of Obornik, Samter, Birnbaum, and Schwerin, contained 69,562 native speakers of German and 90,143 native speakers of Polish.[33] Thus, Polish speakers accounted for approximately 56.5 percent of the population versus 43.5 percent German speakers. This relative distribution of German and minority population was roughly comparable to the conditions found in the electoral district of Memel-Heydekrug, which was split evenly between native speakers of German and Lithuanian. Of the district's 102,622 inhabitants, 50,390 declared German as their mother tongue, 50,139 Lithuanian, and 1760 both.[34] In spite of these cultural similarities, the parliamentary elections of 1903 and 1907 produced noticeably different outcomes.

Table 9. Support for Minority Candidates in Two Electoral Districts in the Reichstag Elections of 1903 and 1907 (First Round)

		Minority Candidate in	
Electoral District	Non-German speakers	1903	1907
Obornik-Samter-Birnbaum-Schwerin	56.5% Polish-speaking	53.8%	52.3%
Memel-Heydekrug	50% Lithuanian-speaking	25.1%	23.2%

Source: *Vierteljahreshefte zur Statistik des Deutschen Reichs*, various issues; *Preußische Statistik*, various issues.

Although the Lithuanian-speaking population of Memel-Heydekrug was almost as strong as the Polish-speaking population of Obornik-Samter-Birnbaum-Schwerin, Lithuanian candidates obtained only half the electoral share of their Polish counterparts. These divergent voting patterns point to the different self-images of Prussia's non-German-speaking minorities.[35] Whereas consciously Polish populations rallied around ethnic candidates, Lithuanian-speaking East Prussians did so to a much smaller extent, and Masurians hardly at all.

In order to ascertain the full significance of such electoral differences, it seems advisable to rule out the influence of other variables. The most logical outside factor would be government interference. Even though one would expect such influence to have been felt universally and not just among the Prusso-Lithuanians, it is worthwhile to follow the continuation of electoral trends in the interwar era, when the tables had been turned and the central government was Lithuanian instead of German.

The census of 1925 confirms that Lithuanian linguistic background, not to mention Lithuanian ancestry, did not translate directly into a Lithuanian national identity. Whereas the German census of 1910 had shown 71,000 German speakers and 67,000 Lithuanian speakers in the Memel region, the first census in the Lithuanian period, which contained a question for nationality, found 59,337 Germans, 37,625 Lithuanians, and 38,404 "Memelites."[36] If one considers that a number of Germans had left the area after its separation from Germany and that Lithuanians from the Grand Duchy had begun to move there, it becomes clear that most local German speakers subscribed to German nationality, whereas many Lithuanian speakers did not identify with the Lithuanian nation and chose the local Memel identity instead.

A look at the interwar voting pattern in the Memel territory further accentuates this national environment. In the six elections to the Memel diet between 1925 and 1938, German-oriented parties consistently gained more than 80 percent of the votes; in 1925, they even exceeded the 90 percent mark.[37]

Table 10. Elections to the Interwar Memel Diet

Year	Total Vote	German Parties Votes	Lithuanian Parties Votes	German Parties Percentage	Lithuanian Parties Percentage
1925	62,517	58,756	3761	94.0	6.0
1927	54,756	45,968	8788	84.0	16.0
1930	49,630	40,813	8817	82.0	18.0
1932	65,767	53,128	12,639	80.8	19.2
1935	67,657	54,917	12,740	81.2	18.8
1938	72,247	62,986	9261	87.2	12.8

Source: Alfred Bohmann, *Menschen und Grenzen* (Cologne, 1970), 3:202.[38]

Compared to the prewar, German period, Lithuanian parties lost further ground, particularly if one focuses on the indigenous population. Under German rule, a considerable share of Lithuanian speakers had supported Lithuanian candidates as an expression of regional cultural identity, without thereby expressing any desire for union with Lithuania. In the interwar era, such apolitical cultural identification with Prusso-Lithuanian traditions no longer seemed possible. Forced to choose between Germany and Lithuania, most Klaipėda Lithuanians opted for the former.

World War II and its aftermath brought the end of German-Lithuanian symbiosis along the river Nyeman. From 1939 to 1945, the territory was ruled by Germany once more. At the end of the war, most locals found themselves transplanted westward along with the other inhabitants of Prussia's historic eastern provinces. Today, the estimated five to ten thousand autochthons of the Klaipėda district form a much smaller share of the population than not only the Lithuanians proper, but also than the Russians.[39] Most of the original inhabitants of this region, Germans and Lithuanians alike, live in the smaller postwar Germany, and to their offspring, Lithuania is no less exotic a country than the various other former Soviet republics. In the pulsating western cities of Bremen and Hamburg, the story of Lena Grigoleit's life at the intersection of German and Lithuanian identity is merely an echo of a distant past.

Their Fathers' God: Religion and National Identity in Upper Silesia

The link between national and religious identity has surfaced repeatedly in this examination of historical European borderlands.[40] Their Protestant heritage limited the receptiveness of Masurians to Polish nationalism, whereas German Catholics in central Poznania proved susceptible to gradual Polonization. It is important to note that this religious identity did not necessarily correlate with active participation in religious life, but can be seen as a cultural phenomenon even more than a theological one. Even in an era of increasing secularization, traditional denominational affiliations continued to influence ethnic and national identity.[41]

In Masuria and Prussian Lithuania, compact regional populations shared history and religion with their German fellow citizens, whereas their linguistic background tied them to the dominant nationalities of neighboring countries. These populations were large enough to be self-contained. Their distinction from potential co-ethnics was not denominational alone. The political response to this multilayered cultural environment is instructive, but the presence of additional variables invites questions as to the true significance of the religious factor. Thus, it is vital to filter out the religious component in a more narrowly circumscribed regional environment, in which religion constitutes the only independent variable. The district of Kreuzburg/Kluczbork provides the ideal setting for such an investigation.

Kreuzburg used to form the northernmost district of German Upper Silesia; today, Kluczbork lies at the northern tip of the Polish voivodeship of Opole. Historical Kreuzburg bordered on Polish territory to the north, on Lower Silesia to the west, and on the Upper Silesian districts of Oppeln and Rosenberg (now Opole and Olesno) to the south and east. Its somewhat peripheral location helps explain its idiosyncrasy within the historical Upper Silesian cultural environment: unlike most of the province, Kreuzburg was predominantly Protestant. In 1900, 31,627 of Kreuzburg's 46,827 inhabitants were Protestant; the resulting percentage of 67.5 percent Protestants was unusual in a province that was more than 90 percent Catholic.[42]

In itself, this religious distinction would not add much to the analysis, which has already shown the perceptual differences between, for example, the Protestant Masurians and the Catholic Poles. What made Kreuzburg unique, however, was the fact that its distinctiveness was almost exclusively denominational. Whereas the historical experience of Protestant Little Lithuanians and Masurians had differed from that of their Catholic colinguals for centuries, the inhabitants of Kreuzburg had partaken in the broader trends of Upper Silesian history. As a consequence, they also shared in a central Upper Silesian characteristic: the interpenetration of German and Polish ethnicity. In turn, the combination of religious idiosyncrasy and cultural normality resulted in another regional specificity: a sizable Polish Protestant population.[43]

In 1900, the district of Kreuzburg was 40 percent German- and 60 percent Polish-speaking.[44] It contained 13,000 German Protestants next to not quite 5,000 German Catholics as well as 18,000 Polish Protestants next to not quite 10,000 Polish Catholics. The 18,000 Polish Protestants constituted almost 40 percent of the district's overall population and formed its single-strongest cultural element. As highlighted above, their overall number was too small and their historical development too interwoven with the rest of Upper Silesia to have given the Polish Protestants of Kreuzburg a distinctiveness comparable to the separate ethnicity of the Masurians. Nonetheless, they demarcated themselves noticeably from other Polish-speaking Silesians.

Firstly, the Polish Protestants of Kreuzburg showed an uncommon tendency towards Germanization. A considerable share of the 13,000 German Protestants of 1900 were the result of fairly recent assimilation. The district's proportion of declared German speakers had grown from 31 to 40 percent during the last decade of the nineteenth century. This development distinguished itself markedly from the linguistic trend in the adjacent, Catholic districts. In Rosenberg, the German share of the population had only grown from 13.5 to 15.3 percent over the same time period, and in the district of Oppeln, it had actually decreased from 18.7 to 18.3 percent.

The Germanization of Kreuzburg's Polish-speaking Protestants continued in the new century and eventually tipped the balance between German and Polish Protestants.

Table 11. Protestants in the District of Kreuzburg by Mother Tongue

	Polish	German
1900	18258	13360
1905	18077	14869
1910	14936	17073

Source: R. Baumgarten, "Evangelische Polen in Posen und Schlesien," *Die Grenzboten* 73:30 (1914): 192.

By the time of World War I, German speakers had surpassed Polish speakers among the district's Protestants, and this shift was not caused by migration but by an ongoing assimilation process. This outright Germanization of many Protestant Polish speakers in Kreuzburg only completed their identification with the Prussian state, however. In addition to—and interconnected with—their religious idiosyncrasy, the inhabitants of Kreuzburg had long demarcated themselves from the rest of Upper Silesia in another important respect: they had a very distinct electoral record.

The largely Catholic province of Upper Silesia constituted a bastion of Germany's Center Party, which claimed the allegiance of much of the country's actively Catholic population. The nationality conflict challenged the sectoral dominance of this party in the Prussian east, where a large proportion of Catholics was Polish-speaking. The Polish electoral movement reached Upper Silesia comparatively late, and the fluid boundaries between Germans and Poles introduced some of the national conflict into the Center Party, whereas it tended to be fought between opposing parties in the more polarized Poznanian environment. Nonetheless, Polish candidates won four and five of Upper Silesia's twelve seats in the two final prewar elections to the German Reichstag. All but one of the remaining seats went to the Center Party; the exception was Kreuzburg-Rosenberg, also referred to as Oppeln One.

Although Rosenberg was heavily Polish Catholic, the electoral district of Kreuzburg-Rosenberg contained a strong Protestant minority of almost 40 percent. About half of the electorate was Polish Catholic, somewhat less than a quarter Polish Protestant; the remaining quarter was German-speaking, predominantly but not exclusively Protestant.[45] Alone among the Upper Silesian districts, Kreuzburg-Rosenberg consistently sent a Conservative to the parliament in Berlin. Only in 1881, the Center Party managed to secure the seat, which was held by the Free Conservatives before and by the Conservatives in all the elections thereafter.[46] To be sure, the unique dominance of the Conservatives, who almost always won an outright majority in the first round of voting and did not depend on a run-off election, was reinforced by an agreement with the Center Party. In exchange for a Conservative withdrawal from unattainable Catholic districts in the area, the Center commonly did not file candidates in the difficult terrain of Kreuzburg.[47] The party's willingness to give up Kreuzburg-Rosenberg merely reflected its appreciation of the district's distinctiveness, however. The failure of Polish candidates to ever win a majority of the more than 70 percent Polish-speaking electorate demonstrates that the local Polish Protestants almost universally sided with the Conservatives, who were the Prussian governmental party *par none*.

In the plebiscite of 1921, Kreuzburg displayed its special character one more time. Although still 47 percent Polish-speaking in the last prewar census of 1910, the district voted 96 percent in favor of remaining part of Germany.[48] This virtual unanimity confirmed that most Polish votes in the combined electoral district of Kreuzburg-Rosenberg had not originated in Kreuzburg but in predominantly Polish-Catholic Rosenberg, where over 30 percent voted for Poland in 1921. Moreover, it put Kreuzburg into a category more reminiscent of Masuria than of the rest of bicultural Upper Silesia. Although the fact that one third of Upper Silesia's Polish speakers preferred Germany over Poland highlights the subjective components of national identity in this border region, a majority did support Polish sovereignty. Among the local Protestants, however, hardly anyone did.

Against the forces of history *and* religion, the Polish national movement could not succeed.

Where the Self Meets the Other: A Southern Styrian Town in the Late Habsburg Period

The transitional identities examined hitherto in this chapter were situated in the Prusso-Polish and Prusso-Lithuanian borderlands. The competition between the German and other Central European national movements was not restricted to the Prussian sphere of influence, however. In fact, the history of the late Habsburg empire has become the classic image of national strife, and a number of important theorists of nationalism and national identity have taken the Habsburg experience as a starting point for their analysis and model-building.[49]

Next to the lands of the Bohemian crown with their protracted competition between Germans and Czechs, the Alpine provinces of Styria, Carinthia, and Carniola formed the second focal point of German-Slavic conflict in the Habsburg Monarchy. The relationship between Germans and Slovenes was not fully as crucial to the viability of the Habsburg state as were German-Czech relations in the wealthy and populous province of Bohemia.[50] Therefore, it has not attracted the same amount of international scholarly attention. For the populations involved, however, this conflict was no less significant, and it offers intriguing insights into the nature of national identity among culturally or politically ambivalent border populations.

The cultural environment in the southeastern Alps was characterized by a gradual movement toward homogenization. Thus, the share of Slovenian speakers fell from 32.74 percent in 1880 to 29.38 percent in 1910 in predominantly German-speaking Styria and, even more noticeably, from 29.72 to 21.24 percent in neighboring Carinthia. In Carniola, by contrast, the share of Slovenian speakers rose from 93.67 to 94.36 percent, with a corresponding reduction of the German presence from 6.15 to 5.36 percent. In the capital city of Ljubljana, the German share dropped from approximately 23 percent in 1880 to less than 15 percent in 1910.[51]

Below the level of this larger trend, however, there were local idiosyncrasies that underscore the potential instability of national sentiment in border regions. What makes this instability particularly interesting is the nature of the measurement in which it expressed itself. The Austrian censuses of the late Habsburg period did not ask people to identify with a cultural or political entity. Instead, they contained a question about an individual's *Umgangssprache*, a term best translated as that person's language of (predominant) daily use, or primary language. Although this question appears to be directed at an objectively defined characteristic, it soon took on distinctly political overtones. Activists on all sides attempted to turn the answer to the linguistic question into a national plebiscite. The consequences of this politicization can be seen in Styrian census results of the late Habsburg period.

The territory of the modern province of Styria had a long history of German-Slavic coexistence. The Alpine Slavs, who had moved into the area soon after the withdrawal of the Romans, had been subjugated by the Bavarians in the early Middle Ages. The territory was integrated into the Frankish kingdom and the Holy Roman Empire that succeeded it. The Babenberg dukes of Austria and their Habsburg successors tied the region ever closer to the Austrian sphere. In the census of 1880, 794,841 Styrians listed their primary language as German and 388,419 as Slovenian, which made the province two-thirds German- and one-third Slovenian-speaking. This linguistic ratio resulted from an overall compilation and did not reflect local conditions, which tended to be more homogenous, with an almost exclusively German-speaking north and a predominantly Slovenian-speaking south.

Many towns and cities in southern Styria had German majorities, however. Much of the region's ethnic strife revolved around these German-speaking urban centers surrounded by rural Slovenes. The specific demographics of southern Styria introduced an element of volatility, which constituted the most noteworthy aspect of the local nationality conflict. In the language statistics of the small town of Šoštanj/Schönstein, this volatility demarcates itself particularly well. In the last four censuses held under Habsburg auspices, the local distribution of German and Slovenian speakers was as follows:

Table 12. Primary Language in Šoštanj/Schönstein 1880-1910

	Total	German	Slovenian
1880	734	118	615
1890	835	410	421
1900	1096	179	908
1910	1257	874	368

Even if one considers the substantial in-migration expressed in the overall population growth, the inconsistency of the results is striking. The citizens of Šoštanj/Schönstein clearly associated primary language with national identification. Their language use could not have vacillated as forcefully as suggested by the census data. They were sufficiently well-versed in both German and Slovenian to see either one as a potential primary language and turned their census replies into conscious political statements. Moreover, many local citizens felt close enough to both national communities to alternate between them. Thus, at a time of protracted conflict between Germans and Slovenes in Austria's Alpine provinces, the inhabitants of Šoštanj/Schönstein would at times be found on the German side, at times on the Slovenian. They would be the self, but they would also be the Other.

Conclusion

This chapter has examined transitional identities in historical Central European borderlands on both an individual and a collective level. Regions as far apart both geographically and politically as northern East Prussia and southern Styria displayed intriguing sociocultural similarities, which illuminate the nature of national identity as it expressed itself at its margins.

In the political and scholarly debate, the cultural idiosyncrasies of the border regions have often been seen in a context of public policy. During the final decades of imperial Germany, to take one important historical setting, one will indeed notice governmental attempts to strengthen the position of German culture and language in the eastern borderlands. The measurable impact of these policies remained small, however, especially vis-à-vis the primarily affected Polish Catholics; when Poznania reverted to Poland after World War I, the region had changed little in overall ethnic composition since Poland's partition in the late 1700s.[52] Instead, the divergent reactions of different minority populations to their political environment highlight the primary importance of broader sociocultural factors. Catholic Polish speakers in a historically Polish territory such as Poznania fully retained a Polish identity under Prussian rule. The Catholic Polish speakers of historically German Upper Silesia were divided by the impact of modern nationalism; one segment of the population adopted a Polish national identity, another segment rejected it. And among the Polish-speaking Protestants in historically German Masuria, the Polish national movement made few inroads.

In some cases, the national development countercaricatured the political setting. The Prussian government had no interest in the assimilation of its German speakers into a different linguistic community, but the Bambergers of central Poznania adopted a Polish identity nonetheless. Similarly, the interwar Lithuanian authorities proved unable to turn the Lithuanian speakers of the Memel territory into conscious members of the Lithuanian nation. Instead, the personal confrontation with Greater Lithuanian authorities and the nationalization policies they pursued seems to have completed the emotional integration of most Memel Lithuanians into the German political sphere.

The border regions were no peaceful multicultural paradise. They were frequently marked by tension and antagonism, but at the same time they constituted a natural zone of transition from one cultural realm to another. There were families with both German and Slavic or Baltic branches; sometimes even siblings chose different sides. Such accumulated knowledge and familiarity across ethnic lines helped to create a border environment in which numerous ties bridged the divide.

On a theoretical plane, the historical border regions between the German-speaking world and its eastern neighbors illuminate the complexity of national identity on the crossroads of language, religion, and history. On a more practical plane, they also alert us to the value of transitional regions as links between larger national communities. The borderlands traditionally contained a zone of contact and passage. Numerous nerve lines tied together different cultural entities, and group identification visibly became a matter of personal choice. Environments such as these created zones of fluid identity. The border populations *understood* their neighbors; they learned from them, transmitted this knowledge on to other members of their respective cultural communities, and thus contributed to a constant flow of information between larger cultural spheres.

There are echoes of such transitional identities in contemporary Upper Silesia, whose regional culture has survived the vicissitudes of twentieth-century European politics better than many comparable border cultures, and arguably along the Austro-Slovenian frontier.[53] On an even smaller scale, isolated remnants of a Masurian and Little Lithuanian culture sphere have weathered the storm, although their political surroundings have been transformed to the point of irrecognizability.[54] But for the most part, the intriguing national ambivalence of these regions is a thing of the past. The removal of the German population from large tracts of East Central Europe has also discontinued the ethnic symbiosis.[55] It is all the more interesting to observe the survival of related phenomena in the Dano-German borderlands.

Notes

1. Although the German-Polish border was discussed extensively in February 1945 at Yalta, the actual political decisions were made during the Potsdam Conference in the summer of the same year.
2. Leszek Kosiński, "Przeobrażenia demograficzne na Ziemiach Zachodnich," in *Przemiany społeczne na Ziemiach Zachodnich*, ed. Paweł Rybicki and Władysław Markiewicz (Poznań, 1967), 78-131; W. W. Kulski, *Germany and Poland* (Syracuse, 1976), 80-81.
3. Christopher Fischer, "Alsace to the Alsatians? Visions and Divisions of Alsatian Regionalism, 1890-1930" (Ph.D. diss., University of North Carolina, 2003).
4. Stephen Harp, *Learning to Be Loyal: Primary Schooling as Nation Building in Alsace and Lorraine, 1850-1940* (DeKalb, Ill., 1998). Among additional recent analyses of Alsace, one could list Samuel Huston Goodfellow, *Between the Swastika and the Cross of Lorraine* (DeKalb, Ill., 1999), David Allen Harvey, *Constructing Class and Nationality in Alsace, 1830-1945* (DeKalb, Ill., 2001), and Günter Riederer, *Feiern im Reichsland: Politische Symbolik, öffentliche Festkultur und die Erfindung kollektiver Zugehörigkeiten in Elsass-Lothringen (1871-1918)* (Trier, 2004).

5. Robert Gary Minnich, *Homesteaders and Citizens: Collective Identity Formation on the Austro-Italian-Slovene Frontier* (Bergen, 1998), and idem, "Die Leute von Ugovizza: Kollektive Identitäten im alpinen Raum," *Historische Anthropologie* 10:1 (2002): 51-75. The village is called Uggowitz in German and Ukve in Slovenian.
6. Gary B. Cohen, *The Politics of Ethnic Survival: Germans in Prague, 1861-1914*, 2d ed. (West Lafayette, Ind., 2006).
7. Jeremy King, *Budweisers into Czechs and Germans: A Local History of Bohemian Politics, 1848-1948* (Princeton, 2002).
8. Pieter M. Judson, *Guardians of the Nation: Activists on the Language Frontiers of Imperial Austria* (Cambridge, Mass., 2006). For a collection of essays on various Central European minorities, see Hans Henning Hahn and Peter Kunze, eds., *Nationale Minderheiten und staatliche Minderheitenpolitik in Deutschland im 19. Jahrhundert* (Berlin, 1999).
9. For an introduction to the Cassubians, see Friedrich Lorentz, Adam Fischer, and Tadeusz Lehr-Spławiński, *The Cassubian Civilization* (London, 1935); Brunon Synak, *Kaszubska tożsamość* (Gdańsk, 1998); Marek Latoszek, ed., *Kaszubi: Monografia socjologiczna* (Rzeszów, 1990); and Heinz Lingenberg, "Die Kaschuben," *Westpreußenjahrbuch* 35 (1985): 123-150.
10. In absolute numbers: 167 German; 204 Polish; 931 German and Polish. In earlier decades, there had been more Polish monolingualism.
11. Although some observers have tried to ascribe the results of the plebiscites to larger international issues such as Poland's military conflict with the Soviet Union, the diversity of the results, which varied from 0.3 percent Polish votes in Leobschütz/Głubczyce to 74 percent in Pless/Pszczyna, and the similarities with the voting patterns in the parliamentary elections advise against primarily external explanations. A good discussion of the issues involved in Upper Silesia can be found in T. Hunt Tooley, *National Identity and Weimar Germany: Upper Silesia and the Eastern Border, 1918-1922* (Lincoln, Nebr., 1997).
12. The original Prussians were a Baltic people related to Lithuanians and Latvians. After their subjugation by the Teutonic Order, they melted together with the new German settlers, creating the German-speaking (East) Prussians; the Prussian language disappeared in the 1600s. The German distinction between the Baltic *Prussen* and the later *Preußen* has no generally understood English equivalent. Earlier attempts by Polish scholars such as Wojciech Kętrzyński to declare the Poles the original inhabitants of Masuria could not be maintained and have largely been abandoned. See Wojciech Kętrzyński, *O Mazurach* (Posen, 1872).
13. The German terms *Kreis*, *Wahlkreis*, and *Regierungsbezirk* are translated as district, electoral district, and governmental district, respectively. The governmental district was the largest of these units; all of East Prussia was divided into two, subsequently three, governmental districts. At the same time, the province contained 17 electoral districts and 37 districts.
14. For the election results, see Gerhard A. Ritter, *Wahlgeschichtliches Arbeitsbuch: Materialien zur Statistik des Kaiserreiches 1871-1918* (Munich, 1980), 67. In the interest of comparison, the inclusion of parts of the governmental district of Gumbinnen into the newly created governmental district of Allenstein by the time of the elections of 1912 has been ignored. The National Liberals were, of course, no less German-oriented than the Conservatives.
15. Hans-Ulrich Wehler, "Zur neueren Geschichte der Masuren," *Zeitschrift für Ostforschung* 11 (1962): 159f. Since candidates were usually not filed in the most marginal districts, not all Polish-leaning voters had the opportunity to support an ethnic can-

didate. At the same time, it should be noted that the Masurian districts also included a small Polish Catholic element. These voters will have largely supported the Polish candidates and would have to be deducted from the total to establish the strictly Masurian contribution. In 1900, the district of Ortelsburg alone contained approximately 4,500 Catholics with Polish or Masurian mother tongue. See Königliches statistisches Bureau, ed., *Preußische Statistik* 177:3 (Berlin, 1902), 358f. For the difficulties faced by the Polish national movement in Masuria, see also Grzegorcz Jasiński, *Mazurzy w drugiej połowie XIX wieku* (Olsztyn, 1994), and Heinrich Mrowka, "Die Anfänge einer polnischen nationalen Bewegung in Masuren," in *Deutsche, Slawen und Balten*, ed. Hans Hecker and Silke Spiller (Lüneburg, 1989), 128-140.

16. The data on religion and language are based on the census of 1900. The electoral district was also known as Gumbinnen Six.
17. Wilhelmine Germany was divided into 397 electoral districts. Candidates had to gain an absolute majority of the ballots cast. If none of the candidates achieved this majority in the first (or main) round of the elections, the two leading candidates competed in a run-off election.
18. Königliches statistisches Bureau, ed., *Preußische Statistik* 177:3 (Berlin, 1902), 177. The distinction made between Masurian and Polish not only by the German authorities, but also by many Masurians, points to their reluctance to identify with matters Polish. Although Masurian contained many German words and had not undergone the homogenization process of standard Polish, it clearly had its roots in a Polish dialectal tradition, and other Masurians did acknowledge the Polish character of their dialect.
19. All the numbers about the East Prussian plebiscite are taken from Sarah Wambaugh, *Plebiscites since the World War* (Washington, D.C., 1933), 1:134. The Allies were less surprised about the basic outcome of the plebiscite than about the crass disparity in the numbers.
20. Max Bär refers to division by nationality, but since the Prussian statistics examined language identification, the table has been titled accordingly.
21. For the cultural orientation of the Bambergers in the early 1800s, see Max Bär, *Die "Bamberger" bei Posen* (Posen, 1882), 35f.
22. Tilsit is now the city of Sovetsk in Russia's Kaliningrad oblast. Most of the information on Lena Grigoleit is taken from Ulla Lachauer, *Paradiesstraße: Lebenserinnerungen der ostpreußischen Bäuerin Lena Grigoleit* (Reinbek, 1996), which combines aspects of an oral history project with a personal memoir.
23. According to Vincas Vileišis, *Tautiniai santykiai Maž. Lietuvoje* (Kaunas, 1935), 237, the community of Bitėnai was home to 427 Lithuanian speakers and 337 German speakers in 1905.
24. For the Memel Convention and Statute, whose regulations formed a frequent topic of debate before the League of Nations, see Thorsten Kalijarvi, *The Memel Statute* (London, 1937).
25. Between 1956 and 1969, another 8,000 Memelites arrived in Germany. See Alfred Bohmann, *Menschen und Grenzen* (Cologne, 1970), 3:215.
26. The exact nature of Lithuanian settlement in northeastern East Prussia used to be an issue hotly debated between German and Lithuanian historians. At the heart of the issue lay questions about the ethnic affiliation of the original Nadrovian, Scalovian, and Sudovian inhabitants of the region (i.e., if they were Prussians or Lithuanians) and about the role of these earlier cultural groups in the later expansion of Lithuanian settlement. At the least, there seems to be increasing agreement about a sizable population movement from Lithuania proper, if not about the question as to what kind of and how many inhabitants they encountered upon their arrival. For some of the major arguments,

see Hans Mortensen and Gertrud Mortensen, *Die Besiedlung des nordöstlichen Ostpreußens bis zum Beginn des 17. Jahrhunderts*, 2 vols. (Leipzig, 1937-38), and Vincas Vileišis, *Tautiniai santykiai Maž. Lietuvoje* (Kaunas, 1935).

27. Königliches Statistisches Bureau, *Preußische Statistik* 177:3 (1902), VIII.
28. Königliches Statistisches Bureau, *Preußische Statistik* 177:3 (1902), VIII. The districts were named for the cities of Memel (now Klaipėda) and Heydekrug (now Šilutė).
29. See the numbers in Ernst-Albrecht Pflieg, *Das Memelland 1920-1939* (Würzburg, 1962), 16 and 244.
30. Strictly speaking, the territory ceded was not demarcated only by the river Memel. Article 28 of the Treaty of Versailles described the relevant stretch of the border as follows: "thence the old frontier of Russia to a point east of Schmalleningken, then the principal channel of navigation of the Niemen (Memel) downstream, then the Skierweth arm of the delta to the Kurisches Haff; thence a straight line to the point where the eastern shore of the Kurische Nehrung meets the administrative boundary about 4 kilometres south-west of Nidden; thence this administrative boundary to the western shore of the Kurische Nehrung." [Fred Israel, ed., *Major Peace Treaties in History, 1638-1967* (New York, 1967), 2:1291f.] For all practical purposes, the river Memel constituted the decisive geographical feature of the boundary.
31. The Lithuanian national movement had traditionally applied the term Little Lithuania/ Lithuania Minor to all the Prussian territories that contained a Lithuanian-speaking population. After World War I, however, the term was also used more narrowly for the Memel territory. The term Klaipėdos kraštas—named after the provincial capital of Klaipėda—has become the dominant designation.
32. In 1898, the Lithuanian candidate Jonas Smalakys won the run-off election in the electoral district of Memel-Heydekrug against the Conservative candidate Count Waldersee with almost 60 percent of the vote. This victory was only achieved because of an alliance with the Liberals, however; in the first round of the elections, Smalakys came in second with 23 percent of the vote. See also Vytautas Žalys, *Kova dėl identito/Ringen um Identität* (Lüneburg, 1993), 13f.
33. The Polish names of these towns/districts are Oborniki, Szamotuły, Międzychód, and Skwierzyna.
34. Königliches Statistisches Bureau, *Preußische Statistik* 177:3 (1902), 166 and 173. The electoral district was also known as Königsberg One.
35. It is these differences in voting pattern that truly confirm the relevance of voting behavior for the assessment of national identity. Initially, one is, of course, inclined to see voting behavior in a broader economic and ideological context and not primarily in a national one. But the fact that candidates who consciously run as minority candidates consistently receive almost the full potential minority vote in Poznania, whereas they consistently receive much less in Prussian Lithuania and in Masuria, regardless of economic similarities, must be seen as an expression of group identity.
36. Walter Hubatsch, "Das Memelland und das Problem der Minderheiten," in *Die deutschen Ostgebiete zur Zeit der Weimarer Republik*, ed. Hermann Conrad (Cologne, 1966), 52.
37. Ernst-Albrecht Pflieg, *Das Memelland 1920-1939* (Würzburg, 1962), 218.
38. The Polish scholar Władysław Wielhorski computed the distribution of German and Lithuanian votes slightly differently. He counted 91 percent German versus 6 percent Lithuanian votes in 1925; 76.7 percent German versus 13.3 percent Lithuanian in 1927; and 75.5 percent German versus 20.5 percent Lithuanian in 1930. [Władysław Wielhorski, "Die Entwicklung der Nationalitätenfrage in Ostpreussen," *Kulturwehr* 11

(1935): 682.] These minor differences, which arise mainly from Wielhorski's separation of the Communist vote, barely change the overall picture, however.

39. By 1970, Russians accounted for 30 percent of the then 140,000 inhabitants of the city of Klaipėda. See Wilfried Schlau, "Der Wandel in der sozialen Struktur der baltischen Länder," in *Die baltischen Nationen*, ed. Boris Meissner (Cologne, 1991), 374.
40. This connection between religion and nationality is, of course, not restricted to the borderlands examined in this essay. The lines between Croats, Serbs, and Bosniaks are essentially drawn along religious lines, and religion competed with history and dialectal tradition in the national distinction between Poles and Ukrainians.
41. This observation does not imply that active religious participation was absent or irrelevant, but that religious identity also had a strong cultural component that continued to influence those who no longer identified as strongly with the theology of their respective religious bodies. At the same time, religion did play an important spiritual role in many of the communities investigated, not least of all the Polish Catholics of Poznania.
42. Königliches Statistisches Bureau, *Preußische Statistik* 177:3 (1902), 386f.
43. The term Polish Protestant serves here as a synonym for Polish-speaking Protestant. It does not imply a Polish national consciousness, as will emerge from the subsequent analysis.
44. Königliches Statistisches Bureau, *Preußische Statistik* 177:3 (1902), XIX.
45. In the census of 1900, the electoral district contained 47,845 Polish-speaking Catholics, 21,804 Polish-speaking Protestants, 15,581 German-speaking Protestants, and 9,331 German-speaking Catholics.
46. The Free Conservatives, or Reich party, were an offshoot of the Conservative party. Its founders had left the Conservatives to support Bismarck's imperial policy when the Conservatives remained more focused on specifically Prussian traditions. After the Conservatives had been integrated more deeply into the Wilhelmine empire, there were few ideological differences between the two conservative parties.
47. See Jürgen Schmädecke, *Wählerbewegung im Wilhelminischen Deutschland* (Berlin, 1995), 1:588.
48. Sigmund Karski, *Albert (Wojciech) Korfanty* (Dülmen, 1990), 314.
49. Notable examples would be Otto Bauer's *Die Nationalitätenfrage und die Sozialdemokratie* (Vienna, 1907) and Karl Renner's *Das Selbstbestimmungsrecht der Nationen* (Vienna, 1918). But a number of theorists of nationalism that do not focus primarily on Austria are also deeply influenced by this country's experience; one might mention Hans Kohn and Eric Hobsbawm in this context.
50. The overall number of Slovenian speakers in the Austrian half of the empire in the census of 1880 was approximately 1.1 million, whereas there were 5.1 million speakers of Czech and Slovak (the latter was not counted separately, but was of little numerical importance). For all the census numbers in this section, see the *Österreichische Statistik* for the years of 1882, 1892, 1902, and 1912, published by the Statistische Zentralkommission in Vienna, and the overviews in Emil Brix, *Die Umgangssprachen in Altösterreich zwischen Agitation und Assimilation* (Vienna, 1982), 436-489, Gerhard Werner, *Sprache und Volkstum in der Untersteiermark* (Stuttgart, 1935), 204f., and Richard Pfaundler, "Die nationalen Verhältnisse in Steiermark am Ausgange des 19. Jahrhunderts," *Statistische Monatschrift* 9 (1906): 401-430.
51. Emil Brix, *Die Umgangssprachen in Altösterreich zwischen Agitation und Assimilation* (Vienna, 1982), 181. Although much of the reduction of the German share derived from the influx of Slovenian speakers into the capital, the absolute numbers of Germans in

Ljubljana (Laibach) stagnated at a time of general population growth and even declined periodically.

52. W. W. Hagen estimated that the percentage of Poles in Poznania rose from 62.9 percent in 1825 to 64.7 percent in 1910. See W. W. Hagen, *Germans, Poles, and Jews* (Chicago, 1980), 324. For additional data and interpretation, see also Eugen von Bergmann, *Zur Geschichte der Entwicklung deutscher, polnischer und jüdischer Bevölkerung in der Provinz Posen* (Tübingen, Germany, 1883); Friedrich Neumann, "Germanisierung oder Polonisierung," *Jahrbücher für Nationalökonomie und Statistik*, n.s., 7 (1883): 457-463; Richard Blanke, *Prussian Poland in the German Empire, 1871-1900* (Boulder, Colo., 1981); and Lech Trzeciakowski, *Kulturkampf w zaborze pruskim* (Poznań, 1970).
53. For a comparative look at contemporary Upper Silesian and Masurian conditions, see Wojciech Łukowski and Tomasz Nawrocki, "Upper Silesia and Masuria in Search of Identity," in *Ethnic Minorities and Ethnic Majority: Sociological Studies of Ethnic Relations in Poland*, ed. Marek S. Szczepański (Katowice, 1997), 107-117. For an introduction to the historical setting in southern Carinthia, see Andreas Moritsch, ed., *Vom Ethnos zur Nationalität: Der nationale Differenzierungsprozeß am Beispiel ausgewählter Orte in Kärnten und im Burgenland* (Vienna, 1991), and Janko Pleterski, *Narodna in politična zavest na Koroškem* (Ljubljana, 1965); for a comparative view, see also Martina Janja Ogris and Werner Platzer, eds., *Kärnten—Slowenien: Belastete Grenze im "neuen Europa"?* (Klagenfurt, 2005).
54. For an introduction to the postwar history of the Masurians, see Andrzej Sakson, *Mazurzy: Społeczność pogranicza* (Poznań 1990); Leszek Belzyt, "Problem weryfikacji polskiej ludności rodzimej na Warmii, Mazurach i Powiślu" (Ph.D. diss., University of Toruń, 1987); and idem, "Zur Frage des nationalen Bewußtseins der Masuren im 19. und 20. Jahrhundert," *Zeitschrift für Ostmitteleuropaforschung* 45:1 (1996): 35-71.
55. In regions with other multiethnic constellations, related phenomena have survived more easily. For a Transylvanian case study, see Margit Feischmidt, *Ethnizität als Konstruktion und Alltagskultur im siebenbürgischen Cluj* (Münster, 2003).

CHAPTER SEVEN

Of Mind and Matter

A Conclusion

The history of Sleswig demonstrates the diversity of identity formation. For centuries, the duchy bridged the divide between Germany and Scandinavia. Through its origins and its rulers, it was tied to the Danish realm. Within this dynastic conglomerate, Sleswig together with Holstein formed a distinct subdivision called the duchies. This entity was governed through the German Chancellery in Copenhagen, reflecting the status of Sleswig as one of the German provinces in the Danish composite monarchy. Below the level of German provincial governance, there were further partitions. Administratively, Sleswig was divided into royal and ducal regions. Linguistically, Sleswig contained Danish, German, and Frisian districts. Finally, the vernacular division was partially reflected in the use of German or Danish in church, school, and court.

The dividing lines sometimes coincided, but more often they did not. In the northernmost districts, the Danish vernacular tradition was echoed in the widespread use of Danish in the public arena. In central Sleswig, on the other hand, the status of the duchy as one of Denmark's German provinces favored the German language also in regions with a historically Danish vernacular tradition. This led to a functional bilingualism, in which the South Jutland dialect dominated in everyday life, whereas the language of religion and education was German.

In the nineteenth century, the new ideology of nationalism challenged such composite polities as Sleswig. At first, both national movements lay claim to the entire duchy. They anchored their image of Sleswig in those aspects that supported their own historical interpretation. The bicultural duchy transformed into the historic Danish border province of South Jutland on the one hand and the northern section of united German Sleswig-Holstein on the other. The respective minorities were destined for toleration at best, assimilation at worst.

Following political setbacks, both national movements eventually appreciated that secure control of half the duchy was preferable to an illusive claim to the whole. Like many other composite territories in an era of mass politics, Sleswig was torn apart by cultural differences. A yet vaguely defined line developed into a substantive boundary. The international border between Germany and Denmark came to separate two clearly demarcated majority populations. Notwithstanding decades of European cooperation, the integrated border region of Sleswig continues to be more disjunct than its historic predecessor two centuries prior.

Yet this politicization of culture did not constitute the only path to identity formation in Sleswig. Not everyone derived his sense of self from objective cultural parameters. At various points in time, segments of the Sleswig population developed subjective self-ascriptions that deviated from their cultural origins. This disconnection between personal language use and national affiliation could express itself in favor of both Denmark and Germany.

The Danish side showed remarkable strength in Flensburg. The largest city in Sleswig had become a center of Low German speech centuries before the rise of nationalism. Among its native citizens, Danish held no relevant position, although it played a role for communication with the Danish heartland and the city's Danish-speaking surroundings. In spite of this German linguistic character, Flensburg developed an ambiguous national orientation. Attachment to the composite monarchy long persisted.

Conditions in Flensburg were countercaricatured by the rural districts of central Sleswig. In those regions, the South Jutland dialect historically dominated, although the public language was German. When the royal government tried to reinforce Danish by making it the language of education and the church in the mid 1800s, popular discontent further eroded Danish dialect use. Even those areas where Danish speech survived frequently identified with a German-oriented Sleswig-Holsteinism.

Identities in the German-Danish borderlands displayed many variations, corresponding to divergent theoretical models. A core population on both sides of the border gave credence to ethnocultural and instrumentalist approaches. Under the impact of intellectual elites, these regional majorities transformed their established cultural background into a modern political identity. The persistence of Danish identity in Prussian-ruled North Sleswig shows the resilience of cultural allegiances. In spite of half a century of increasingly onerous foreign domination, the minority held on to most of its membership and actually deepened its commitment. Decades earlier, the political mobilization of German speakers in Sleswig and Holstein had challenged the Danish composite monarchy.

Next to this traditional identity rooted in politicized culture, the borderlands brought forth a more subjective sense of self. Giving true meaning to Renan's image of the nation as a daily plebiscite, a minority of Sleswigers formed their national identity in opposition to their linguistic background and environment. Diverse political, economic, and cultural factors weighed heavier than their medium of communication. For some, this choice had no significant repercussions. For others, it became the most critical decision of their lives.

The different expressions of subjective identity are exemplified most visibly by the interwar and postwar Danish communities in South Sleswig. The discrepancies revolve around the intergenerational depth of national identification. The old minority was defined by families with historical ties to Danish traditions. Their relationship to German identity was less central to their self-identification. It did not matter so much whether Germany was seen as the vanguard of culture and progress or as an international pariah. What mattered was being Danish.

In this respect, the historic Danish minority resembled its German counterpart in the north. This community does not define itself predominantly by language either. Here, too, identification with the minority derives from family tradition; it is subjective, but with an objective component. The relevant factor is the sense of being German rather than the desire not to be Danish. In fact, mirroring the good fortunes of Denmark's image in the world, Danish identity has increasingly positive connotations among German North Sleswigers. They are not Germans because they want to escape an undesirable Danish identity, but their collective memory binds them to an identity that they experience as more cumbersome than that of their Danish neighbors.

The postwar Danish community in Germany displays the most diverse composition. In addition to the identities of traditional Danish speakers and conscious converts to the Danish cultural sphere, it also displays another form of subjective identification. One segment of Sleswig society chose to identify with the Danish national tradition without fully assuming it. This particularly subjective form of identity is reminiscent of immigrant societies, where it has been described by the American sociologist Herbert Gans. Gans rejects the notion that third- or fourth-generation European Americans have truly retained or regained their ancestral ethnicity.[1] He concedes a renewed interest in ethnic self-identification and the embrace of visible symbols of a particular ethnic culture. Yet he does not see this development as an expression of reemerging immigrant ethnicity. Instead, Gans maintains that the average member of American ethnic groups is less interested in substantive participation in ethnic life—be it cultural or organizational—than in the preservation of an ethnic identity in a psychological sense. This identity is purely self-chosen and voluntary; it is assumed by some and rejected by others.

Although Gans described ethnic identity among the descendants of European immigrants in North America, his findings are relevant for the national self-identification along the Danish-German border as well. One segment of the South Sleswig populace chose to identify with the Danish minority without truly internalizing its cultural codes. Ephemeral minority members restricted their involvement to the more painless aspects of minority life. Just like many Euro-American ethnics, these minority members consider this identity as a part of personal self-realization; it is meant to entail emotional enrichment, not sacrifice.

What makes identities in Sleswig so multilayered is that their different expressions exist side by side. The prewar Danish minority consisted primarily of a prenational regional populace that transformed an established parochial perspective into a modern mass identity. Yet from the very beginning, it also contained German speakers who consciously chose the Danish side, such as Christian Paulsen and many of his fellow Flensburgers. The German minority, in turn, arose among Danish speakers who attached greater importance to their affiliation with the German-speaking south of the duchies than to their linguistic background. The interwar Danish minority in South Sleswig formed its mirror image. In the postwar era, however, the latter's numbers swelled with new members who visibly converted to Danish nationality and others who took this step only symbolically. And whereas the postwar German minority in North Sleswig has not been able to attract many converts, some of its younger members, too, have been gravitating toward a noncommittal minority affiliation that is primarily symbolic in nature. Thus, several layers of identity coexist within individual communities.

These composite identities are not a uniquely Sleswigian phenomenon. The analysis of German-Slavic and German-Baltic borderlands further confirms that culture does not consist of language alone but encompasses a wide array of mores, traditions, and attitudes. The Sleswig case, however, is especially illustrative of the interplay of mind and matter, of personal identification and cultural realities. Its findings lead us back to the theoretical discussion in the introduction of this study. Torn between an essentialist definition that inappropriately reifies it and a radical constructionism that deprives it of relevant substance, identity has become problematic as an analytical category. Rather than abandoning the concept altogether, however, I would advocate a different approach.[2] The Sleswig experience highlights the inherent duality of identity, which relies on both objective and subjective elements. Social identity is not an essential prerequisite of individual existence—it can be embraced or rejected, as well as change in both salience and character. Culture, language, and citizenship do not inherently determine national orientation, but require a conscious policy of national mobilization. At the same time, this process of nationalization cannot fully succeed in a subjectivist vacuum. Without an eventual incorporation of concrete cultural and political elements, constructed self-identifications tend to remain ephemeral phenomena that are largely symbolic in nature. The analytical usefulness of the concept of identity depends on its ability to encompass both its cultural-political and its identificational components.

The German-Danish borderlands draw attention to the composite nature of national identity. Not that these findings can be transferred indiscriminately to other political environments. The analysis of border identities supplements and refines the broader literature on nationalism rather than invalidates it. The duchy of Sleswig was torn apart by its cultural divisions, confirming the role of language and culture in the forming of national identities. Yet on both sides of the border, national minorities developed a sense of self not rooted in language. By drawing attention to its dual nature, the Sleswig experience adds an important facet to the interpretation of national identity.

Notes

1. Gans expresses his views succinctly in "Symbolic Ethnicity: The Future of Ethnic Groups and Cultures in America," in *On the Making of Americans*, ed. Herbert Gans (Philadelphia, 1979), 193-220.
2. The former was suggested in Rogers Brubaker and Frederick Cooper, "Beyond 'Identity'," *Theory and Society* 29:1 (2000): 1-47.

TIMELINE

811	The river Eider forms border between Frankish and Danish realms.
1232	Abel becomes duke in the south of Jutland (Sleswig).
1326	Constitutio valdemariana gives Sleswig independent position within Danish realm.
1386-1459	Schauenburg dynasty from adjacent German territory of Holstein rules in Sleswig. Increases German influence in Sleswig.
1460	Joint noble representatives of Sleswig and Holstein elect Denmark's King Christian I duke of Sleswig and count of Holstein. In exchange, the Treaty of Ribe stipulates close ties between Sleswig and Holstein and autonomy from the Danish kingdom.
1474	Holstein elevated to duchy.
1658	Treaty of Copenhagen grants the duke of Gottorp sovereignty for his possessions in Sleswig.
1721	King Frederik IV of Denmark reincorporates the former Gottorp possessions in Sleswig.
1800s	Emergence of modern national movements among both German- and Danish-oriented Sleswigers.

1848-1850	Revolutionary wave in Europe leads to establishment of provisional Sleswig-Holstein government. Civil war between Sleswig-Holstein and royal Danish governments divides Germans and Danes.
1852	Second London Protocol largely reestablishes the constitutional status quo from before the civil war.
1864	Danish king has to cede all rights in Sleswig and Holstein following defeat in German-Danish war.
1867	Schleswig-Holstein becomes Prussian province following Prussia's defeat of Austria in 1866.
1871	Schleswig-Holstein enters newly founded German empire as Prussian province.
1920	Sleswig divided between Germany and Denmark as a consequence of World War I and subsequent plebiscites.
1940-1945	Denmark, including North Sleswig, occupied by Germany.
1945	Germany's defeat in World War II leads to liberation of Denmark and increases Danish sympathies in South Sleswig.
1949	Schleswig-Holstein, including the southern half of Sleswig, becomes member state of Federal Republic of Germany.
1955	Bonn-Copenhagen Declarations secure minority rights on both sides of the border. Gradual decline of national discord.

BIBLIOGRAPHY

PRIMARY SOURCES

Archival Sources

Schleswig, Landesarchiv Schleswig-Holstein

Abteilung 301 Oberpräsidium

809	Reichstagswahlen Allgemeines
2308-2313	Nordschleswigsche Geistlichkeit
2326	Deutscher Verein für das nördliche Schleswig
2384	Verbot gewisser Farben und Konkarden
2385	Verein für deutsche Friedensarbeit in der Nordmark
2390	Veränderungen des nationalen Besitzstandes in Nordschleswig
2437-2439	Ausweisungen aus den Kreisen Hadersleben, Tondern, Apenrade, Sonderburg, Flensburg Stadt und Flensburg Land
2961-2963	Naturalisierungsgesuche dänischer Optanten
5654	Die schleswig-holsteinischen Landesfarben

Abteilung 309 Regierungspräsidium

35244	Dänenagitation in der 2. und 3. Zone
35252	Friesenbewegung
35284	Dänische Jugendagitation
35302	Regelung der Minderheitenrechte
35311	Pol. Tätigkeit des Cornelius Petersen

Abteilung 400.1 Schleswig-Holsteinische Handschriften

512	Petersen, Ulrich. "Beschreibung der Stadt Schleswig."

Copenhagen, Rigsarkivet

Ministeriet for Hertugdømmet Slesvig
Nyere Sprogsager (1850-61)

Kongehusarkivet
Christian VIII
273 (1837-1847) Sager vedr. slesvigske forhold

Aabenraa, Landsarkivet for Sønderjylland

Den slesvig-holstenske Provinsialregering
I Alm. Sager
4 (1840-1850) Sager vedr. udførelsen af sprogreskriptet af 14.5.1840
5 (1840-1848) Diverse Sager vedr. undervisning i dansk og tysk i skolerne i hertugdømmet Slesvig

Printed Sources

Periodicals

Amtsblatt der königlichen Regierung zu Schleswig
Chronologisk Samling af de udkomne Love og Bekjendtgjørelser for Hertugdømmet Slesvig/Chronologische Sammlung der ergangenen Verordnungen und Verfügungen für die Herzogthümer Schleswig und Holstein
Flensborg Avis
Kieler Blätter
Kraks Blå Bog
Der Nordschleswiger
Sydslesvigsk Årbog
Zeitschrift des Königlich-Preußischen Statistischen Landesamts

Other Printed Sources

Aktstykker betreffende det Tydske Forbunds Intervention i Hertugdømmet Holsteen. Copenhagen, 1852.

Beda. *Opera historica.* With an English translation by J. E. King. 2 vols. Reprint. London, 1962.

Boysen, Didrik, and Jasper Boysen. *Schleswig-Holsteinischer historischer Kirchen- und Schul-Almanach auf das Jahr 1801*. Schleswig, 1801.

Danckwerth, Caspar. *Newe Landesbeschreibung der zwey Herzogthümer Schleswig und Holstein.* N. P., 1652.

Deutscher Schul- und Sprachverein für Nordschleswig, ed. *Materialien zur Geschichte Schleswigs.* Aabenraa, Denmark, 1976.

Diercks, Willy, ed. *Flüchtlingsland Schleswig-Holstein: Erlebnisberichte vom Neuanfang 1945-1950.* Heide, Germany, 1997.

Doederlein, Ludwig, ed. *Taciti Germania.* Erlangen, 1850.

Fabricius, Knud, and Johannes Lomholt-Thomsen, eds. *Flensborgeren, Professor Christian Paulsens dagbøger.* Copenhagen, 1946.

Falck, Nicolaus. *Das Herzogthum Schleswig in seinem gegenwärtigen Verhältnis zu dem Königreich Dänemark und zu dem Herzogthum Holstein.* Schleswig, 1816.

________. *Die historischen Landes-Rechte in Schleswig und Holstein urkundlich.* Kiel, 1842.

________, ed. *Sammlungen zur nähern Kunde des Vaterlandes in historischer, statistischer und staatswirthschaftlicher Hinsicht.* 3 vols. Altona, Germany, 1819-1825.

Fink, Troels. *Forhandlingerne mellem Danmark og Tyskland i 1955 om de slesvigske mindretal.* Copenhagen, 2001.

Flensburger Arbeitskreis für Stadt- und Regionalforschung, ed. *Quellen zur Geschichte Schleswig-Holsteins.* 4 vols. Kiel, 1980-1987.

Friis, Aage, ed. *Det nordslesvigske spørgsmaal, 1864-1879: Aktstykker og breve til belysning af den danske regerings politik.* 6 vols. Copenhagen, 1921-1948.

Göbell, Walter, ed. *Die Schleswig-Holsteinische Kirchenordnung von 1542.* Neumünster, Germany, 1986.

Hamre, Jørgen, and Johann Runge, eds. *Barn og ung i Sydslesvig 1900-1982.* 2 vols. Flensburg, 1986.

Hansen, Johann Friederich. *Staatsbeschreibung des Herzogthums Schleswig.* Ed. by Anton Friderich Busching. Hamburg, 1758.

Hanssen, H. P. *Fra krigstiden: Dagbogsoptegnelser.* 2 vols. Copenhagen, 1924.

________. *Et tilbageblik.* 4 vols. Copenhagen, 1928-1934.

Hegewisch, Dietrich Hermann. "Schreiben an einen Freund über die Folgen, die aus der Vereinigung verschiedener Völker entstehen können." Mit Einleitung und Nachtrag, betreffend das Verhältnis der Sprachen in den Herzogtümern Schleswig und Holstein, von Prof. Falck. *Kieler Blätter* II (1816): 74-140.

Henningsen, Lars N., ed. *Dagbøger fra Sydslesvig 1999.* Flensburg, 2000.

________. *Da Sydslesvig gik af lave: Erindringer fra sindelagsskiftets år.* Flensburg, 2003.

________. *Bonn-Erklæringen og de unge: Elevberetninger fra Duborg-Skolen 2005.* Flensburg, 2005.

Institut für Regionale Forschung und Information and Institut for grænseregionsforskning, eds. *Der nationale Gegensatz/De nationale modsætninger, 1800-1864.* Flensburg, 1984.

Institut für schleswig-holsteinische Zeit- und Regionalgeschichte and Institut for grænseregionsforskning, eds. *Der nationale Gegensatz/De nationale modsætninger, 1914-1933.* Aabenraa and Flensburg, 2001.

Israel, Fred, ed. *Major Peace Treaties in History, 1638-1967.* 4 vols. New York, 1967.

Jensen, Hans Nicolai Andreas. *Versuch einer kirchlichen Statistik des Herzogthums Schleswig.* 4 vols. Flensburg, 1840-1842.

________ . *Angeln.* Flensburg, 1844.

Johannsen-Bojesen, Karin. "Som vi ser os selv: Uddrag af samtaler med 60 sydslesvigere." *Grænseforeningens årbog* (1981): 3-81.

Komiteen for den slesvigske Subskription, ed. *Den danske sag i den slesvigske stænderforsamling 1842.* Copenhagen, 1842.

Lachauer, Ulla. *Paradiesstraße: Lebenserinnerungen der ostpreußischen Bäuerin Lena Grigoleit.* Reinbek, Germany, 1996.

Lornsen, Uwe Jens. *Ueber das Verfassungswerk in Schleswigholstein.* Kiel, 1830.

Meyersahm, Hans. *Die Vertretung der einzelnen Parteien in Schleswig-Holstein bei den Reichstagswahlen seit 1867.* Kiel, 1912.

Nordfriesischer Verein für Heimatkunde und Heimatliebe, ed. *13.000 Nordfriesen an den Minderheitenkongreß in Genf.* Husum, 1926.

Paulsen, Christian. *Über Volksthümlichkeit und Staatsrecht des Herzogthums Schleswig.* Kiel, 1832.

________ . *Samlede mindre skrifter.* 3 vols. Copenhagen, 1857-1859.

Pedersen, Christiern. *Danske skrifter.* Published by C. J. Brandt and Theodor Fenger. 5 vols. Copenhagen, 1850-1856.

Pedersen, Karen Margrethe, et al. *Vi bor i Sønderjylland: Sprog og kultur i lokalsamfundet.* Aabenraa, Denmark, 1993.

Petersen, Cornelius. *Das schleswigsche Volk.* Flensburg, 1919.

________ . *Det slesvigske spørgsmaal og det slesvigske folk.* Copenhagen, 1919.

________ . *Entgegnung auf Herrn Julius Momsens Erwiderung.* Flensburg, 1919.

________ . *Die friesische Bewegung.* Tønder, 1920.

________ . *Uve Jens Lornsen Däne?* Tønder, 1920.

________ . *Parlamentarismens Sammenbrud.* Copenhagen, 1922.

Pontoppidan, Erik. *Det Danske Sprogs Skiæbne udi Sønder-Jylland.* Copenhagen, 1745.

Prahl, Else, et al., eds. *Karl Otto Meyer og Flensborg Avis.* Flensburg, 1988.

Schmidt, Ernst. *Briefwechsel der Brüder Grimm mit nordischen Gelehrten*. Berlin, 1885. Reprint, Wallruf, Germany, 1974.

Schubert, Lars, and Johann Runge, eds. *Barn og ung i Flensborg 1920-1945*. Flensburg, 1977.

Sørensen, H. E. *Mellem dansk og tysk: Sønderjyder fortæller III*. Skærbæk, 1987.

Statistisches Landesamt Schleswig-Holstein, ed. *Beiträge zur historischen Statistik Schleswig-Holsteins*. Kiel, 1967.

________. *Das Flüchtlingsgeschehen in Schleswig-Holstein infolge des Zweiten Weltkriegs im Spiegel der amtlichen Statistik*. Kiel, 1974.

Stemann, C. L. E. von. *Schleswigs Recht und Gerichtsverfassung im siebenzehnten Jahrhundert*. Flensburg, 1855.

Interview

Siegfried Matlok. Interview by author. Tape recording. Aabenraa, Denmark, 27 May 2004.

SECONDARY LITERATURE

Achelis, Thomas Otto. "Deutsche und dänische Gottesdienste im Herzogtum Schleswig." *Schriften des Vereins für Schleswig-Holsteinische Kirchengeschichte*, 2d ser., 10 (1949): 79-102.

Adler, J. G. C. "Die Volkssprache in dem Herzogthum Schleswig seit 1864." *Zeitschrift der Gesellschaft für Schleswig-Holstein-Lauenburgische Geschichte* 21 (1891): 1-135.

________ . "Die Volkssprache in dem vormaligen Herzogtum Schleswig auf Grund der Sprachenzählung vom 1. Dezember 1905." *Zeitschrift der Gesellschaft für Schleswig-Holsteinische Geschichte* 45 (1915): 55-85.

________ . *Die sprachlichen Verhältnisse in Schleswig.* Flensburg, 1923.

Adriansen, Inge, and Broder Schwensen. *Fra det tyske nederlag til Slesvigs deling 1918-1920.* Aabenraa and Flensburg, 1995.

Adriansen, Inge, and Immo Doege, eds. *Dansk eller tysk? Billeder af national selvforståelse i 1920.* Aabenraa, Denmark, 1992.

Ægidius, Jens Peter. *Christian Flor: Pædagogen, politikeren, folkeoplyseren.* Odense, 1994.

Allchin, Arthur Macdonald. *N. F. S. Grundtvig: An Introduction to his Life and Work.* Aarhus, 1997.

Allen, C. F. *Haandbog i fædrelandets historie.* Copenhagen, 1840.

________ . *Det danske Sprogs Historie i Hertugdømmet Slesvig eller Sønderjylland.* 2 vols. Copenhagen, 1857-1858.

Alnor, Karl. *Handbuch zur schleswigschen Frage.* 4 vols. Neumünster, Germany, 1926-1939.

Alvarez, Robert R. "The Mexican-US Border: The Making of an Anthropology of Borderlands." *Annual Review of Anthropology* 24 (1995): 447-470.

Andersen, H. Hellmuth. *Danevirke og Kovirke: Arkæologiske undersøgelser 1861-1993.* Aarhus, 1998.

Andersen, Heine, and Lars Bo Kaspersen, eds. *Klassisk og moderne samfundsteori.* 2d ed. Copenhagen, 2000.

Andersen, Mette Lund. *Grænsen i hverdagen – grænsen i hovedet.* Aabenraa, Denmark, 2004.

Anderson, Benedict. *Imagined Communities: Reflections on the Origins and Spread of Nationalism.* London, 1983.

Andresen, Sigfred. *Sydslesvig - grænselandet mellem dansk og tysk.* Flensburg, 1989.

Anthias, Floya, and Nira Yuval-Davis, eds. *Woman—Nation—State.* London, 1989.

Applegate, Celia. *A Nation of Provincials: The German Idea of Heimat.* Berkeley, Calif., 1990.

Armstrong, John. *Nations before Nationalism.* Chapel Hill, N.C., 1982.

Arteaga, Alfred, ed. *An Other Tongue: Nation and Ethnicity in the Linguistic Borderlands.* Durham, 1994.

Asiwaju, Anthony Ijaola. *Western Yorubaland Under European Rule, 1889-1945: A Comparative Analysis of French and British Colonialism.* London, 1976.

________ , ed. *Transfrontier Regionalism: Perspectives on the European Union and Post-Colonial Africa with Special Reference to Borgu.* Ibadan, Nigeria, 1999.

Asiwaju, Anthony Ijaola, and Peter O. Adeniyi, eds. *Borderlands in Africa: A Multidisciplinary and Comparative Focus on Nigeria and West Africa.* Lagos, 1989.

Banac, Ivo, and Katherine Verdery, eds. *National Character and National Ideology in Interwar Eastern Europe.* New Haven, Conn., 1995.

Bankwitz, Philip C. F. *Alsatian Autonomist Leaders 1919-1947.* Lawrence, Kans., 1978.

Bantelmann, Albert, et al. *Geschichte Nordfrieslands.* 2d ed. Heide, Germany, 1996.

Bär, Max. *Die "Bamberger" bei Posen.* Posen, 1882.

Barth, Fredrik, ed. *Ethnic Groups and Boundaries.* Boston, 1969.

Bauer, Otto. *Die Nationalitätenfrage und die Sozialdemokratie.* Vienna, 1907.

________ . *Werkausgabe.* Edited by Arbeitsgemeinschaft für die Geschichte der österreichischen Arbeiterbewegung. 9 vols. Vienna, 1975-1980.

Baumgarten, R. "Evangelische Polen in Posen und Schlesien." *Die Grenzboten* 73:30 (1914): 189-192.

Becker-Christensen, Henrik. *Dansk mindretalspolitik i Nordslesvig.* Aabenraa, Denmark, 1984.

________ . *Det tyske mindretal i Nordslesvig 1920-1932.* 2 vols. Aabenraa, Denmark, 1990.

________ . *Byen ved grensen: Tønder 1920-1970.* Aabenraa, Denmark, 1993.

________ , ed. *Grænsen i 75 år: 1920-1995.* Aabenraa, Denmark, 1995.

Becker-Christensen, Henrik, and Ulrich Lange, eds. *Geschichte Schleswigs vom frühen Mittelalter bis 1920.* Aabenraa, Denmark, 1998.

Belzyt, Leszek. "Problem weryfikacji polskiej ludności rodzimej na Warmii, Mazurach i Powiślu." Ph.D. diss., University of Toruń, 1987.

________. "Zum Verfahren der nationalen Verifikation in den Gebieten des ehemaligen Ostpreußens 1945-1950." *Jahrbuch für die Geschichte Mittel- und Ostdeutschlands* 39 (1990): 247-269.

________. "Zur Frage des nationalen Bewußtseins der Masuren im 19. und 20. Jahrhundert." *Zeitschrift für Ostmitteleuropaforschung* 45:1 (1996): 35-71.

Berdichevsky, Norman. *The Danish-German Border Dispute: Aspects of Cultural and Demographic Politics 1815-2001*. Bethesda, Md., 2002.

Bergmann, Eugen von. *Zur Geschichte der Entwicklung deutscher, polnischer und jüdischer Bevölkerung in der Provinz Posen*. Tübingen, 1883.

Beyer, Hans. "Der Friese Cornelius Petersen und 'Bondens Selvstyre': Ein dänisches Beispiel zur Problematik der Landvolkbewegung zwischen beiden Weltkriegen." *Zeitschrift für Agrargeschichte und Agrarsoziologie* 10 (1962): 212-230.

Bjerrum, Anders. "Sprogskiftet i Sydslesvig og dets Årsager." *Danske Folkemål* 32 (1990): 1-35.

________. "Om de danske dialekter i Sønderjylland." *Sønderjyske Årbøger* (1953): 101-124.

Blanke, Richard. "Upper Silesia, 1921: The Case for Subjective Nationality." *Canadian Review of Studies in Nationalism* 2 (1975): 241-260.

________. *Prussian Poland in the German Empire (1871-1900)*. Boulder, Colo., 1981.

________. *Orphans of Versailles: The Germans in Western Poland, 1918-1939*. Lexington, Ky., 1993.

________. *Polish-Speaking Germans? Language and National Identity among the Masurians since 1871*. Cologne, 2001.

Blatt, Lothar. *Die rechtliche Behandlung der dänischen Minderheit in Schleswig-Holstein von 1866 bis 1914*. Husum, Germany, 1980.

Bock, Karl Nielsen. *Niederdeutsch auf dänischem Substrat: Studien zur Dialektgeographie Südostschleswigs*. Copenhagen, 1933.

Boehm, Carl. *Die jüngere politische und kulturelle Entwicklung der dänischen nationalen Minderheit in der Bundesrepublik Deutschland und der deutschen nationalen Minderheit im Königreich Dänemark unter besonderer Berücksichtigung des friesischen Bevölkerungsteils in der Bundesrepublik*. Hamburg, 1991.

Bohmann, Alfred. *Menschen und Grenzen*. 3 vols. Cologne, 1969-1970.

Bohn, Robert, Uwe Danker, and Jørgen Kühl, eds. *Nationale mindretal i det dansk-tyske grænseland 1933-1945*. Aabenraa, Denmark, 2001.

Bracker, Jochen. "Die dänische Sprachpolitik 1850-1864 und die Bevölkerung Mittelschleswigs." *Zeitschrift der Gesellschaft für Schleswig-Holsteinische Geschichte* 97 (1972): 127-225; 98 (1973): 87-213.

Brakas, Martin, ed. *Lithuania Minor*. New York, 1976.

Brandt, Otto. *Geschichte Schleswig-Holsteins*. 8th ed. Kiel, 1981.

Braunmüller, Kurt, and Willy Diercks, eds. *Niederdeutsch und die skandinavischen Sprachen*. Heidelberg, 1993.

Breuilly, John. *Nationalism and the State*. New York, 1982.

Brix, Emil. *Die Umgangssprachen in Altösterreich zwischen Agitation und Assimilation*. Vienna, 1982.

Brix, Theodor. *Nordschleswig und die Selbsterniedrigung Deutschlands*. Berlin, 1902.

Brownlie, Ian, ed. *African Boundaries: A Legal and Diplomatic Encyclopedia*. London, 1979.

Brubaker, Rogers. *Nationalism Reframed: Nationhood and the National Question in the New Europe*. Cambridge, Mass., 1996.

________ . *Ethnicity without Groups*. Cambridge, Mass., 2004.

Brubaker, Rogers, and Frederick Cooper. "Beyond 'Identity'." *Theory and Society* 29:1 (2000): 1-47.

Brunner, Zbigniew, et al., eds. *Atlas Samochodowy Polski*. Warszawa, 1967.

Bruns, Inken. *Von der Feindschaft zur Kooperation: Die deutsche Minderheit eines dänischen Dorfes von 1920-1990*. Münster, 1995.

Bruun, Daniel, ed. *Danmark: Land og Folk*. 5 vols. Copenhagen, 1919-1922.

Bucken-Knapp, Greg, and Michael Schack, eds. *Borders Matter: Transboundary Regions in Contemporary Europe*. Aabenraa, Denmark, 2001.

Bucur, Maria, and Nancy M. Wingfield, eds. *Staging the Past: The Politics of Commemoration in Habsburg Central Europe, 1848 to the Present*. West Lafayette, Ind., 2001.

Bundgård Christensen, Claus, Niels Bo Poulsen, and Peter Scharff Smith. *Under hagekors og Dannebrog: Danskere i Waffen SS*. Copenhagen, 1998.

Buruma, Ian. *The Wages of Guilt: Memories of War in Germany and Japan*. London, 1994.

Byram, Michael. *Minority Education and Ethnic Survival: Case Study of a German School in Denmark*. Clevedon, England, 1986.

Callesen, Gerd. *Die Schleswig-Frage in den Beziehungen zwischen dänischer und deutscher Sozialdemokratie von 1912 bis 1924*. Aabenraa, Denmark, 1970.

Carr, William. *Schleswig-Holstein 1815-48: A Study in National Conflict*. Manchester, England, 1963.

Cedergreen Bech, Svend. *Dansk biografisk leksikon*. 3d ed. 16 vols. Copenhagen, 1979-1984.

Chavez, Linda. *Shadowed Lives: Undocumented Immigrants in American Society.* Fort Worth, 1992.

Christensen, Jan Hyldal. "'Die neue Entwicklung in Dänemark hat begonnen': Det tyske mindretal i Nordslesvig 1945-47." *Sønderjyske Årbøger* (2004): 87-132.

Christensen, Lorenz. "Hjemmetyskheds-Problemet." *Sønderjyske Årbøger* (1929): 220-254.

Christiansen, Flemming, and Ulf Hedetoft, eds. *The Politics of Multiple Belonging: Ethnicity and Nationalism in Europe and East Asia.* Aldershot, England, 2004.

Christiansen, Karl O. *Mandlige landssvigere i Danmark under besættelsen.* Copenhagen, 1950.

________ . *Landssvigerkriminaliteten i sociologisk belysning.* Copenhagen, 1955.

Cieślak, Tadeusz. "Die Kaschuben als soziales und politisches Problem am Ende des 19. und Anfang des 20. Jahrhunderts." *Letopis* 25 (1978): 31-38.

Clausen, H. N. *Slesvigeren Christian Ditlef Paulsens livshistorie i omrids.* Copenhagen, 1857.

Clausen, H. V. "Folkesproget i Sønderjylland." *Sønderjyske Årbøger* (1892): 182-212; (1893): 89-105.

________ . *Nordslesvig 1863-93: Den nationale stilling på landet.* Flensburg, 1894.

________ . *Sønderjylland: En geografisk skitse.* Copenhagen, 1905.

________ . *Før afgørelsen.* Copenhagen, 1918.

Clausen, Otto. *Flurnamen Schleswig Holsteins.* 2d, enl. ed. Rendsburg, Germany, 1988.

Cohen, Gary B. *The Politics of Ethnic Survival: Germans in Prague, 1861-1914.* 2d ed. West Lafayette, Ind., 2006.

Cole, John W., and Eric R. Wolf. *The Hidden Frontier: Ecology and Ethnicity in an Alpine Valley.* New York, 1974.

Connor, Walker. *The National Question in Marxist-Leninist Theory and Strategy.* Princeton, N.J., 1984.

________ . *Ethnonationalism.* Princeton, N.J., 1994.

________ , ed. *Mexican-Americans in Comparative Perspective.* Washington, D.C., 1985.

Conrad, Hermann, et al., eds. *Die deutschen Ostgebiete zur Zeit der Weimarer Republik.* Cologne, 1966.

Conze, Werner. *Ostmitteleuropa: Von der Spätantike bis zum 18. Jahrhundert.* Munich, 1992.

Davidson, Basil. *The Black Man's Burden: Africa and the Curse of the Nation-State.* London, 1992.

Davis, Horace B. *Toward a Marxist Theory of Nationalism.* New York, 1978.

Degn, Christian. *Schleswig-Holstein: Eine Landesgeschichte.* 2d ed. Neumünster, Germany, 1995.

Doege, Immo. "Die deutsche Minderheit in Nordschleswig und ihre dänische Umwelt." *Grenzfriedenshefte* 1985/4 (1985): 205-221.

Döring, Joachim, et al., eds. *Friesen, Sachsen und Dänen: Kulturen an der Nordsee, 400-1000.* Franeker, Netherlands, 1996.

Dralle, Lothar. *Die Deutschen in Ostmittel- und Osteuropa.* Darmstadt, 1991.

Elklit, Jørgen. *Folketællingen 1845: Metodiske problemer ved databehandlingen af et folketællingsmateriale.* Aarhus, 1970.

________. "Nationalt tilhørsforhold og holdninger til EF." *Sønderjyske Årbøger* (1974): 180-203.

Elklit, Jørgen, Johan Peter Noack, and Ole Tonsgaard. "Om måling af nationalt tilhørsforhold i Nordslesvig." *Økonomi og Politik* 46:4 (1972): 375-395.

________. *Nationalt tilhørsforhold i Nordslesvig: Resultater fra en interviewundersøgelse.* Aarhus, 1978.

Elklit, Jørgen, and Ole Tonsgaard. "The Policies of Majority Groups towards National Minorities in the Danish-German Border Region: Why the Differences?" *Ethnic and Racial Studies* 6:4 (1983): 477-491.

________. "Elements for a Structural Theory of Ethnic Segregation and Assimilation." *European Journal of Political Research* 12:1 (1984): 89-100.

Engberg, Jens. *Det slesvigske spørgsmål 1850-1853.* Copenhagen, 1968.

Engsnap, Knud B. *Sprog og ideologi i Sydslesvig.* Flensburg, 1984.

Fassmann, Heinz, and Rainer Münz. "European East-West Migration, 1945-1992." *International Migration Review* 28:3 (1994): 520-538.

Feischmidt, Margit. *Ethnizität als Konstruktion und Alltagskultur im siebenbürgischen Cluj.* Münster, 2003.

Feldbæk, Ole, ed. *Dansk identitetshistorie.* 4 vols. Copenhagen, 1991-1992.

Fink, Troels. *Rids af Sønderjyllands historie.* Copenhagen, 1943.

________. "Den kirkelige sproggrænse." *Sønderjyske Årbøger* (1964): 275-285.

________. *Otte foredrag om Danmarks krise 1863-64.* Aarhus, 1964.

________. *Da Sønderjylland blev delt.* 3 vols. 2d ed. Aabenraa, Denmark, 1979.

Fischer, Christopher. "Alsace to the Alsatians? Visions and Divisions of Alsatian Regionalism, 1890-1930." Ph.D. diss., University of North Carolina, 2003.

Forstreuter, Kurt. "Die Anfänge der Sprachstatistik in Preußen und ihre Ergebnisse zur Litauerfrage." *Zeitschrift für Ostforschung* 2 (1953): 329-352.

Frederiksen, Bjarne. *Danmarks Sydslesvigpolitik efter det tyske sammenbrud i 1945.* Munksgaard, Denmark, 1971.

Fussing, Hans, ed. *Til Knud Fabricius.* Copenhagen, 1945.

Gans, Herbert, ed. *On the Making of Americans.* Philadelphia, 1979.

Gellner, Ernest. *Thought and Change.* London, 1964.

________ . *Nations and Nationalism.* Oxford, 1983.

________ . *Encounters with Nationalism.* Oxford, 1994.

Gesellschaft für Schleswig-Holsteinische Geschichte und Verein für Lübeckische Geschichte und Altertumskunde, eds. *Biographisches Lexikon für Schleswig-Holstein und Lübeck.* 12 vols. to date. Neumünster, Germany, 1970-.

Göhring, Martin, and Alexander Scharff, eds. *Geschichtliche Kräfte und Entscheidungen: Festschrift zum fünfundsechzigsten Geburtstage von Otto Becker.* Wiesbaden, 1954.

Gónzalez, Nancie L. *Dollar, Dove and Eagle: One Hundred Years of Palestinian Migration to Honduras.* Ann Arbor, Mich., 1992.

Goodfellow, Samuel Huston. *Between the Swastika and the Cross of Lorraine: Fascisms in Interwar Alsace.* DeKalb, Ill., 1999.

Gradus, Yehuda, and Harvey Lithwick, eds. *Frontiers in Regional Development.* Lanham, Md., 1994.

Grau, Andreas. *De Danske i Sydslesvig – Tyskerne i Nordslesvig.* 2d. ed. Sønderborg, Denmark, 1935.

Gregersen, Hans Valdemar. *Plattysk i Sønderjylland: En undersøgelse af fortyskningens historie indtil 1600-årene.* Odense, 1974.

________ . *Slesvig og Holsten før 1830.* Copenhagen, 1981.

Gribsvad, Frode. "Hvad fortæller retsprotokollerne om retssproget i Nordslesvig?" In *Afhandlinger tilegnede rigsarkivar Axel Linvald,* 122-128. Copenhagen, 1956.

Grimm, Jacob. *Geschichte der deutschen Sprache.* 3d ed. Leipzig, 1868.

Groß, Bernd, and Peter Schmitt-Egner. *Europas kooperierende Regionen: Rahmenbedingungen und Praxis transnationaler Zusammenarbeit deutscher Grenzregionen in Europa.* Baden-Baden, 1994.

Gudme, A. C. *Schleswig-Holstein.* Kiel, 1833.

Hagen, William W. *Germans, Poles, and Jews: The Nationality Conflict in the Prussian East, 1772-1914.* Chicago, 1980.

Hahn, Hans Henning, and Peter Kunze, eds. *Nationale Minderheiten und staatliche Minderheitenpolitik in Deutschland im 19. Jahrhundert.* Berlin, 1999.

Hall, John A., ed. *The State of the Nation: Ernest Gellner and the Theory of Nationalism.* Cambridge, England, 1998.

Hansen, Ernst Siegfried. *Kurier der Heimat: Das Spiel um Schleswig zwischen Kapitulation und Programm Nord.* Bielefeld, 1955.

________ . *Disteln am Wege: Von der Besetzung Dänemarks bis zu den Bonner Erklärungen.* Bielefeld, 1957.

Hansen, Hans Peter. *Schleswig: Eine kurze geschichtliche Übersicht.* Flensburg, 1921.

Hansen, Niles. *The Border Economy: Regional Development in the Southwest.* Austin, 1981.

Hansen, Reimer. "Was bedeutet 'up ewig ungedeelt'? Das Ripener Privileg von 1460 im deutsch-dänischen Nationalkonflikt des 19. Jahrhunderts." *Grenzfriedenshefte* 1996/4 (1996): 215-232.

Harp, Stephen L. *Learning to Be Loyal: Primary Schooling as Nation Building in Alsace and Lorraine, 1850-1940.* DeKalb, Ill., 1998.

Hartmann, Stefan. "Zur nationalpolnischen Bewegung und zur preußischen Politik in Masuren vor dem Ersten Weltkrieg." *Zeitschrift für Ostforschung* 42:1 (1993): 40-83.

Harvey, David Allen. *Constructing Class and Nationality in Alsace, 1830-1945.* DeKalb, Ill., 2001.

Haubrichs, Wolfgang, and Reinhard Schneider, eds. *Grenzen und Grenzregionen.* Saarbrücken, 1994.

Hauser, Oswald. *Preußische Staatsräson und nationaler Gedanke.* Neumünster, Germany, 1960.

Hayes, Carlton. *The Historical Evolution of Modern Nationalism.* New York, 1931.

Hecker, Hans, and Silke Spieler, eds. *Deutsche, Slawen, und Balten: Aspekte des Zusammenlebens im Osten des Deutschen Reiches und in Ostmitteleuropa.* Bonn, 1989.

Hector, Kurt. *Die politischen Ideen und Parteibildungen in den schleswigschen und holsteinischen Ständeversammlungen 1836-1846.* Neumünster, Germany, 1938.

Henningsen, Lars N. *Kirke og folk i grænselandet: Dansk kirke i Sydslesvig 1921-1996.* Flensburg, 1996.

________ . "Dänische und deutsche Kirche im Grenzland seit 1920." *Grenzfriedenshefte* 1996/1 (1996): 5-22.

________ . "Lutherske kirker mellem dansk og tysk: Omrids af Sønderjyllands kirkehistorie efter reformationen." *Sønderjyske Årbøger* (2004): 133-170.

Henningsen, Lars N., Martin Klatt, and Jørgen Kühl. *SSW: Dansksindet politik i Sydslesvig 1945-1998.* Flensburg, 1998.

Hermann, Arthur. "Das Nationalbewußtsein der litauischen Lutheraner in Preußisch-Litauen und in Litauen." *Baltisches Jahrbuch* 3 (1986): 64-80.

________ . "Die Besiedlung Preußisch-Litauens im 15.-16. Jahrhundert in der deutschen und litauischen Historiographie." *Zeitschrift für Ostforschung* 39 (1990): 321-341.

Herrmann, Hayo. "Situation und Entwicklung der deutsch-dänischen Grenzräume und insbesondere des Grenzraumes Sønderjylland-Schleswig." *Grenzfriedenshefte* 53:3 (2005): 227-236.

Herzog, Lawrence A., ed. *Shared Space: Rethinking the U.S.-Mexico Border Environment.* La Jolla, Calif., 2000.

Herzog, Robert. *Die Volksdeutschen in der Waffen-SS.* Tübingen, 1955.

Hinderling, Robert, and Ludwig M. Eichinger, eds. *Handbuch der mitteleuropäischen Sprachminderheiten.* Tübingen, 1996.

Hirschhausen, Ulrike von, and Jörn Leonhard, eds. *Nationalismen in Europa: West- und Osteuropa im Vergleich.* Göttingen, 2001.

Hjelholt, Holger. *Sønderjylland under Treårskrigen.* 2 vols. Copenhagen, 1959-1961.

Hobsbawm, Eric. *Nations and Nationalism since 1780.* Cambridge, England, 1990.

Hobsbawm, Eric, and Terence Ranger, eds. *The Invention of Tradition.* Cambridge, England, 1983.

Hoensch, Jörg K. *Geschichte Böhmens: Von der slavischen Landnahme bis zur Gegenwart.* 3d ed. Munich, 1997.

Höffken, Martin. *Die "Kieler Erklärung" vom 26. September 1949 und die "Bonn-Kopenhagener Erklärungen" vom 29. März 1955 im Spiegel deutscher und dänischer Zeitungen.* Frankfurt, 1994.

Hoffmann, Erich. *Die Herkunft des Bürgertums in den Städten des Herzogtums Schleswig.* Neumünster, Germany, 1953.

________. *Die heiligen Könige bei den Angelsachsen und den skandinavischen Völkern.* Neumünster, Germany, 1975.

________. *Königserhebung und Thronfolgeordnung in Dänemark bis zum Ausgang des Mittelalters.* Berlin, 1976.

________. "Historische Voraussetzungen für die Herausbildung der heutigen deutsch-dänischen Staatsgrenze." *Zeitschrift der Gesellschaft für Schleswig-Holsteinische Geschichte* 106 (1981): 9-29.

________. "Die Entstehung des nordschleswigschen Deutschtums." *Schriften der Heimatkundlichen Arbeitsgemeinschaft für Nordschleswig* 51 (1985): 5-20.

________. "Nicolaus Falck und die Schleswig-Holsteinische Frage." *Zeitschrift der Gesellschaft für Schleswig-Holsteinische Geschichte* 111 (1986): 143-155.

Hoppe-Kossack, Andrea. *Aufgaben und Möglichkeiten der nationalen Minderheiten im deutsch-dänischen Grenzraum.* Flensburg, 1993.

Hroch, Miroslav. *Social Preconditions of National Revival in Europe.* Cambridge, England, 1985.

________. "From National Movements to the Fully-Formed Nation: The Nation-Building Process in Europe." *New Left Review* 198 (1993): 3-20.

Hubatsch, Walter. "Masuren und Preußisch-Litthauen in der Nationalitätenpolitik Preußens 1870-1920." *Zeitschrift für Ostforschung* 14 (1965): 641-670; 15 (1966): 1-55.

Hutchinson, John. *The Dynamics of Cultural Nationalism.* London, 1987.

Institut Nordostdeutsches Kulturwerk, ed. *Zwischen Staatsnation und Minderheit: Litauen, das Memelland und das Wilnagebiet in der Zwischenkriegszeit.* Lüneburg, 1993.

Isbary, Gerhard. *Problemgebiete im Spiegel politischer Wahlen am Beispiel Schleswigs*. Bad Godesberg, 1960.

Jahnke, Carsten. "'dat se bliven ewich tosamende ungedelt': Neue Überlegungen zu einem alten Schlagwort." *Zeitschrift der Gesellschaft für Schleswig-Holsteinische Geschichte* 128 (2003): 45-59.

Japsen, Gottlieb. *Den nationale udvikling i Åbenrå 1800-1850.* Aabenraa, Denmark, 1961.

________. *Det dansksprogede skolevæsen i Sønderjylland indtil 1814.* Tønder, Denmark, 1968.

________. "Betragtninger over den danske bevægelse i Nordslesvig." *Sønderjyske Årbøger* (1973): 63-75.

________. *Dansk og tysk i Sønderjylland fra 1864 til vore dage.* Copenhagen, 1979.

________. *Pastor Jacobsen fra Skærbæk og hans foretagender.* Aabenraa, Denmark, 1980.

________. *Den fejlslagne germanisering: Den tyske forening for det nordlige Slesvig*. Aabenraa, Denmark, 1983.

Jasiński, Grzegorz. *Mazurzy w drugiej połowie XIX wieku: Kształtowanie się świadomości narodowej*. Olsztyn, 1994.

Jeismann, Karl-Ernst, ed. *Zur Geschichte und Problematik der deutsch-dänischen Beziehungen von der Wikingerzeit bis zur Gegenwart/Det dansk-tyske forholds historie og problemer fra vikingetiden til nutiden.* Braunschweig, 1984.

Jensen, Johannes. *Nordfriesland in den geistigen und politischen Strömungen des 19. Jahrhunderts (1797-1864).* Neumünster, Germany, 1961.

Jensen, Niels Lyhne, ed. *A Grundtvig Anthology. Selections from the Writings.* Cambridge, 2000.

Jessen, Franz von. *Haandbog i det slesvigske spørgsmaals historie*. 3 vols. Copenhagen, 1935-1938.

________, ed. *Haandbog i det nordslesvigske spørgsmaals historie*. Copenhagen, 1901.

Jessen, Hanns Christian, ed. *Faarhus 1945-1949: Straflager für die deutsche Minderheit in Dänemark.* Husum, Germany, 1987.

Jessen-Klingenberg, Manfred. "Rückzug aus der Nation in die Region: Aus dem Schriftwechsel dreier Schleswig-Holsteiner 1946." *Grenzfriedenshefte* 1996/3 (1996): 131-144.

________. "Schleswig-Holsteins Geschichtsschreibung und das Nationalitätenproblem in Schleswig von 1864 bis 1940." *Grenzfriedenshefte* 1997/3 (1997): 165-192.

________. *Standpunkte zur neueren Geschichte Schleswig-Holsteins.* Malente, Germany, 1998.

Johnsen, Axel. *Dannevirkemænd og Ejderfolk: Den grænsepolitiske opposition i Danmark 1920-1940.* Flensburg, 2005.

Johnsen, Axel, and Birgitte Thomsen, eds. *19 myter i Sønderjyllands historie.* Aabenraa, Denmark, 2002.

Jørgensen, Adolf Ditlev. *Fyrretyve fortællinger af fædrelandets historie.* Copenhagen, 1882.

Judson, Pieter M. *Guardians of the Nation: Activists on the Language Frontiers of Imperial Austria.* Cambridge, Mass., 2006.

Jürgensen, Kurt. *Die Gründung des Landes Schleswig-Holstein nach dem Zweiten Weltkrieg: Der Aufbau der demokratischen Ordnung in Schleswig-Holstein während der britischen Besatzungszeit, 1945-1949.* Neumünster, Germany, 1998.

Kalijarvi, Thorsten. *The Memel Statute.* London, 1937.

Kappeler, Andreas, ed. *The Formation of National Elites.* Aldershot, 1992.

Kardel, Harboe. *Fünf Jahrzehnte in Nordschleswig.* Aabenraa, Denmark, 1971.

Karski, Sigmund. *Albert (Wojciech) Korfanty.* Dülmen, 1990.

Kearney, Michael. "The Local and the Global: The Anthropology of Globalization and Transnationalism." *Annual Review of Anthropology* 24 (1995): 547-565.

Kedourie, Elie. *Nationalism.* 4th ed. London, 1993.

________, ed. *Nationalism in Asia and Africa.* London, 1971.

Kętrzyński, Wojciech. *O Mazurach.* Poznań, 1872.

King, Jeremy. *Budweisers into Czechs and Germans: A Local History of Bohemian Politics, 1848-1948.* Princeton, 2002.

Klatt, Martin. *Flygtningene og Sydslesvigs danske bevægelse 1945-1955.* Flensburg, 2001.

Klose, Olaf, and Erich Hoffmann, eds. *Geschichte Schleswig-Holsteins.* 8 vols. to date. Neumünster, Germany, 1958-.

Knudsen, Anne. "Slesvig—et skoleeksempel." *Fortid og Nutid* (1994): 173-180.

Köster, Adolf. *Der Kampf um Schleswig.* Berlin, 1921.

Krieger, A. F., ed. *Antislesvigholstenske fragmenter.* 16 vols. Copenhagen, 1848.

Kühl, Jørgen. *På vej mod den slesvigske model: Mindretallene i det dansk-tyske grænseland 1955-1995.* Aabenraa, Denmark, 1996.

________. "Zusammenleben von Mehrheit und Minderheit: Das deutsch-dänische Grenzland als Beispiel." *Grenzfriedenshefte* 1996/3 (1996): 188-203.

________. *The "Schleswig Experience": The National Minorities in the Danish-German Border Area.* Aabenraa, Denmark, 1998.

________. *The National Minorities in the Danish-German Border Region.* Aabenraa, Denmark, 2003.

________, ed. *En europæisk model? Nationale mindretal i det dansk-tyske grænseland 1945-2000.* Aabenraa, Denmark, 2002.

Kühl, Jørgen, and Marc Weller, eds. *Minority Policy in Action: The Bonn-Copenhagen Declarations in a European Context, 1955-2005.* Flensburg and Aabenraa, 2005.

Kulski, Władisław W. *Germany and Poland.* Syracuse, N.Y., 1976.

Kurlander, Eric. "Multicultural and Assimilationist Models of Ethnopolitical Integration in the Context of the German *Nordmark*, 1890-1933." *The Global Review of Ethnopolitics* 1:3 (2002): 39-52.

Kürti, László, and Juliet Langman, eds. *Beyond Borders: Remaking Cultural Identities in the New East and Central Europe.* Boulder, Colo., 1997.

La Cour, Vilhelm, Knud Fabricius, Holger Hjelholt, and Hans Lund, eds. *Sønderjyllands Historie: Fremstillet for det danske Folk.* 5 vols. Copenhagen, 1931-1933.

Landeszentrale für politische Bildung Schleswig-Holstein, ed. *Minderheiten im deutsch-dänischen Grenzbereich.* Kiel, 1993.

Lange, Ulrich, ed. *Geschichte Schleswig Holsteins: Von den Anfängen bis zur Gegenwart.* Neumünster, Germany, 1996; 2d, enlarged ed., 2003.

Lassen, Aksel. *Valg mellem tysk og dansk: Hundrede års folkevilje i Sønderjylland.* Aabenraa, Denmark, 1976.

Latoszek, Marek, ed. *Kaszubi: Monografia socjologiczna.* Rzeszów, 1990.

Laur, Wolfgang. "Die sprachlichen Verhältnisse in Angeln in ihrer geschichtlichen Entwicklung." *Jahrbuch des Angler Heimatvereins* 17 (1954): 50-73.

Lauridsen, Peder. "Vort folks sydgrænse." *Sønderjyske Årbøger* (1893): 28-50, 106-148, 253-289.

________. *Da Sønderjylland vaagnede.* 8 vols. Copenhagen, 1909-1922.

Lebeck, Anders. *Tyve Aars Elever: Den nordslesvigske Skoleforenings Virksomhed fra 1894-1913.* Haderslev, 1914.

Lenzing, Hilke. "Die deutsche Volksgruppe in Dänemark und das nationalsozialistische Deutschland (1933-1939): Ein Beitrag zur Problematik deutscher Volksgruppen während des Dritten Reiches." Ph.D. diss., University of Bonn, 1973.

Leppien, Jörn-Peter. *Martin Rade und die deutsch-dänischen Beziehungen 1909-1919*. Neumünster, Germany, 1981.

Linde-Laursen, Anders, and Jan Olof Nilsson, eds. *Nationella identiteter i Norden: Ett fullbordat projekt?* Stockholm, 1991.

Lindstrøm, Anders Ture. *Landet Slesvig-Holstens historie i hovedtræk 1945-1954*. Flensburg, 1975.

Lingenberg, Heinz. "Die Kaschuben." *Westpreussen-Jahrbuch* 35 (1985): 123-150.

Lorek, Sabine. *Rechtsabrechnung—Retsopgør: Politische Säuberung nach dem Zweiten Weltkrieg in Nordschleswig*. Neumünster, Germany, 1998.

Lorentz, Friedrich, Adam Fischer, and Tadeusz Lehr-Spławiński. *The Cassubian Civilization*. London, 1935.

Lund, Hans. "Træk af den danske sønderjyske presses historie 1864-1914." *Sønderjyske Årbøger* (1934): 1-12.

Lundgreen-Nielsen, Flemming, ed. *På sporet av dansk identitet*. Copenhagen, 1992.

Lundgreen-Nielsen, Kay. *The Polish Problem at the Paris Peace Conference: A Study of the Policies of the Great Powers and the Poles, 1918-1919*. Odense, 1979.

Lyngby, Kristen Jensen. *Bidrag til en sønderjysk sproglære*. Copenhagen, 1858.

Mackeprang, Mouritz. *Nordslesvig 1864-1909*. Copenhagen, 1910.

________, ed. *Tønder gennem tiderne*. 2 vols. Tønder, Denmark, 1943-1944.

Marstrand, Vilhelm. *Grænsespørgsmaalet belyst fra administrative handels- og samfærdselstekniske synspunkter*. Copenhagen, 1919.

Marti, Roland, ed. *Sprachenpolitik in Grenzregionen*. Saarbrücken, 1996.

Mártinez, Oscar J. *Border People: Life and Society in the U.S.-Mexico Borderlands*. Tucson, Ariz., 1994.

________, ed. *Across Boundaries: Transborder Interaction in Comparative Perspective*. El Paso, Tex., 1986.

________, ed. *U.S.-Mexico Borderlands: Historical and Contemporary Perspectives*. Wilmington, Del., 1996.

Matlok, Siegfried. "Von den Schatten der Vergangenheit verfolgt." *Grenzfriedenshefte* 1978/1 (1978): 18-26.

________. "Dänemark zwischen Skepsis und Hoffnung." *Grenzfriedenshefte* 1979/2 (1979): 73-83.

______, ed. *Dänemark in Hitlers Hand*. Husum, Germany, 1988.

Mehnert, Gottfried. *Die Kirche in Schleswig-Holstein: Eine Kirchengeschichte im Abriß*. Kiel, 1960.

Meinecke, Friedrich. *Weltbürgertum und Nationalstaat: Studien zur Genesis des deutschen Nationalstaats*. Munich, 1907.

Meissner, Boris. *Die baltischen Nationen.* 2d ed. Cologne, 1991.

Mensing, Otto. "Das Plattdeutsche in Schleswig und die neue Bewegung." In *Schleswig-Holsteinisches Jahrbuch 1921*, ed. Ernst Sauermann, 76-80. Hamburg, 1921.

Miles, William. *Hausaland Divided: Colonialism and Independence in Nigeria and Niger.* Ithaca, N.Y., 1994.

Minnich, Robert Gary. *Homesteaders and Citizens: Collective Identity Formation on the Austro-Italian-Slovene Frontier.* Bergen, 1998.

________. "Die Leute von Ugovizza: Kollektive Identitäten im alpinen Raum." *Historische Anthropologie* 10:1 (2002): 51-75.

Mogensen, Carsten R. *Dansk i hagekorsets skygge: Det tredie rige og det danske mindretal i Sydslesvig 1933-1939.* Flensburg, 1981.

Mørch, Søren. *Den sidste Danmarkshistorie.* Copenhagen, 1996.

Moritsch, Andreas, ed. *Vom Ethnos zur Nationalität.* Vienna, 1991.

Mortensen, Hans. "Einwanderung und innerer Ausbau in den Anfängen der Besiedlung des Hauptamtes Ragnit." *Acta Prussica* (1969): 67-76.

Mortensen, Hans, and Gertrud Mortensen. *Die Besiedlung des nordöstlichen Ostpreußens bis zum Beginn des 17. Jahrhunderts.* 2 vols. Leipzig, 1937-1938.

Munske, Horst Haider, ed. *Handbuch des Friesischen/Handbook of Frisian Studies.* Tübingen, 2001.

National identitet: Fem foredrag om dansk og tysk identitetsfølelse i grænselandet. Aabenraa, Denmark, 1994.

Neubach, Helmut. "Die Nationalitätenverhältnisse in der Provinz Schlesien im Spiegel der letzten Reichstagswahlen vor dem 1. Weltkrieg (1912)." *Oberschlesisches Jahrbuch* 1 (1985): 57-83.

________. "Die Nationalitätenverhältnisse in der Provinz Posen im Spiegel der letzten Reichstagswahl vor dem Ersten Weltkrieg (1912)." *Zeitschrift für Ostforschung* 35:1/2 (1986): 141-159.

Neumann, Friedrich. "Germanisierung oder Polonisierung." *Jahrbücher für Nationalökonomie und Statistik,* n.s., 7 (1883): 457-463.

Neureuter, Ferdinand. "Die Kaschuben." *Mickiewicz Blätter* 13 (1968): 228-242.

Nickelsen, Hans Christian. *Das Sprachbewußtsein der Nordfriesen in der Zeit vom 16. bis ins 19. Jahrhundert.* Bredstedt, Germany, 1982.

Nielsen, Hans Frede. *The Germanic Languages: Origins and Early Dialectal Interrelations.* Tuscaloosa, Ala., 1989.

________. *Guldhornsindskriften fra Gallehus: Runer, sprog og politik.* Odense, 2002.

Noack, Johan Peter. *Det tyske mindretal i Nordslesvig under besættelsen.* Copenhagen, 1975.

________. *Det danske mindretal i Sydslesvig 1920-1945.* 2 vols. Aabenraa, Denmark, 1989.

________. *Det sydslesvigske grænsespørgsmål 1945-1947.* Aabenraa, Denmark, 1991.

________. "Als die Grenze 'fest lag': Der Grenzstreit nach dem Zweiten Weltkrieg." *Grenzfriedenshefte* 1996/1 (1996): 23-41.

________. *Det danske mindretal i Sydslesvig 1948-55.* 2 vols. Aabenraa, Denmark, 1997.

Nonnenbroich, Karl Friedrich. *Die dänische Minderheit in Südschleswig unter besonderer Berücksichtigung des SSW.* Kiel, 1972.

Nugent, Paul, and Anthony I. Asiwaju, eds. *African Boundaries: Barriers, Conduits, and Opportunities.* London, 1996.

Nyberg, Magda. "Den sproglige udvikling i Sønderjylland efter Genforeningen." *Sønderjyske Årbøger* (1995): 261-290.

Nyholm, Asger. *Nationale og religiøse brydninger i Tønder på sprogreskripternes tid.* Aabenraa, Denmark, 1958.

Ogris, Martina Janja, and Werner Platzer, eds. *Kärnten—Slowenien: Belastete Grenze im "neuen Europa"?* Klagenfurt, 2005.

Ortmann, Anja. *Die Dänen in Schleswig-Holstein: Zur Soziologie einer Minderheit.* Göttingen, 1996.

Paetau, Rainer, and Holger Rüdel, eds. *Arbeiter und Arbeiterbewegung in Schleswig-Holstein im 19. und 20. Jahrhundert.* Neumünster, Germany, 1987.

Pauseback, Paul-Heinz. *Übersee-Auswanderer aus Schleswig-Holstein.* Husum, Germany, 2000.

Pedersen, Karen Margrethe. *Mødet mellem sprogene i den dansk tyske grænseregion.* Aabenraa, Denmark, 1986.

________. *Sprachliche Vielfalt in einer Grenzregion.* Aabenraa, Denmark, 1994.

________. *Dansk sprog i Sydslesvig.* 2 vols. Aabenraa, Denmark, 2000.

Peters, L. C., ed. *Nordfriesland: Heimatbuch für die Kreise Husum und Südtondern.* Husum, 1919. Reprint, Kiel, 1975.

Petersen, Carl. "Nicolaus Falck und die Entstehung des schleswig-holsteinischen Gedankens." *Jahrbuch der Schleswig-Holsteinischen Universitätsgesellschaft* (1926): 1-111.

________. "Nicolaus Falck und die schleswig-holsteinische Bewegung." *Kieler Blätter* (1939): 237-253.

________. "Nikolaus Falcks politische Wandlung in den Jahren der Reaktion (1819-1934)." *Zeitschrift der Gesellschaft für Schleswig-Holsteinische Geschichte* 67 (1939): 243-288.

Petersen, Jakob. "Sprogforeningens Udvikling gennem 50 År." In *Aarsberetning 1929-30*, ed. Sprogforeningen, 5-52. Aabenraa, Denmark, 1930.

________. *En kort oversigt over folketingsvalgene fra 1920-1935*. Aabenraa, Denmark, 1939.

Petersen, Søren Ryge. *Dansk eller tysk? En undersøgelse af sprogforholdene i en flersproget sydslesvigsk kommune i 1973*. Flensburg, 1975.

Pfaundler, Richard. "Die nationalen Verhältnisse in Steiermark am Ausgange des 19. Jahrhunderts." *Statistische Monatschrift* 11 (1906): 401-430.

________. "Die Grundlagen der nationalen Bevölkerungsentwicklung Steiermarks." *Statistische Monatschrift* 11 (1907): 557-592.

Pflieg, Ernst-Albrecht. *Das Memelland 1920-1939: Deutsche Autonomiebestrebungen im litauischen Gesamtstaat*. Würzburg, 1962.

Pleterski, Janko. *Narodna in politična zavest na Koroškem*. Ljubljana, 1965.

Pontoppidan Thyssen, Anders, ed. *Herrnhuter-samfundet i Christiansfeld*. 2 vols. Aabenraa, Denmark, 1984.

Prescott, John Robert Victor. *Political Frontiers and Boundaries*. London, 1987.

Prisching, Manfred, ed. *Identität und Nachbarschaft: Die Vielfalt der Alpen-Adria Länder*. Vienna, 1994.

Ramirez, José, ed. *Att forska om gränser*. Stockholm, 2001.

Rasmussen, Carsten Porskrog, Inge Adriansen, and Lennart S. Madsen, eds. *De slesvigske hertuger*. Aabenraa, Denmark, 2005.

Rasmussen, Troels. *Den dansk-tyske traktat 1922*. Aabenraa, Denmark, 1996.

Ratjen, Henning. *Zur Erinnerung an Nicolaus Falck*. Kiel, 1851.

Renan, Ernest. *Qu'est-ce qu'une nation?* Paris, 1882.

Renner, Karl. *Das Selbstbestimmungsrecht der Nationen*. Vienna, 1918.

Rerup, Lorenz. *Grænsen: Fra grænsekamp til sameksistens*. Albertslund, Denmark, 1969.

________. *Slesvig og Holsten efter 1830*. Copenhagen, 1982.

Rheinheimer, Martin. *Die Dorfordnungen im Herzogtum Schleswig: Dorf und Obrigkeit in der Frühen Neuzeit*. 2 vols. Stuttgart, 1999.

Riecken, Claas. *Nordfriesische Sprachforschung im 19. Jahrhundert*. Bredstedt, Germany, 2001.

Riederer, Günter. *Feiern im Reichsland: Politische Symbolik, öffentliche Festkultur und die Erfindung kollektiver Zugehörigkeiten in Elsass-Lothringen (1871-1918)*. Trier, 2004.

Ritter, Alexander, ed. *Kolloquium zur Sprache und Sprachpflege der deutschen Bevölkerungsgruppen im Ausland*. Flensburg, 1985.

Ritter, Gerhard A. *Wahlgeschichtliches Arbeitsbuch: Materialien zur Statistik des Kaiserreiches, 1871-1918*. Munich, 1980.

Rohweder, Jürgen. *Sprache und Nationalität: Nordschleswig und die Anfänge der dänischen Sprachpolitik*. Glücksburg, Germany, 1976.

Rolfs, Claus. *Geschichte des Kirchspiels und Fleckens Hoyer.* Preetz, Germany, 1926.

Rosenthal, Harry K. "National Self-Determination: The Example of Upper Silesia." *Contemporary History* 7:3-4 (1972): 231-241.

Rösler, Michael, and Tobias Wendl, eds. *Frontiers and Borderlands: Anthropological Perspectives*. New York, 1999.

Ross, Stanley, ed. *Views Across the Border.* Albuquerque, 1978.

Runge, Johann. *Christian Paulsens politische Entwicklung: Ein Beitrag zur Analyse der Entwicklung des dänischen Bewußtseins in der ersten Hälfte des 19. Jahrhunderts im Herzogtum Schleswig.* Neumünster, Germany, 1969.

________ . "Die dänische Minderheit in Südschleswig und ihre deutsche Umwelt." *Grenzfriedenshefte* 1985/4 (1985): 222-234.

Rybicki, Paweł, and Władysław Markiewicz, eds. *Przemiany społeczne na Ziemiach Zachodnich.* Poznań, 1967.

Sach, August. *Das Herzogtum Schleswig in seiner ethnographischen und nationalen Entwicklung*. 3 vols. Halle, 1896-1907.

Sahlins, Peter. *Boundaries: The Making of France and Spain in the Pyrenees.* Berkeley, Calif., 1989.

Sakson, Andrzej. *Mazurzy: Społeczność pogranicza.* Poznań, 1990.

Salomon, Kim. *Konflikt i grænselandet: Sociale og nationale modsætninger i Sønderjylland 1920-33.* Copenhagen, 1980.

Schäfer, Thomas. *Die Schleswig-Holsteinische Gemeinschaft 1950-1958.* Neumünster, Germany, 1987.

Scharf, Claus, and Hans-Jürgen Schröder, eds. *Politische und ökonomische Stabilisierung Westdeutschlands 1945-1959: Fünf Beiträge zur Deutschlandpolitik der westlichen Alliierten.* Wiesbaden, 1977.

________ . *Die Deutschlandpolitik Großbritanniens und die Britische Zone 1945-1949.* Wiesbaden, 1979.

Scharff, Alexander. *Schleswig-Holstein in der deutschen und nordeuropäischen Geschichte.* Stuttgart, 1969.

________ . *Wesen und Bedeutung der schleswig-holsteinischen Erhebung 1848-1850.* Neumünster, Germany, 1978.

Scheel, Otto. *Nordschleswig im schleswig-holsteinischen Gedanken.* Kiel, 1927.

Schmädecke, Jürgen. *Wählerbewegung im Wilhelminischen Deutschland.* 2 vols. Berlin, 1995.

Schultz Hansen, Hans. *Det nordslesvigske landbrug og den danske bevægelse 1880-1914.* Aabenraa, Denmark, 1985.

________ . *Danskheden i Sydslesvig 1840-1918 som folkelig og national bevægelse*. Flensburg, 1990.

________ . "Den danske bevægelse i Sønderjylland ca. 1838-50." *Historie*, n.s., 18:3 (1990): 353-395.

________. *Det sønderjyske landbrugs historie 1830-1993*. Aabenraa, Denmark, 1994.

________. "Schleswigsche Identität in den 1840er Jahren: Ein historischer Begriff wird aktuell." *Grenzfriedenshefte* 1997/4 (1997): 239-252.

________. *"Dansk jord på danske hænder": Foreningen Landeværnet og den nationale jordkamp i Sønderjylland 1927-2002*. Aabenraa, Denmark, 2002.

________. *Hjemmetyskheden i Nordslesvig 1840-1867*. 2 vols. Aabenraa, Denmark, 2005.

Schultz Hansen, Hans, and Henrik Skov Kristensen, eds. *Sønderjylland under krig og besættelse 1940-1945*. Aabenraa, Denmark, 2003.

Schütt, Otto. *Die Geschichte der Schriftsprache im ehemaligen Amt und in der Stadt Flensburg bis 1650*. Flensburg, 1919.

________. "Flensburgs Sprache." In *Schleswig-Holsteinisches Jahrbuch 1921*, ed. Ernst Sauermann, 63-67. Hamburg, 1921.

Schwalm, Eberhardt. *Volksbewaffnung 1848-1850 in Schleswig-Holstein: Vorarbeiten zu einer Psychologie und Soziologie der Schleswig-Holsteinischen Erhebung*. Neumünster, Germany, 1961.

Schwensen, Broder, Gerhard Paul, and Peter Wulf, eds. *Ausgebürgert. Ausgegrenzt. Ausgesondert: Opfer politischer und rassischer Verfolgung in Flensburg 1933-1945*. Flensburg, 1998.

________. *Zwischen Konsens und Kritik: Facetten kulturellen Lebens in Flensburg 1933-1945*. Flensburg, 1999.

Seefried-Gulgowski, Ernst. *Von einem unbekannten Volke in Deutschland: Ein Beitrag zur Volks- und Landeskunde der Kaschubei*. Berlin, 1911.

Selk, Paul. *Die sprachlichen Verhältnisse im deutsch-dänischen Sprachgebiet südlich der Grenze: Eine statistisch-geographische Untersuchung*. 2 vols. Flensburg, 1937-1940.

Sestoft, Leif. *Drømmen om Danmark: Det danske Flensborgs blomstring og fald 1830-1875*. Flensburg, 2002.

Sievers, Kai Detlev. *Die Köllerpolitik und ihr Echo in der deutschen Presse 1897-1901*. Neumünster, Germany, 1964.

________, ed. *Beiträge zur Frage der ethnischen Identifikation des Bundes Deutscher Nordschleswiger*. Flensburg, 1975.

Silvert, Kalman, et al., eds. *Expectant People: Nationalism and Development*. New York, 1962.

Smith, Anthony D. *Theories of Nationalism*. 2d ed. New York, 1983.

________. *The Ethnic Origins of Nations*. Oxford, 1986.

________. *National Identity*. London, 1991.

________. "The Problem of National Identity: Ancient, Medieval and Modern?" *Ethnic and Racial Studies* 17:3 (July 1994): 375-395.

________. *Nationalism and Modernism: A Critical Survey of Recent Theories of Nations and Nationalism.* London, 1998.

________, ed. *Ethnicity and Nationalism.* Leiden, 1992.

Snyder, Louis. *The Meaning of Nationalism.* New Brunswick, N.J., 1954.

Søndergaard, Bent. *Fra tysk børnehave til tysk eller dansk skole - myte og realitet.* Aabenraa, Denmark, 1988.

Spear, Thomas, and Richard Waller, eds. *Being Maasai: Ethnicity and Identity in East Africa.* London, 1993.

Spener, David, and Kathleen Staudt, eds. *The U.S.-Mexico Border: Transcending Divisions, Contesting Identities.* Boulder, Colo., 1998.

Stalin, Joseph. *The Essential Stalin: Major Theoretical Writings, 1905-1952.* Edited by Bruce Franklin. Garden City, N.Y., 1972.

Steefel, Lawrence. *The Schleswig-Holstein Question.* Cambridge, Mass., 1932.

Steensen, Thomas. *Die friesische Bewegung in Nordfriesland im 19. und 20. Jahrhundert.* 2 vols. Neumünster, Germany, 1986.

________. *Friesische Sprache und friesische Bewegung.* Husum, Germany, 1996.

________, ed. *Nationalsozialismus in Nordfriesland.* Bredstedt, Germany, 1993.

Steensen, Thomas, and Alistair Walker, eds. *Friesen heute.* Bredstedt, Germany, 1990.

Steg, Christian Jepsen. "De blakkede: National indifference og neutralitet i Nordslesvig 1890-1940." *Sønderjyske Årbøger* (2004): 67-86.

Stehr, Rudolf. "Neubeginn und kritische Rückschau: Erlebnisse, Erfahrungen, und Betrachtungen aus Jahrzehnten in Nordschleswig und Kopenhagen." *Schriften der heimatkundlichen Arbeitsgemeinschaft für Nordschleswig* 43/44 (1981): 5-113.

Stender-Petersen, Ole. *Det sønderjyske spørgsmål og skolebøgerne.* Copenhagen, 1998.

Stenz, Christian. "Det danske Sprogs Stilling i Mellemslesvig 1946." *Sønderjyske Årbøger* (1947): 153-191.

Stoddard, Ellwyn R. "Border Studies as an Emergent Field of Scientific Inquiry: Scholarly Contributions of U.S.-Mexico Borderland Studies." *Journal of Border Studies* 1 (1986): 1-33.

Strassoldo, Raimondo. "Regionalism and Ethnicity: The Case of Friuli." *International Political Science Review* 6:2 (1985): 197-215.

________. *Lingua, identità, autonomia: Ricerche e riflessioni sociologiche sulla questione friulana.* Udine, 1996.

Strassoldo, Raimondo, and Giovanni Delli Zotti, eds. *Cooperation and Conflict in Border Areas.* Milano, 1982.

Svalastoga, Kaare, and Preben Wolf. *En by ved grænsen.* Copenhagen, 1963.

Svane, Inger. "Vælgerforeningen og de dansksinnede nordslesvigeres politik 1906-1910." *Sønderjyske Årbøger* (1973): 76-198.

Synak, Brunon. *Kaszubska tożsamość*. Gdańsk, 1998.

Szczepański, Marek, ed. *Ethnic Minorities and Ethnic Majority: Sociological Studies of Ethnic Relations in Poland.* Katowice, 1997.

Tägil, Sven. *Deutschland und die deutsche Minderheit in Nordschleswig: Eine Studie zur deutschen Grenzlandpolitik 1933-1939.* Stockholm, 1970.

________, ed. *Ethnicity and Nation Building in the Nordic World.* Carbondale, Ill., 1995.

Tamm, Ditlev. *Retsopgøret efter besættelsen.* Copenhagen, 1984.

Tardieu, André, and Franz von Jessen. *Slesvig paa fredskonferencen, januar 1919-januar 1920.* Copenhagen, 1926.

Thodberg, Christian, and Anders Pontoppidan Thyssen, eds. *N F S Grundtvig, Tradition and Renewal: Grundtvig's Vision of Man and People, Education and the Church, in Relation to World Issues Today.* Copenhagen, 1983.

Thorsen, Peder Kristian. *Afhandlinger og Breve.* 3 vols. Copenhagen, 1927-1930.

Thorsen, Svend. *Delt efter anskuelser: Den politiske partidannelses forløb i Sønderjylland efter genforeningen i 1920.* Copenhagen, 1970.

Thurau, Harald, ed. *Festschrift für Otto Scheel: Beiträge zur deutschen und nordischen Geschichte.* Schleswig, 1952.

Tiedje, Johannes. *Die Zustände in Nord-Schleswig.* Marburg, 1909.

________. "Die nationale Schichtung Schleswigs." In *Schleswig-Holsteinisches Jahrbuch 1921*, ed. Ernst Sauermann, 16-23. Hamburg, 1921.

Toft, Gösta. *Die bäuerliche Struktur der deutschen Volksgruppe in Nordschleswig.* Flensburg, 1982.

Trzeciakowski, Lech. *Kulturkampf w zaborze pruskim.* Poznań, 1970.

Unverhau, Henning. *Untersuchungen zur historischen Entwicklung des Landes zwischen Schlei und Eider im Mittelalter.* Neumünster, Germany, 1990.

________. *Gesang, Feste und Politik: Deutsche Liedertafeln, Sängerfeste, Volksfeste und Festmähler und ihre Bedeutung für das Entstehen eines nationalen und politischen Bewußtseins in Schleswig-Holstein 1840-1848.* Frankfurt, 2000.

Urcioli, Bonnie. "Language and Border." *Annual Review of Anthropology* 24 (1995): 525-546.

Ureland, P. Sture, ed. *Sprachkontakte im Nordseegebiet.* Tübingen, 1978.

Ureland, P. Sture, and Iain Clarkson, eds. *Scandinavian Language Contacts.* Cambridge, England, 1984.

Verein für Schleswig-Holsteinische Kirchengeschichte, ed. *Schleswig-Holsteinische Kirchengeschichte.* Vol. 4, *Orthodoxie und Pietismus.* Neumünster, Germany, 1984.

Vileišis, Vincas. *Tautiniai Santykiai Maž. Lietuvoje.* Kaunas, 1935.

Vogel, Klaus A. *Der Kreis um die Kieler Blätter (1815-1821).* Frankfurt, 1989.

Vollertsen, Nils. *SPD, Socialdemokratiet og det danske mindretal.* Odense, 1983.

________ . *Det danske mindretal.* Odense, 1994.

________ . *Sydslesvig: En landsdel i nationalt opbrud 1945-1948.* Odense, 1994.

Volquardsen, Sönnich. "Initiator im Verborgenen: Cornelius Petersen und der Friesisch-schleswigsche Verein." *Nordfriesland* 103/104 (1993): 30-32.

Waitz, Georg. *Schleswig-Holsteins Geschichte.* 3 vols. Göttingen, 1851.

Wambaugh, Sarah. *Plebiscites since the World War.* 2 vols. Washington, D.C., 1933.

Weber, Eugen. *Peasants into Frenchmen: The Modernization of Rural France, 1870-1914.* Stanford, Calif., 1976.

Wegner, Bernd. *Hitlers politische Soldaten.* Paderborn, 1982.

Wehler, Hans-Ulrich. "Zur neueren Geschichte der Masuren." *Zeitschrift für Ostforschung* 11 (1962): 147-172.

Weitling, Günter. *Die Heimdeutschen: Ursprung, Geschichte und Wesen.* Aabenraa, Denmark, 1990.

Werner, Gerhard. *Sprache und Volkstum in der Untersteiermark.* Stuttgart, 1935.

Wetzel, Jürgen. *Theodor Lehmann und die nationale Bewegung in Schleswig-Holstein 1859-1862.* Neumünster, Germany, 1971.

Wielhorski, Władysław. "Die Entwicklung der Nationalitätenfrage in Ostpreussen." *Kulturwehr* 11 (1935): 673-698.

Wiell, Stine. *Kampen om oldtiden/Der Kampf um die Vorgeschichte.* Aabenraa, Denmark, 2000.

Wilson, Thomas M., and Hastings Donnan, eds. *Border Identities: Nation and State at International Frontiers.* Cambridge, England, 1998.

Windmann, Horst. *Schleswig als Territorium: Grundzüge der Verfassungsentwicklung im Herzogtum Schleswig von den Anfängen bis zum Aussterben des Abelschen Hauses 1375.* Neumünster, Germany, 1954.

Winge, Vibeke. *Dänische Deutsche - deutsche Dänen: Geschichte der deutschen Sprache in Dänemark 1300-1800 mit einem Ausblick auf das 19. Jahrhundert.* Heidelberg, 1992.

Witt, Jann Markus, and Heiko Vosgerau, eds. *Schleswig-Holstein von den Ursprüngen bis zur Gegenwart.* Hamburg, 2002.

Wódz, Kazimiera, ed. *Regional Identity—Regional Consciousness: The Upper Silesian Experience.* Katowice, 1995.

Wolff, Larry. *Inventing Eastern Europe: The Map of Civilization on the Mind of the Enlightenment.* Stanford, Calif., 1994.

Wolff, Stefan. *Disputed Territories: The Transnational Dynamics of Ethnic Conflict Settlement.* New York, 2003.

________ , ed. *Ethnic German Minorities in Europe*. New York, 2000.

Yndigegn, Carsten. *Unge og regional identitet: Forventninger og instilling til livsbetingelser og livsmuligheder i den dansk-tyske grænseregion.* Aabenraa, Denmark, 2003.

Žalys, Vytautas. *Kova dėl identiteto / Ringen um Identität.* Lüneburg, 1993.

Zeh, Jürgen. *Die deutsche Sprachgemeinschaft in Nordschleswig: Ein soziales Gebilde im Wandel.* Stuttgart, 1982.

INDEX